1981

THE
KODÁLY
CONTEXT

THE
KODÁLY
CONTEXT:
Creating an Environment
for Musical Learning

LOIS CHOKSY

PRENTICE-HALL, INC., Englewood Cliffs, New Jersey 07632

Library of Congress Cataloging in Publication Data

Choksy, Lois.
    The Kodály context.

    1. School music—Instruction and study. 2. Kodály,
Zoltán, 1882–1967. I. Kodály, Zoltán, 1882–1967.
II. Title.
MT1.C536   780′.7   80-22149
ISBN 0-13-516674-8
ISBN 0-13-516666-7 (pbk.)

Editorial/production supervision and interior design: Robert Hunter
Cover design: Maureen Olsen
Manufacturing buyer: Harry P. Baisley

Printed in the United States of America

10 9 8 7 6 5 4 3 2 1

PRENTICE-HALL INTERNATIONAL, INC., *London*
PRENTICE-HALL OF AUSTRALIA PTY. LIMITED, *Sydney*
PRENTICE-HALL OF CANADA, LTD., *Toronto*
PRENTICE-HALL OF INDIA PRIVATE LIMITED, *New Delhi*
PRENTICE-HALL OF JAPAN, INC., *Tokyo*
PRENTICE-HALL OF SOUTHEAST ASIA PTE. LTD., *Singapore*
WHITEHALL BOOKS LIMITED, *Wellington, New Zealand*

To
Erzébet Szőnyi
Teacher, Colleague, Friend

Contents

PREFACE   *xv*

ACKNOWLEDGMENTS   *xix*

1 KODÁLY: AN OVERVIEW   *3*

Kodály: The Man Behind "The Method"   *3*
The Kodály Method   *6*
Suggested Reading   *11*

part I
Kodály Practice and the Young Child

2 KODÁLY AND EARLY CHILDHOOD MUSIC   *15*

Child-developmental Characteristics in Music   *16*
A Proposed Music Program for Young Children   *17*

In-tune Singing   *17*
Movement   *22*
Beat, Metric Accent, Rhythm   *24*
The Comparatives   *29*
  Faster-Slower   *29*
  Softer-Louder   *30*
  Higher-Lower   *31*
Timbre   *33*
Memory Training   *34*
Inner Hearing   *35*
Listening to Music   *36*
Conclusion   *36*
Suggested Assignment   *38*
Suggested Reading   *39*

**3   MOVEMENT AND DANCE
IN KODÁLY PRACTICE**   *40*

Movement in Hungary   *40*
Historic Roots of Dance in America   *41*
Movement and the Young Child   *44*
  Circle Games and Dances   *46*
    Acting-out games   *46*
    Partner-choosing games   *46*
    Chase games   *47*
    Winding games   *47*
    Double circle games   *47*
  Line Games and Dances   *48*
  Other Game Forms   *49*
Movement and Creativity   *49*
  One Possible Skill-Teaching Sequence in Movement,
    Singing Games and Dances   *49*
Suggested Assignments   *52*
Suggested Reading   *52*
Sources for Further Information   *52*

part II
Kodály for Older Students

INTRODUCTION TO PART II   55

4 BEGINNING A KODÁLY PROGRAM WITH OLDER STUDENTS   57

Rationale   57
First-year Skill Teaching-Learning Order   61
In-tune Singing   62
Rhythmic Learning   64
Melodic Teaching   67
Meter and Measure   72
Reading Music   73
Suggested Assignment   74
Suggested Reading   74

5 UNDERSTANDING MUSIC THROUGH PERFORMING AND CREATING: A KODÁLY APPROACH TO MUSIC LISTENING   75

Improvisation   77
    Some Ways to Encourage Rhythmic Improvisation   78
    Some Ways to Encourage Melodic Improvisation   79
    Development of Compositional Skills   85
Listening to Music   86
    Using Standard Compositional Techniques
        with a Known Folk Song   90
    Selecting Music for Listening Experience   94

A Series of Listening Experiences Using Bach's "The Little Fugue in G Minor" *95*

Suggested Assignments *96*

6 APPLYING KODÁLY PRINCIPLES IN THE TRAINING OF CHORAL GROUPS *98*

The Singers *98*

Auditioning *99*

Choosing the singers *99*

Voice range *99*

Rhythmic ability *100*

Sightsinging *101*

Ear ability *101*

Musical memory *101*

Audition techniques *102*

The cambiata voice *103*

Organizing *105*

Routines *107*

Student accompanists *107*

Rehearsing *107*

In-tune singing *108*

Music reading *108*

Inner hearing *110*

Memory training *111*

Following the director *111*

The Singing *112*

Vocal Technique and Enunciation *112*

Inner hearing *113*

Singing posture *114*

Breathing *115*

Jaw, throat, tongue *116*

Vowel and consonant sounds *117*

The Sung *120*

Budget your time *122*

Performance *122*

Selecting Music for Choir   123
  A Part-Singing Hierarchy   124
  Ostinati   125
  Descants   127
  Two-hand singing   128
  Canons   128
  Root singing of the I, IV, and V chords as an
    accompaniment to songs   130
  Two-part singing in contrary motion or imitative   134
  Three-part singing of music in which there are canonic
    and descant-like parts   135
  Two-part singing that is harmonic in character   136
  Chording with folk songs   137
  Three-part harmonic singing   138
  Part songs with unusual or dissonant harmonies   139
  Unison singing   139
Searching for New Music   140
Suggested Assignments   142
Suggested Reading   143

part III
Planning for Musical Learning

INTRODUCTION TO PART III   147

7 CONSTRUCTING CURRICULUM VIA KODÁLY PRINCIPLES   149

The Purpose of Curriculum Construction
    and Evaluation   150
The Teacher: Changing Teaching Behavior   150
The Learner: Facilitating the Learning Process and Evaluating
    Whether Students Have Learned What the Curriculum
    Established for Them to Learn   151

The Content   *152*

Goals for Music Education   *153*

Instructional Objectives   *154*

A Curriculum Construction Outline   *155*

A Long-Range Teaching Plan for Making Children Consciously
      Aware of a New Melodic or Rhythmic Element   *156*

Suggested Assignment   *162*

Suggested Reading   *163*

8 PLANNING AND SEQUENCING FOR MUSICAL LEARNING—LONG RANGE TO INDIVIDUAL LESSON   *164*

One Possible Order for Teaching Musical Concepts
      and Skills   *166*

Planning for Musical Learning   *170*

Outline for a 30-Minute Lesson   *172*

Songs (Arranged by the Position of the ♩. ♪ Figure)   *174*

Summary   *178*

Suggested Assignment   *178*

9 PROBLEMS IN KODÁLY PRACTICE, UNIQUE TO AMERICAN SCHOOLS AND MATERIALS   *179*

The $\frac{6}{8}$ Problem   *179*

What Is Compound Meter? How Is It Different from Simple
      Meter? What Concept Should Children Hold of
      Compound Meter?   *182*

When Should $\frac{6}{8}$ Be Taught?   *182*

The Triple Meter Problem   *186*

Problems Involved in Teaching Low *la* and *ti*   *187*

Duration Syllable Terminology   *190*

Rhythm Names Developed by Pierre Perron   *191*

Suggested Assignments   *192*

10 AMERICAN FOLK MUSIC FOR TEACHING   *193*

Anglo-American   *195*
Black-American   *198*
Musical Characteristics of American Folk Music   *199*
Choosing Folk Songs for Teaching   *200*
    Folk Song Collections   *203*
Suggested Reading   *204*

Appendices

INTRODUCTION TO THE APPENDICES   *209*

A   SONGS TO ACCOMPANY CHAPTER 2   *211*

B   SONGS TO ACCOMPANY CHAPTER 3   *218*

C   SONGS TO ACCOMPANY CHAPTER 4   *236*

D   SONGS TO ACCOMPANY CHAPTER 7   *254*

E   SONGS TO ACCOMPANY CHAPTER 8   *258*

F   SONGS TO ACCOMPANY CHAPTER 10   *265*

G   EXISTING KODÁLY PROGRAMS AND ORGANIZATIONS   *275*

ALPHABETIC LIST OF SONGS   *279*

Preface

Richard Kapp, the distinguished composer and conductor said [1] of Kodály teaching practice that it is not a "concept" but rather "a *context; a space in which things occur.*" He elaborated:

> The single immutable lesson at the heart of Kodály's legacy [is that]: each human being is the source of his own musical experience—indeed of his entire human experience—and as such, has the capacity to choose to share with others and in the experience of others. The greater the "sourcing," the more one is impelled to seek and use and play with further means of experiencing and sharing. Immersion in the game of musical language is complete at every point in time and as the language expands within us, the facility to use it as *our* instrument and extension expands accordingly. Repertoire, the so-called musical elements, everything we include in our definitions of music, becomes an extension of the completion of our experience of what we do and what we encounter. Every experience completed creates more space for experience to occur, *context,* if you will—so that the Great Walls and Maginot Lines are not the barriers to experience we thought them to be. The cycle of experience, creation of space, and experience within space is never-ending and always complete.

[1] Delivered as the keynote address to the annual conference of the Organization of American Kodály Educators, Oakland, California, April, 1979; used by permission.

It is from this insight of Dr. Kapp that I have taken the title of this book, for, to me, Kodály classrooms are truly "a space in which things occur."

For 3 years I had the good fortune to be associated with a program in the schools of the San Jose (California) Unified School District, where, for a time, as many as 3000 children were receiving daily music taught via Kodály principles—taught by music specialists trained intensively in Kodály pedagogy. What those talented teachers provided for the children under their tutelage was truly a musical context—a space in which to experiment, to discover, to grow in music.

One criticism sometimes leveled at Kodály practice is that it is rigid, that it is too narrowly defined in scope and sequence. Yet it is this very rigidity, this knowledge of where one is, where one is going, and how one is going to get there, that makes it possible for the Kodály teacher to create an environment in which musical development can take place.

A researcher who spent many hours evaluating the San Jose Project observed that the existence of well-defined methods and specific teaching sequence seemed, in reality, not to inhibit but to free the Kodály teacher to concentrate on providing a setting conducive to learning. Indeed, the many people who visited this project were struck by the atmosphere permeating every class—the total involvement of the children in the task at hand, the lack of discipline problems, the self-assurance of the students, the total absence of self-consciousness or fear as they dealt with new skills, new experiences, that cycle of experience—creation of space—experience within space, spoken of so eloquently by Dr. Kapp.

This book has grown largely from my work with the teachers in the San Jose Project. All of these teachers used my first book [2] as a basic guide, all had been with me for at least a year of graduate study. However, in a concentrated teaching situation, such as we faced in San Jose, numerous questions arose; questions of sequencing, of materials, of aspects of the pedagogy either not treated or inadequately treated in *The Kodály Method*. It was to answer these questions, and others, that I undertook the writing of this volume. While I have included enough basic information in it so that a teacher may use it without previous Kodály exposure, it is actually intended as a companion volume to *The Kodály Method*.

I should like to thank all the fine teachers of the San Jose Project for their many contributions; particularly, Mary Esposito and Karen Gruber, the first project teachers, and Kathleen Cain and Kathleen

[2] Lois Choksy, *The Kodály Method* (Englewood Cliffs, New Jersey: Prentice-Hall, Inc., 1974).

Jamison who collected and tested with children many of the singing games and dances included in this book.

I wish to express my appreciation also to Holy Names College where for 5 years I enjoyed teaching talented graduate students who came with Ford Foundation Fellowships to develop Kodály teaching skills. The teaching–learning was often a two-way street. I learned much from them.

To Sister Mary Alice Hein, Director of the Kodály Program at Holy Names College and friend of long standing, I offer thanks for the opportunity she gave me to be part of this truly innovative teacher-training program from its inception. This unique experience has greatly influenced my thinking and writing.

Last, but certainly not least, I wish to thank my husband who has acted as critic and sounding board throughout the preparation of this manuscript.

LOIS CHOKSY
Department of Fine Arts
University of Calgary
Calgary, Alberta, Canada

Acknowledgments

Grateful acknowledgment is made to Boosey & Hawkes, Inc. for permission to reprint copyrighted material vital to the writing of this book. In particular, I would like to thank them for permission to reprint the following: Exercise No. 48 from *333 Elementary Exercises* by Zoltán Kodály © 1963 by Boosey & Hawkes, Inc.; "Old Abram Brown" from *Friday Afternoon Songs* by Benjamin Britten © 1936; the arrangement of "Rain, Rain, Go Away" from *Bicinia Americana* by E. Szőnyi (in press); "Ladybird," chorus music for SSA, Octavo 5674 by Zoltán Kodály © 1966.

"Trail to Mexico" from *Folk Songster* by Leon and Lynn Dallin. William C. Brown & Co., Dubuque, Iowa, 1967. Used by permission of the authors.

"John Randolph," "There Was a Little Oak," and "Black Is the Color" from *80 English Folksongs from the Southern Appalachians* by Cecil Sharp and Maud Karpeles. Copyright © 1968 by Faber Music Ltd., London. Used by permission of the publisher.

From *Folksongs of Alabama,* collected by Byron Arnold: "Oh, Johnny," pp. 6–7; "Take Yo' Feet Out de Sand," p. 145; "Remember Me," p. 155. Copyright © 1950 by The University of Alabama Press. Used by permission.

The melody line of "Soundings" from *Steamboatin' Days* by Mary Wheeler by permission of Louisiana State University Press, copyright © 1944.

The melody and words of "The Good Old Man," from *Old Songs and Singing Games* by Richard Chase by permission of Dover Publications, Inc., New York, copyright © 1972.

"Fed My Horse in a Poplar Trough" from *English Folksongs from the Southern Appalachians* (Cecil Sharp) by permission of Oxford University Press, London, copyright © 1966.

"Bye, Baby Bunting" from *Two-Part American Songs* edited by Mark Williams. Copyright © 1977 by Southern Music Company, San Antonio, Texas. Used by permission.

"Rattlesnake," "Shady Grove," and "John Henry" from *Folksongs of North America* by Alan Lomax. Copyright © 1975 by Doubleday & Co., Garden City, New York. Used by permission of the publisher.

"Mary L. MacKay" from *Songs and Ballads from Novia Scotia* by Helen Creighton. Copyright © 1933 by Dent & Sons, Toronto. Used by permission of Miss Creighton.

Singing is the foundation of music in all things.

GEORG PHILIPP TELEMANN
(1681–1767)

*Try to sing, however small your voice, from written
music without the aid of an instrument.*

ROBERT SCHUMANN
(1810–1856)

*If one were to attempt to express the essence of this
education in one word, it could only be*—singing.

ZOLTÁN KODÁLY
(1882–1967)

THE
KODÁLY
CONTEXT

chapter 1

Kodály:
An Overview

KODÁLY: THE MAN BEHIND "THE METHOD"

Zoltán Kodály is known as a twentieth-century composer. Less well known is that he was, also, a many-faceted scholar: ethnomusicologist, linguist, educator, author, and philosopher.

Kodály was born in Kecskemét, a small town in central Hungary, on December 16, 1882, and spent his childhood in the small villages of Hungary—a childhood that no doubt influenced the great love he held for the Hungarian countryside to the day he died. His father, an amateur musician, encouraged the young child's early interest in music. Kodály was composing by the time he was in secondary school. After completing his secondary-school education, Kodály simultaneously entered The Franz Liszt Academy (the country's most prestigious institution of music), where he studied composition, and the University of Hungary, where he took a degree in Hungarian and German and, later, earned a Doctor of Philosophy degree in linguistics.

At that time Hungary was tied politically and economically to Austria and the Hapsburg monarchy. The music of the Hungarian upper classes was Viennese music. German was the language spoken by educated Hungarians. The massive peasant population spoke Hungarian, to be sure, and had a music of its own—a Hungarian music, but this "Hungarian music" went unvalued and largely unnoticed by both professional musicians and the Hungarian ruling class, who made up the concert audiences.

Kodály and his friend and colleague, composer Béla Bartók, turned their backs on this "foreign" music culture in the early 1900s and began to search for the ancient roots of Hungarian music. They made their first folk-song collecting expedition in 1905 and, a year later, arranged and published twenty of the songs they found. Their work was ridiculed by the existing power structure at the Academy, which saw such music as uncultured.

To understand the reaction of their colleagues at the Academy one must realize that before Kodály and Bartók appeared on the musical scene, Hungarian composers had simply imitated the compositional styles and techniques of the other European composers of their times. The operas written by Erkel are reminiscent of those of Verdi. The piano pieces of Liszt did not differ greatly in style from those of Schumann or Brahms. Even the "nationalistic" music (the *Hungarian Fantasy* and the *Hungarian Rhapsodies* of Liszt, for example) that was presented as "Hungarian" music was actually gypsy music arranged and orchestrated in the style of the German masters.[1]

The young Kodály consciously and deliberately set about to free Hungarian art music from the German-Austrian influences that had dominated it for two centuries. His compositions, ranging from arrangements of folk songs to large orchestral and choral works, used the pentatony, the modes, the characteristic rhythms, and the melodic turns he had discovered in Hungarian folk music.

It was the true Hungarian folk idiom, known so well to Kodály through his many collecting expeditions, on which he based his creative work. In rapid succession he produced his *Nine Piano Pieces* (1909), *String Quartet #1* (1909), *Sonata for Violoncello* (1915), *Seven Piano Pieces* (1918), *String Quartet #2* (1918), and *Trio Serenade* (1920). 1910 marked the beginning of Kodály's recognition in Hungary and abroad as a composer.

It was his *Psalmus Hungaricus* (1923), acknowledged as one of the true masterpieces of the twentieth century, that first brought him world acclaim. This magnificent choral work, which recalls melodically the quality of the old Hungarian songs, is set to a poetic paraphrase of the 55th Psalm by the sixteenth-century Hungarian poet Mihály Vég.

Kodály used actual folk tunes he had collected in a number of his works, *Dances of Marosszék* (1930) and *Dances of Galanta* (1933), for example. The latter is a set of variations on eighteenth-century folk melodies from the region where he spent his childhood years.

However, Kodály's genius is most evident in his choral music. In

---

[1] Authentic Hungarian folk music bears no relationship melodically and little relationship rhythmically to the music of the gypsies, even that of the Hungarian gypsies. This is not to say that gypsy music is without worth; simply that it is not Hungarian.

addition to the aforementioned *Psalmus Hungaricus,* his *Mátra Pictures* (1931), *Songs of Karád* (1934), *Jesus and the Traders* (1934), and *The Peacock* (1937) are all masterworks of choral writing.

No mention of Kodály's works would be complete without including his two works for stage, inspired by folk themes, *Háry János* (1927) and *Spinning-Room* (1932). The former, composed in folk style, but not using actual folk music, is a marvelously humorous romp concerning the relationship between the peasant "folk" and the "gentry" in the Viennese Imperial Court during the Napoleonic Wars. The latter work uses beautiful old Hungarian folk songs to tell a tale of Hungarian peasant life.

Kodály continued composing throughout his long life. Later years saw his *Budavari Te Deum* (1936), his *Peacock Variations* (1938), the *Concerto for Orchestra* (1939), and his *Symphony* (1961).

A significant part of Kodály's creative life was devoted to composing for children and young music students; children's choruses: "Whitsunday," "Ladybird," "Christmas Dance of the Shepherds," "Norwegian Girls," and many others; exercises to encourage musicianship: "Let Us Sing Correctly," "15 Two-part Exercises," "333 Elementary Exercises In Sight-singing," "33 Two-part Singing Exercises," "44 Two-part Singing Exercises," and "55 Two-part Singing Exercises." He composed volumes of two- and three-part songs in Hungarian folk style, arranged from easy to difficult: "Bicinia Hungarica," vols. I–IV, and "Tricinia." He also composed for the very young: "50 Nursery Songs" and "Pentatonic Music," vols. I–IV.

During his protracted career as composer, Kodály continued to be interested in folk music and to work actively for its collection and preservation. He wrote two important books on the subject: *Erdélyi Magyarság (Transylvanian Hungarians),* written in collaboration with Bartók and published in 1921, and *A Magyar Népzene (The Folk Music of Hungary),* published in 1937. The scholarly analysis of folk song in this latter work has caused it to receive worldwide notice in the field of ethnomusicology.

Operating under the leadership and direction of Kodály, The Folk Song Research Group, a division of the Hungarian Academy of Sciences, published five massive volumes of Hungarian folk songs, categorized and analyzed. More than 50,000 folk songs are included in the work *Corpus Musicae Popularis Hungaricae.*[2] This work realized a hope and plan Kodály had held since the earliest days of his folk-song collecting expeditions.

Kodály was a highly literate man, well and widely read, and a prolific author on musical subjects ranging from sensitive essays, such as one

---

[2] Zeneműkiadó, vol. I (Budapest, 1951); Akadémiai Kiadó, vols. II–V (1952, 1955, 1959, 1966).

written on the death of Debussy, to articles such as his "Hundred Year Plan" in which he projected Hungarian music education to the year 2000.[3]

In later years Kodály was president of the Hungarian Academy of Sciences, president of the International Folk Music Council, and honorary president of the International Society for Music Education.

In spite of all this, he never lacked time to visit the schools, to advise teachers of children, or to listen to a children's choir. On the day he died, March 6, 1967, he was to have made one of his many elementary school visits.

Children sang at his funeral—a fitting tribute to one who felt that,

> No one is too great to write for the little ones; indeed, one must do his best to be great enough for them.

THE KODÁLY METHOD

What evolved in Hungary under Kodály's guidance, in actuality, is not a method at all, but a life-permeating philosophy of education of which only the pedagogical principles may be said to have "method."

Kodály's educational philosophy, as gleaned through his writings, is:

1. *That true musical literacy—the ability to read, write, and think music— is the right of every human being.*

Without literacy today there can be no more a musical culture than there can be a literary one. . . . the promotion of music literacy is as pressing now as was the promotion of linguistic literacy between one and two hundred years ago. In 1690 . . . [the] idea that everybody could learn to read and write his own language was at least as bold as the idea today that everybody should learn to read music. Nevertheless, this is something no less possible.[4]

. . . it may well be hoped that by the time we reach the year 2000 every child that has attended the primary school will be able to read music fluently.[5]

A five year plan should be fixed for the complete extermination of [musical] illiteracy. In five years it would be possible to achieve a situation where everyone could read at a level appropriate to his age.[6]

---

[3] Some of these many articles, talks, and essays are available in English in *The Selected Writings of Zoltán Kodály* (London: Boosey & Hawkes Music Publishers Ltd., 1974).

[4] Zoltán Kodály, from the Preface to *Musical Reading and Writing*, by Erzsébet Szőnyi (1954).

[5] Zoltán Kodály, "A Hundred Year Plan," Énekszó XIV (1947).

[6] Zoltán Kodály, "After the First Solfege Competition" (Budapest, 1949).

2. *That, to be internalized, musical learning must begin with the child's own natural instrument—the voice.*

It is a long accepted truth that singing provides the best start to music education; moreover, children should learn to read music before they are provided with any instrument.[7]

Even the most talented artist can never overcome the disadvantages of an education without singing.[8]

Individual singing plus listening to music . . . develops the ear to such an extent that one understands music one has heard with as much clarity as though one were looking at a score; if necessary . . . one should be able to reproduce such a score.[9]

If one were to attempt to express the essence of this education in one word, it could only be—*singing*.[10]

Singing without any instrument, free singing, is the really deep training of the child's musical faculties.[11]

3. *That the education of the musical ear can be completely successful only if it is begun early—in kindergarten and the primary grades—even earlier, if possible.*

. . . the years between three and seven are educationally much more important than the later ones. What is spoiled or omitted at this age cannot be put right later on. In these years man's future is decided practically for his whole lifetime.[12]

It is at the kindergarten . . . that the first laying of foundations, the collecting of first, decisive musical experiences begins. What the child learns here, he will never forget: it becomes his flesh and blood.[13]

4. *That, as a child possesses a mother-tongue—the language spoken in his home—he also possesses a musical mother-tongue in the folk music of that language. It is through this musical mother-tongue that the skills and concepts necessary to musical literacy should be taught.*

A person can have only one mother-tongue—musically, too.[14]

. . . the musical education of Hungarian children must be founded on Hungarian music.[15]

---

[7] Kodály, Preface to *Musical Reading*, Szőnyi (1954).

[8] *Ibid.*

[9] *Ibid.*

[10] Zoltán Kodály, from the Introduction to *Musical Education in Hungary*, F. Sándor, ed. (1969).

[11] Zoltán Kodály, "The Popularization of Serious Music," Lecture (1946).

[12] Zoltán Kodály, "Music in the Kindergarten," Lecture (1940).

[13] *Ibid.*

[14] *Ibid.*

[15] *Ibid.*

. . . folk songs are never to be omitted . . . if for no other reason, for keeping alive . . . the sense of the relationship between language and music. For, after all, the most perfect relationship between language and music is to be found in the folk song.[16]

. . . the soul of the child should be nursed on the mother's milk of the ancient Magyar musical phenomenon; . . . a child should not be allowed to learn any other language apart from his mother-tongue until he has consciously mastered this latter, . . . A child nurtured on mixed music will not feel musically at home anywhere, . . .[17]

5. *That only music of unquestioned quality—both folk and composed— should be used in the education of children.*

. . . whatever "lessons" are contained in music which is worthless from an artistic point of view, these works are harmful from the pedagogical aspect, too.[18]

Of foreign music: only masterpieces! There are plenty of them.[19]

Strangely enough, children learn what is good much more easily than what is bad. This, too, is a criterion, Masters! [20]

[The aim of Hungarian music education is] to make the masterpieces of world literature public property, to convey them to people of every kind and rank.[21]

Kodály did not involve himself greatly in developing the pedagogy, the "method," through which his concept was to be achieved. This he delegated to his colleagues, friends, and students. He did express strong feelings on the importance of using moveable-*do solfa* in musical training and the value of pentatony as the starting point for musical instruction. On the use of *solfa,* he said:

. . . solmization, I think, should even precede acquaintance with musical notation. . . . Successions of syllables are easier and more reliably memorized than letters; in addition, the syllable indicates the tonal function and, by memorizing the interval, we develop our sense of the tonal function.[22]

. . . sol-fa needs [to] be continued right up to the highest grade of tuition in both singing and instrumental work, in order that we should read music in the same way that an educated adult will read a book: in silence, but imagining the sound.[23]

[16] Zoltán Kodály, "Ancient Traditions—Today's Musical Life," Lecture (1951).

[17] Zoltán Kodály, "Hungarian Music Education," Lecture (1945).

[18] Kodály, "Music in Kindergarten" (1940).

[19] Zoltán Kodály, "Children's Choirs," Zenei Szemle III (1929).

[20] *Ibid.*

[21] Kodály, "A Hundred Year Plan" (1947).

[22] Zoltán Kodály, *Let Us Sing Correctly* (London: Boosey & Hawkes, 1941).

[23] Kodály, Preface to *Musical Reading,* Szőnyi (1954).

On pentatony, he said:

> The pentatonic [folk songs] are particularly suited to the kindergarten. It is through them that children can achieve correct intonation soonest, for they do not have to bother with semitones. Even for children of eight–nine years of age, semitones and the diatonic scale are difficult, not to mention the chromatic semitones. This latter is difficult even at the secondary school.[24]

> Nobody wants to stop at pentatony. But, indeed, the beginnings must be made there; on the one hand, in this way the child's biogenetical development is natural and, on the other, this is what is demanded by a rational pedagogical sequence.[25]

The system of music education that developed under Kodály's guidance drew on the best of educational thought, past and present, from around the world. From England, where Kodály had visited and been impressed with the quality of choral singing, came the use of movable-*do solfa* (in which *do* is the tonic in major and *la* is the tonic in minor) and a system of hand signs devised originally by John Spencer Curwen (1816–1880). Later, these were somewhat modified and are used today in Hungary as follows:[26]

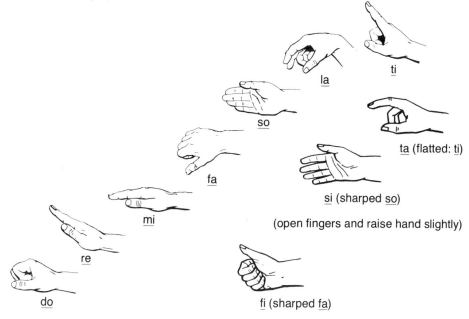

la

ti

so

ta (flatted: ti)

fa

si (sharped so)

mi

(open fingers and raise hand slightly)

re

do

fi (sharped fa)

[24] Kodály, "Music in Kindergarten" (1940).

[25] Kodály, "A Hundred Year Plan" (1947).

[26] These and other techniques mentioned later are treated more fully in: Lois Choksy, *The Kodály Method* (Englewood Cliffs, New Jersey: Prentice-Hall, Inc., 1974).

Kodály, in his writing, has made no specific reference to the use of hand signs. As a part of the methodology, they first appeared in print in Hungary in a book written by Jenő Ádám at Kodály's request.[27] Today hand signs are used by all music teachers in the Singing Primary Schools of Hungary. They not only present a visualization in space of tonal relationships but also appear to establish memory of pitch patterns much more securely than if they are not used.[28]

A system of rhythm syllables—a way of expressing duration aloud correctly—was adapted from the work of French musician and teacher Emile-Joseph Chevé (1804–1864) to aid the reading and writing of rhythms:

These are widely used in Hungary only at the early stages of music instruction. By fourth grade, children can usually read melodies in correct rhythm without first chanting the rhythm.

From Switzerland, certain aspects of the work of Emile Jaques-Dalcroze in eurhythmics were incorporated: stepping the beat, clapping rhythms, performing rhythmic ostinati, rhythmic movement of various kinds. However, unlike Dalcroze practice elsewhere, no piano is used in the Hungarian classroom. The child moves to his own singing.

The teaching–learning process that evolved in the Hungarian schools drew heavily on the work of other educators: Pestalozzi in Switzerland, Kestenberg in Germany; and in many ways foreshadowed the work of Piaget.

Much musical experience precedes symbolization. The teaching order is always sound to sight, concrete to abstract.

At the lowest level the sequencing of concepts is structured to follow child-developmental patterns, beginning with the simplest two- and three-note tunes and simple rhythms of early childhood and adding to them only as the child's readiness is demonstrated.

At later stages, sequence is also suggested by the frequency of occurrence of a particular melodic turn or rhythmic figure in the folk music that comprises the instructional material; and still later, by the need to deal with the complexities of art music.

The pedagogical order for each new learning at each level is *hearing, singing, deriving, writing, reading, creating.*

[27] Jenő Ádám, *Módszeres Énektanítás A Relative Sozlmizáció Alapján* [*Method of Singing Tuition Based on Relative Solmization*] (Budapest: 1944).

[28] See the 1973 doctoral dissertation of Arpad Darazs (Columbia University).

What has made Kodály's ideas so significant in the world of music education? It is just *that*: they are ideas. They are the embodiment of something much larger than a bag of tricks by which to teach. If one were to take away rhythm duration syllables and hand signs, if one removed all the visual aids that have become appendages to the "method"—the felt staves, the sticks, the "flying notes"—if one removed even the *solfa, the ideas would remain*:

- That music literacy is something everyone can and should enjoy.
- That singing is the foundation of all music education.
- That music education must begin with the very young.
- That the folk songs of a child's own culture is his musical mother-tongue and should be the vehicle for early instruction.
- That only music of the highest artistic value (folk and composed) should be used in teaching.

Any pedagogical technique may be misused in the hands of a poor teacher; a philosophy such as the one bequeathed to the world by Zoltán Kodály cannot be.

SUGGESTED READING

The Selected Writings of Zoltán Kodály (London: Boosey & Hawkes Music Publishers Ltd., 1974).

ERZSEBÉT SZŐNYI, *Kodály's Principles in Practice* (London: Boosey & Hawkes Music Publishers Ltd., 1973).

JACQUOTTE RIBIÈRE-RAVERLAT, *Musical Education in Hungary* (Paris: Alphonse Leduc et Cie., 1971) .

FRIGYES SÁNDOR, Ed., *Musical Education in Hungary* (London: Boosey & Hawkes Music Publishers Ltd., 1969).

LOIS CHOKSY, *The Kodály Method* (Englewood Cliffs, New Jersey: Prentice-Hall, Inc., 1974).

KODÁLY
PRACTICE AND
THE YOUNG CHILD

chapter 2

Kodály and Early Childhood Music

What age is early childhood? It may be the three-, four-, or five-year-old in a nursery school situation or it may also include the six-year-old in an area without kindergartens. The steps necessary to bring young children, three-year-olds or six-year-olds, to music are essentially the same. The developmental stages through which the children will pass in acquiring the skills necessary for musical performance—singing, moving, playing, and creating—are the same.

Of course, the six-year-old may have a bit wider singing range than the three-year-old, just as he has a larger speaking vocabulary, but the range is still quite limited and, unless the child comes from a musical family, he may actually be less able musically at six than at three. It is a curious phenomenon that the older children are when they first come to music the more difficult it is to teach them. Anyone who has ever tried to sing with a group of fifth-grade boys who have never had music before is well aware of this fact.

Three-, four-, five-, and six-year-olds are generally open and inquiring. Authorities tell us that the child learns most quickly during the first five years of life. Daily, the child acquires new skills, grows physically, intellectually, socially, and emotionally. His world broadens as he moves from the close family circle to a wider environment that includes other children, other adults. He begins to develop a sense of sex identification and increasingly to pattern behaviors on examples set by others. He is imaginative and creative in play. Attention span, although brief, becomes longer. Very self-concerned at three, the child develops more positive attitudes toward group activities at ages four, five, and six. Abstractions are not easy for the young child. He can think and react best in concrete terms. Physically, large muscles are better developed than small ones. The child becomes increasingly more aware of his body position in space, of itself and in relation to others.

Musically, precise rhythmic movement may present problems for the child initially and he may also have difficulties with pitch matching. The rhythm of the child's natural, self-created chants is duple; it may be either simple or compound duple, it may even shift in the middle of a chant from simple to compound. The tunes the child creates while playing tend to be rather plaintive, in a slow tempo, and sung on an approximation of a minor third or combinations of untuned minor thirds and major seconds. The child's natural singing range (when singing in a head voice, not droning) generally lies between D above middle C and the A or B above, although cultural differences may affect this range.[1] The child's self-started tunes almost always begin with a descending interval and he can rarely sing half-steps in tune.[2]

The implication of these developmental characteristics of early childhood should be far-reaching. They are not recent discoveries, and yet, if one peruses the music textbooks intended for use in kindergarten and nursery schools, it is possible to find example after example of unsingable songs with ranges of an octave or even a 10th, of songs built on ascending scale patterns, of songs in $\frac{3}{4}$ meter. A publisher, once questioned as to why his kindergarten music books had so much material musically unsuitable for young children, answered: "Children don't buy books—teachers do."

That was some time ago. There has been little improvement in school music texts since then, but considerable improvement in teachers. Many teachers have learned to pick and choose musical materials with

[1] There has been some research with young black children that indicates that their early comfortable singing range may be somewhat lower (unpublished conference report, Organization of American Kodály Educators, Pittsburgh, 1976), and with Navajo Indian children that indicates that their early singing range is very high with no evidence of pitch problems (J. Jaccard, "Indian Children," Show Low Schools, Arizona). For the former group this may be a result of the chest voice used in Gospel singing, while the latter may result from the falsetto ceremonial singing of Navajo men.

[2] These musical characteristics of young children have been reported repeatedly by people working in the field: Katalin Forrai, Director of Early Childhood Education in Hungary; Hani Kyoto, Director of the Kodály Institute in Japan; H. Moog, U.S.A.; Ruth Fridmann, Argentina; A. Atanasova, Bulgaria. Also see: Gladys Moorhead and Donald Pond, *Music of Young Children*, vols. 1–4 (Santa Barbara, California: Pillsbury Foundation for Advanced Music Education, 1941–1951).

children in mind and with an understanding of what children can do and what they should learn to do if music is to become a meaningful part of their lives.

What should a music program for the preschool or first-grade youngster include?

1. First, unaccompanied singing. Singing, because the voice is the instrument the child was born with and singing with it is as natural an activity as speaking. Unaccompanied singing, because any accompaniment tends to cover the young child's voice. The child needs to hear his own voice and the voices of the children around him.

2. Moving to music. First, free, expressive movement, then, gradually, the more precise movement of singing games and dances, and, finally, the highly specific movement of responding correctly to beat.

3. Work on developing skills in rhythm and beat. Feel for beat through games, stepping the beat, stamping accent, clapping beat and rhythm patterns, echo-clapping patterns clapped by the teacher and other children. Inventing his own rhythm patterns, clapping or playing rhythm ostinati to familiar songs.

4. Discriminating between comparatives: faster from slower tempi, softer from louder dynamics, higher from lower pitches, different timbres or tone colors. In other words, becoming familiar with the qualities that make music expressive.

5. Ear training and musical memory: the ability to think musical sound and to recall what one has heard.

6. Listening skills. The development of focused listening.

Very young children may be helped in developing a relatively high level of musical concepts and skills in all of the above areas—singing, moving, rhythm, the comparatives, musical memory, inner hearing, and listening—if these skills and concepts are approached through play activities.

IN-TUNE SINGING

In order to sing in tune a child must first hear the sound he is to produce, then, having that sound in mind, produce it vocally, and, last, distinguish whether the sound produced is the same as the sound previously heard. Most children do this to a greater or lesser degree automatically; but there are always a few for whom the process seems to break down at some point. For these, individual help must be given. Nothing less will suffice.

The child who is droning rather than producing a musical sound, the child who is singing at a pitch much lower than that of classmates, must be taught to focus on the sound of a model (teacher or other student) and to try to match that sound. The child must then determine whether what he sang was the same as or different from the singing of the model, and, if different, how different (higher or lower). This process of focusing and matching can only take place in a one-to-one situation. The whole class can be involved in listening and evaluating, but the child with the pitch problem is the one who, in the end, must recognize that problem and act to correct it.

It is absolutely imperative that the teacher in such a situation make mistakes an acceptable part of learning. The child who cannot sing in tune must be made to feel by every action, word, and look that the class and the teacher accept that child as a person, while work continues on the skill. With the example of the teacher before them, young children can be very supportive of each other. Acceptance or rejection must not be fastened to skill performance, or children will be afraid to try anything. The beginner should be helped to realize that correct performance is not achieved without practice.

The teacher must, however, be alert to faulty or incorrect performance. He should never say: "Fine! Fine!" if the performance is not fine. How can the child hope to conquer a problem if he has never been made aware that it exists? It is up to the teacher to help the child, first to perceive, and then to correct the problem.

To this end there are a number of techniques that have proven helpful with young children.

1. Research indicates that the earliest musical interval usually produced by young children is an approximation of a minor third. This being the case, it would seem likely that the out-of-tune singer would be helped by being given a variety of singing experiences using this interval. For example:

  a. Songs built entirely on *so-mi* or *la-so-mi:* "Oliver Twist." (See Appendix A)
  b. Games or individual response activities built on the minor third: "Lemonade."

2. The "oo" seems to be an easier vowel sound for finding pitch than others. Games or songs in which the individual child is called upon to sing a simple response on "oo" may be successful where responses sung on words have not been.

Examples:

1. Cuckoo games.
2. "Skin and Bones."

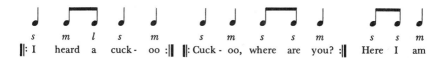

3. The child who is not singing in tune has sometimes not distinguished between the speaking and singing voice. That child's singing is performed on a speech-pitched drone. Some speech therapists have suggested that to correct this it proves helpful to have the child feel the teacher's throat during speaking and singing and then feel his own. (The difference is more noticeable in women's and children's throat movement than in men's.) The teacher may also focus on the difference between speech sounds and singing sounds by saying: "This is my speaking voice"; then singing on a minor-third interval: "This is my singing voice." Several children may repeat the two phrases after the teacher. After each performance, the class should evaluate whether the speech sounds and singing sounds were actually different.[3]

One technique frequently practiced, which seems to hinder rather than aid development of in-tune singing, is that of pitching the teacher's voice where the child's is, trying gradually to step the pitch higher until it matches that of the rest of the class. The problem seems to occur because the child is either droning or singing in a deep-chest voice. A gradual step-by-step rise in pitch is impossible using the drone or chest voice.

4. It is much easier for the child to hear and produce a sharply different sound, i.e., a head tone at a much higher pitch than he has been singing, particularly, if that sound is fastened to something he does not think of as singing. For instance, using the rhyme "Engine, Engine, Number 9," the child could perform a train whistle at the end: "oo-oo-oo."

so-mi-so

Different children in the class could try being the train whistle to see who can make the highest sound. Later, when the child with pitch problems is performing the whistle in a clear head voice, the teacher might have him use the whistle sound to find a starting pitch before singing.

---

[3] This technique has been used successfully for many years by Betty Bertaux, Director of The Children's Chorus of Maryland.

5.   The volume at which children sing is another important factor in fostering in-tune singing. Often the child singing most loudly in a class situation is the one most out of tune. The child is singing so loudly that he cannot hear the others, more in tune, around him. Children sing in tune more easily if they are instructed to sing softly. The young child generally cannot produce a good singing tone loudly.

6.   Tempo also affects the quality of children's singing. Bright, fast ditties are far more teacher- than child-oriented. Even the simple three-note songs of early childhood are often sung by teachers at a tempo too fast for children. A short song may be over before the child with pitch discrimination difficulty has found his first note. Songs should be sung very slowly and clearly for and with young children.

7.   Small-range songs are better for aiding the development of in-tune singing than are larger-range songs. If a child cannot sing three notes in tune there is little point to performing music with an octave range.

8.   The hum is an invaluable tool for establishing pitch awareness. While one hears the voices of others through sound waves, one's own voice is conducted to his hearing principally through vibration of bone and muscle tissue. This sensation is intensified in a hummed sound. The teacher should give the pitch on a neutral vowel ("loo") and the class should *hum* it before singing.

9.   It frequently helps to sing into the right ear of a child with pitch problems. Many times the child's voice will slide to the correct pitch when he hears it so directly given. Also useful are hollow telephone-shaped listening devices like those used by speech teachers. The child covers the left ear with the hand, listens to the pitch, then produces it into the mouthpiece. The sound is carried more directly to his hearing with the device than if it is not used. While the latter technique is useful only in a private one-to-one setting with a child, the former may be practiced in the classroom with the whole class singing. The teacher simply walks among the children as they sing, listening and giving specific help where needed. Unfortunately, the child's voice quite often slides back down when the teacher moves away. However, if the procedure is frequently repeated, a change in the child's ability to correctly reproduce given pitches does take place.

It is important that the singing be done into the *right* rather than the *left* ear. There has been much research in recent years into laterality. One such study, with far-reaching implications, was reported by A. A. Tomatis.[4]

---

[4] A. A. Tomatis, "The Role of Music in the Field of Audio-psycho-phonology," Third International Kodály Symposium (London, Ontario, Canada: 1976).

The two ears do not have the same function . . . one of them has the job of directing all vocal emission. (Tomatis named this the *leading ear*.)

He stated further:

. . . the characteristics of a musical ear concern only the right ear . . . the only one which controls the act of speaking and singing.[5]

10. It sometimes happens that a whole class seems to sing out of tune. When this occurs the probability is that the teacher has not taken the steps necessary to establish the starting pitch firmly before allowing the class to begin singing. The teacher should:

a. sing a complete phrase to recall the song to the children and to estab-lish the tempo
b. give the starting note on "loo" while the children listen
c. have the children hum the same pitch
d. listen to the class intently, i.e., physically portray a listening attitude. (This encourages children to listen also)
e. indicate the beginning of the song with a conducting gesture

All this takes only a few moments, but it can be the difference between good and poor class singing.

11. It is important also that once the class thoroughly knows a song the teacher stop singing with them on that song. Vocal independence can be encouraged only by allowing children to sing without the support of an adult voice.

12. Last, the young voices must not be accompanied by piano at any time. Few instruments offer a worse model for singing than the piano. The model for a voice should properly be another voice, child's or teacher's.

To summarize, in-tune singing may be encouraged by:

1. Singing many songs and games built on the minor third.
2. Using the vowel sound "oo."
3. Focusing on the differences between speech sounds and singing sounds, physiologically and aurally.
4. Using a siren sound or train-whistle sound to move the child's voice to a head tone.
5. Singing softly.
6. Singing slowly and clearly.
7. Choosing only songs of small range (five or six notes).

[5] The present author questions whether the right ear *is* the leading ear in left-handed children.

8. Having the children use the hummed sound to begin the songs.
9. Singing directly into the child's right ear.
10. Establishing the starting pitch firmly before class singing.
11. Having children sing alone and evaluate their own singing.
12. Singing without accompanying instruments; particularly, without piano.

There are a number of competency levels through which a child with real pitch problems must move in learning to sing in tune. At the beginning the child may not be able to voice a musical tone at all. Later, with encouragement and practice, that child may be able to sing a minor third, but it may be at a pitch considerably lower than the one given. Finally, the child will be able to match the third at the given pitch. This does not necessarily mean he will now always sing in tune or be able to sing whole songs in tune. That takes still more practice. But, if there is no voice damage or physical impairment and if the child is given sufficient opportunity to hear his own voice with that of the model he is trying to match, he will sing in tune eventually.

As with any group of any age, the level of performance will vary from individual to individual. Teachers must be aware of this and expect it. Each child's musical growth should be measured in terms of his own starting point, not in terms of some mythical average five- or six-year-old child. A child who learns, in the course of a year, to sing accurately songs that have a wide range and complicated rhythms has undoubtedly made great musical growth. The child who has never been able to distinguish between higher and lower pitches and who suddenly begins singing three-note tunes with relative correctness (albeit a fourth lower than the rest of the class) *also* has made great musical progress.

The extent to which we tend to ignore the development of individual singing was brought sharply into focus a few years ago when the preliminary findings of the National Assessment in Music were released. They showed that across the United States hardly *any* child tested could sing "America" all the way through in tune. This is not a condition music teachers should allow to continue.

MOVEMENT

A second important area of instruction in early childhood music is movement. Movement with the very young child in a Kodály context means moving to the child's own singing. The child's body relates more easily and naturally to self-produced music than to music from an external source, instruments or records.

If one examines collections of young children's game songs (those created *by* children, not those created by adults *for* children), they are full of imagery and imagination. They are highly conducive to creative movement. For example: "Get Your Feet Out the Sand"

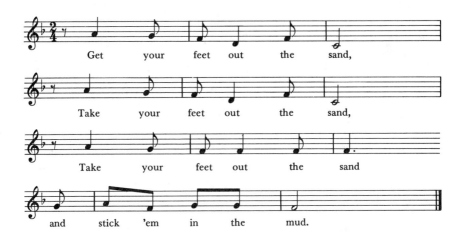

Songs such as this have limitless possibilities, they are open-ended. They do not require a specific dance formation. They can be performed by thirty children or by one child. They *can* be structured (as a circle game, for example) but they do not of themselves *have* structure. One may use them to encourage imaginative free rhythmic response.

The first structured movement to use with young children is the circle game or dance. Young children do not form circles easily or automatically. Some years ago one could be relatively sure that with older and younger children playing games together, the older ones would teach circle formation to the younger ones. Today it is a formation that must be carefully prepared and taught.[6] The child must understand both the shape of the circle overall, and his own spatial relationship *in* the circle— it is really a matter of perception.

One technique which helps this along is for the teacher to take a ball of yarn into the class. Have the children watch the teacher slowly step a circle, dropping yarn behind while stepping. Then have the chil-

---

[6] One reason for this is that today children's leisure-time activities have become so organized by adults that the children no longer have time for their own spontaneous games during which circle formation would, after some time, become automatic. Spending long hours in front of the television set is also a contributing factor toward this loss of spontaneity in children's self-composed games.

dren, a few at a time, take places around the circle, toes on the yarn. (No one may change places once toes have been placed on the yarn.)

The procedure should be followed for three or four class periods. Then one day the teacher should "forget" the yarn and tell the children just to "imagine" it. The teacher should still step the outline of the circle before having the children come up. After this is done successfully, the children should be able to make and maintain a circle formation independently. If a circle becomes lopsided or too small, the teacher should place responsibility for correcting the formation on each individual child. "Look at our circle! Look at your place in it! What can you do to make it better?"

Children's circle games involve several different kinds of movement and several degrees of social skill. Movement and dance will be dealt with more completely in Chapter 3.

In performing singing games and dances children gradually begin to respond more accurately to basic beat. Most games are in duple meter (very few English-language children's games are in triple). However, we do not rely primarily on this material for *teaching* beat, accent, and rhythm. They are very good for *feeling* beat, but many are musically too complex for teaching, i.e., for focusing on and *identifying* beat.

BEAT, METRIC ACCENT, RHYTHM

Let us examine the most basic of all music skills: the ability to correctly identify and perform the beat in music.

There are various learning levels the teacher can expect to see as the young child attempts to acquire this skill. Obviously, at the lowest level the child is unable in any way to show a feeling for beat. This is unusual even in a child of three. Next, a child will probably respond bodily to the fastness or slowness of music—not a specific response to beat at all, but to tempo (for example, a three-year-old bouncing to the music of a park band). Body tapping of some sort to the beat is generally the next level of ability, and, finally, after much practice, the child is able accurately to step to the beat. Much later, the child will be able to step to the beat while clapping rhythm patterns. Children will *progress through these developmental levels at different rates.* In any given class, there may be children at *each* of these levels of development at one time.

This is not the whole story, however. At each of these four levels, (a) unable, (b) gross response, (c) smaller bodily response, (d) highly specific response, there are other factors to consider.

One of these is the *familiarity* of the musical material being used. The child who can successfully step the beat to a song he knows well does not necessarily do the same for music he has never heard before. That requires a much higher level of skill development.

Still another factor is the degree of *dependence* or *independence* with which the skill is performed. A child learning a new skill needs a *model* initially—a teacher or fellow student who has mastered the skill.

The steps toward independence involve:

1. performing the skill within a group situation with a leader
2. performing the skill within a group, but without a leader
3. performing the skill alone

It is this last step—performing alone—that is most often omitted by teachers, yet it is the *most important* step if musical independence is one of the goals of music education.

The materials for teaching beat, metric accent, and rhythm may be classified into three groups. All are duple in meter. Materials from the three categories are used concurrently, but the teaching purpose of each is different.

First, there are those songs, games, and dances that have a pronounced feeling of duple stress, but have complicated rhythm patterns—dotted rhythms, syncopation, etc. ("Wind the Bobbin," "Mighty Pretty Motion," "Walk, Daniel.") Many of the singing games and dances given in the next chapter fall into this category. They are often very good for feeling and stepping beat and metric accent, but are musically too complex for the child successfully to be able to identify, diagram, and label beat specifically.

The second category is that of rhymes and verses. This is a rich and frequently overlooked source for teaching beat.

Queen, Queen Caroline,
    Washed her hair in turpentine,
Turpentine made it shine.
    Queen, Queen Caroline.

Bee, Bee, Bumblebee
    Stung a bear upon his knee,
Stung a pig upon the snout.
    I declare that you are out.

Many nursery rhymes may be useful:

    Baa, Baa, black sheep
        Have you any wool?
    Yes, sir! Yes, sir!
        Three bags full.

    Pease porridge hot,
        Pease porridge cold,
    Pease porridge in a pot,
        Nine days old.

These are all in simple duple meter. However, there are many examples in ⁶⁄₈ which also give a strong duple feeling:

Hickory, Dickory, Dock,　　　　　Jack and Jill
　　The mouse ran up the clock.　　　　Went up the hill
　　. . .　　　　　　　　　　　　. . .

These, like the singing games, are good for feeling the beat, but they are not useful for making concepts about beat conscious knowledge to young children. They are too rhythmically complex for this purpose. They must, however, be part of every child's repertory. English is a language spoken in compound meter; to neglect the rote performance of compound-meter rhymes and songs with young English-speaking children is to ignore the most characteristic rhythmic and metric flow of the mother-tongue. This diametrically opposes the philosophy of Kodály.

The third materials category is children's folk songs and singing games in simple duple meter, absolutely within the young child's singing range and with no rhythmic elements other than quarter notes, eighth notes in pairs, and quarter rests. These comprise the core of teaching songs for beat, metric accent, and rhythm patterns. To adults they may sound dull and repetitious. Children love their repetition. It is this quality that makes them easy to sing.

The songs in this group should be ordered for teaching purposes by the rhythm of the first four beats. These songs may be taught in any order by rote to children, but when the teacher is ready to focus on a specific rhythm pattern with the class, he must have a number of examples, beginning with that pattern, from songs well-known by the children.

This core of songs should include some that begin with four quarter notes, in order to establish very firmly the feeling of one step to one sound as children walk the beat.

SNAIL, SNAIL

Snail, Snail,　　Snail, Snail,　　go　a - round and　'round and 'round.

When beat is being performed with absolute accuracy the teacher may identify one sound on one beat as "ta" and show its symbol "I."

Teaching of patterns other than four quarter notes may follow in an order based upon the frequency of the pattern in the song material and the musical complexity of the pattern. The simplest and most common pattern in young children's music is ♩ ♩ ♫ ♩ :

BLUE BELLS

Blue - bells,   Cock-le - shells,   Ee - vy I - vy   O - ver

While singing songs beginning with this pattern the children should:

1. step the beat
2. clap the rhythm
3. step the beat and clap the rhythm at the same time

The teacher should maintain an audible beat and have the class sing and clap the rhythm to only the first phrase of one song to discover:

1. Is there any beat with more than one sound?
2. Which beat?
3. How many sounds are there on the third beat?

Repeated singings are advisable between questions.

If the children respond accurately to these questions, the teacher may label the two sounds "ti–ti" and show the symbol for them as "⊓".

If the children do not respond correctly, there has not been sufficient preparation. More songs should be taught, sung, stepped, and clapped.

Once ⊓ has been identified on the third beat in songs, it is important to move on quickly to other placements in the measure. Otherwise, the children become so attached to "ta ta ti-ti ta" that it may be their response to all patterns shown or heard.

Although it is less frequent in the song material than some other patterns, ♩ ♫ ♩ ♩ should be the second rhythm taught, since it involves only one new idea—that two sounds may occur on a beat other than the third.

Bye,   Ba - by Bunt - ing

The procedure for teaching it and the questions to be asked are the same as for ♩ ♩ ♫ ♩:

1. Are there any beats with more than one sound?

2. Which beat?

3. How many sounds?

The next conceptual level introduces two sounds occurring on more than one beat in a pattern:

Ring   A- round the   Ro - sy

Again, the same questions as above must be asked.

All patterns of quarter notes and eighth notes should be introduced in this same way; moving from singing, to expressing the beat physically, to clapping the rhythm and identifying how many sounds occur on each beat.

The process is to move from the performed sound to the analysis of that sound, and only then to the visual representation—the symbol for that sound.

The quarter rest (𝄽) is presented in much the same way, with the children discovering that there is one beat with *no* sound.

Bow - wow - wow

Who's   dog art thou?

Metric accent can be taught as soon as children are tapping and stepping beat accurately. Even five-year-olds can feel stressed beats and express them physically. One technique employed successfully by Mary Esposito, Kodály Specialist in the San Jose schools, is to have children remove one shoe and step the beat beginning on the other foot while singing "Deedle Deedle Dumpling." The result is an accented beat where it should be, and much fun for the children.

The importance of teaching children early to distinguish between stressed and unstressed beats cannot be overemphasized. On this skill rests all future understanding of meter.

The pace at which a five- or six-year-old can move through rhythm skill material is breathtaking. The teacher must be on guard not to be so taken with successes in this area that he neglects other areas, such as in-tune singing, where growth is less obvious and sometimes seems so much less encouraging.

THE COMPARATIVES

The comparatives (high-low, soft-loud, fast-slow, and to a lesser degree, different timbres) are those elements in which concepts always involve comparison.

— This song was sung more *softly* than that one; that one was *louder.*
— This tune sounds better *faster;* that one should be *slower.*
— This note (sound) is *higher;* that one is *lower.*
— This instrument produces one kind of sound; that one, another.

Faster-Slower

Because they deal with relatives rather than absolutes, the comparatives are among the easiest of musical concepts for young children to grasp. Even three-year-olds have no difficulty demonstrating faster and slower tempi; chanting "Engine, Engine Number 9" while play-acting a train going up a high hill (slowing down), coming down the other side (speeding up), and pulling into a station (gradually coming to a stop).

Faster and slower in the context of specific beat is more difficult. It can be comprehended only after beat is firmly established *and* is being performed correctly. The children must understand that although the beat is steady and unchanging throughout one performance of a song, it may become faster or slower for the performance of another song, or even for a second performance of the same song. The most appropriate tempo for a song should be drawn from the children.

In teaching faster-slower comparison, the following technique may be useful. The teacher establishes and maintains a steady beat at a moderate tempo. The children sing a familiar song, tapping the beat with the teacher.

Teacher: "Listen to my tempo." (Tap 8 beats noticeably faster than before.)

Children sing and tap the beat for the same song at the new tempo.

Teacher: "Was my new beat faster or slower than before?"

Children reply.

Teacher: "Listen to my new tempo." (This time tap the beat noticeably slower than at the first performance of the song.)

Children sing and tap the beat, following the new tempo.

Teacher: "Was my new beat faster or slower than before?"

Children reply.

When the class can do this accurately, individual children should be asked to sing, following various tempi established by the teacher. The rest of the class should listen intently to determine whether the child singing alone stayed exactly on the beat and followed the new tempo correctly.

When children can identify and perform a variety of tempi, the only remaining skill in this area is that of discriminating which tempo is appropriate to a given song.

Teacher: "What beat shall we use for this march? How fast do our feet step in a parade?" or "How fast shall we sing this lullaby? What tempo will help the baby go to sleep?"

Softer-Louder

Softer-louder is a somewhat more complex concept. The terms *softer* and *louder* should be taught through songs. The teacher should elicit from the children whether a softer or a louder singing voice is appropriate to each particular song or part of a song. For example: [7]

"Hey, Betty Martin"
 — How should we sing the verse that says "tiptoe, tiptoe"?
 — How shall we sing the verse that says "stamp-stamp"?
"Night Herding Song"
 — What are some of the problems facing cowboys? (stampedes, etc.)
 — How should the cowboys sing to the cattle to calm them down at night?
"Old Mr. Rabbit"
 — How would you sing if you were mad at the rabbit?
 — How would you sing if you were sneaking up, trying to catch the rabbit?

[7] Taken from lessons taught by Robin Goodfellow.

The soft-loud and fast-slow comparatives are not thoroughly learned unless the children can combine them successfully. They might sing "Poor Little Kitty Cat"

— softly and very slowly
— loudly and faster
— softly and faster
— loudly and slower

This kind of activity should be done both by the class as a whole and by individual children. The teacher can be sure of each child's level of understanding only by having each child perform alone at some time.

Higher-Lower

Of the comparatives, higher-lower is the most difficult to teach. It presents a unique problem because of inexact language usage. Children do not really have difficulty singing in a higher voice or a lower voice if given a model to imitate by the teacher's voice. However, if *told* what to do, they frequently confuse "high" with "loud" and "low" with "soft." The reason is semantic. In spoken English, pitch terminology is often used to express volume or direction: "Turn that TV *down lower* (for softer). Turn the radio *up higher* (for louder)." The result of such language usage is that when children come to a highly specific musical meaning of the terms "higher" and "lower" they are confused.

There are ways to alleviate this confusion, if not to eliminate it altogether. First, the musical concept *softer-louder* should have been taught thoroughly before introducing the terms *higher-lower*. If children have repeatedly demonstrated their ability to sing a song softer or louder when requested to do so by the teacher, they are less likely to confuse these terms with pitch terms later. In addition, the teacher must be careful to refer to pitches using only the pitch terminology "higher and lower" and asking:

not: "Can you make your voice go up (down)?"
but: "Can you make your voice go higher (lower)?"
not: "Does the tune go up or down here?"
but: "Does the tune go higher or lower here?"

Any inconsistency in a teacher's use of these terms makes learning more difficult for children. There is a specific musical meaning attributed to *higher-lower* that differs greatly from the meaning in daily speech. Children can understand and correctly use those terms in a musical context only if they are used correctly by the teacher.[8]

As with in-tune singing, to which it bears an obvious relationship, the skill of distinguishing higher from lower pitches is attained by young children only after they have moved through several learning stages. Some children move through these stages quickly, with little or no help from the teacher. Many, however, need much guidance in order to acquire the skills necessary for pitch discrimination.

At the earliest stage, the teacher may simply lead the children to sing some songs in higher and some in lower keys within their comfortable range. It is not necessary to draw attention to these key changes. Later, the group can be led to perform the *same* song at a higher and then at a lower key placement. At this time the teacher should ask: "Was our song higher or lower the second time we sang it?" This activity should be repeated frequently, until the children are secure in the correctness of their responses.

At a more advanced level, when the class has sung a song they know well, the teacher might say: "Johnny, would you sing it alone for us; and sing it beginning at a higher (lower) place?" If Johnny understands the musical use of the terms higher and lower (assuming that he can sing in tune), he will be able to do so.

Only after the above activities are easy for the children, should the teacher focus on higher and lower pitches within one song. Choosing a song containing a very obvious high and low—an octave jump—encourage the children to show, with large arm movement, where the tune is highest and lowest:

    s,   s   s,   s,   s   s   s,
    The first one, the sec-ond one

From the octave move to the perfect 5th:

           s   s   d
    Flea died, Johnny cried, Tee hee hee

Finally, incorporate the minor third and major second intervals that make up most of the early childhood songs:

    s   l   s   m
    Bounce high, Bounce low

---

[8] Dr. David Woods, Professor of Music at Iowa State University, has suggested that with older students we might more accurately refer to sound wave frequency. Higher notes would become "sounds of higher frequency," lower notes, "sounds of lower frequency." In today's electronic world, this approach has much to commend it.

Have the children both show with motions and express with the words "higher" and "lower" where the tune moves higher and where it moves lower.

The steps toward intervallic identification, in increasing specificity, are:

1. This way of singing this song is higher (lower) than the way we sang it before.
2. In this song this pitch is the highest, that pitch the lowest. (The example must contain an obvious highest and lowest.)
3. In this interval this is the higher (lower) of these two pitches.

When children have reached this last level of pitch discrimination, simplified notation may be introduced. Pictorial symbols (stars for "Starlight, Starbright," snails for "Snail, Snail") may be placed by children on a felt board in a pattern that graphically represents the higher and lower pitches they are singing. Later, the teacher should assess the children's ability to distinguish higher from lower pitches by singing random four-note patterns. First on octaves, then 5ths, and last, minor thirds, having individual children place felt cutouts or magnetic objects on a board to represent the order of higher and lower sounds. For example, the teacher might sing on *loo*:

1. 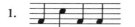   2.

One child at the board would move four symbols to show which sounds were relatively higher and which lower:

1.    2.

When most children in a class can do this accurately, the teacher may begin to fasten *solfa* to the minor third sound. This level of proficiency in intervallic hearing is not common in American school children below the age of six, even when they have had extensive kindergarten musical experience.

TIMBRE

Although musical timbre may seem a very advanced concept to teach the very young, it is not uncommon for a five- or six-year-old to be able to recognize the singing voice of every classmate, as well as a number of instrumental sounds, through timbre. By making a game of voice recognition the teacher may encourage this ability. Numerous children's games are based on hiding some object which the child who is "it" must then find. It is easy to add on a simple call–response to these games. For example:

	s m m s s
Call (by "it"):	"Who has the but-ton?"
	s m m s s
Response (by one with button):	"I have the but-ton."

Have the child who is "it" hide his eyes during the game and call–response. The child must then name who has the button (or key, or handkerchief) simply by voice recognition. At the beginning many mistakes are made. Within a matter of days the children become so adept at recognizing each other's voices that it becomes necessary for the child answering to disguise his voice.

Instruments may be used in a similar way. The child with eyes closed must determine which rhythm instrument is being played, solely by its sound. Tone blocks and sticks, or hand drum and bongos, have a very similar sound, but children quickly learn to distinguish between them aurally.

Children should be encouraged to experiment with sound sources. What kind of sound does an empty box make when struck? A string tied to a board when plucked? A string tied to a board over an empty box? Basic principles of sound may emerge from such experimentation.

MEMORY TRAINING

At the preschool and first-grade levels, when children appear to have difficulty remembering songs, it may be due to the way in which the songs are initially taught. Musical memory is a learned skill and one that children can be led to acquire. The rote song process, properly practiced, can greatly aid the acquisition of this skill. This process, as practiced by many Kodály teachers, is as follows:

1. The teacher sings the entire song, musically, giving attention to phrasing and dynamics.
2. Teacher and children discuss any words or meanings that may not be clear to the children.
3. The teacher sings the first phrase *while the children listen.*
4. The children echo the first phrase *while the teacher listens.*

5. The teacher sings the second phrase *while the children listen.*
6. The children sing the second phrase *while the teacher listens.*
7. The teacher sings both the first and second phrases *while the children listen.*
8. The children sing back both the first and second phrases *while the teacher listens.*

The same process is followed for the third and fourth phrases (the usual children's song being four phrases in length). At that point:

9. The teacher sings the entire song again while the children listen, singing along *inside their heads.* (Concentration may be improved if the children close their eyes.)
10. The children sing the entire song *alone.* The teacher listens and gives voice help only where there is uncertainty.

The most pertinent point about this process is that children *listen* when the teacher sings and teacher *listens* when the children sing. It is this highly-focused listening, combined with repetition, that makes the difference between a song well-learned and one half-learned.

Another technique to aid memory training is to give only one part of a song—the melody or the rhythm—and to ask the class to identify the song and sing it back. For example, instead of telling the children what the next song is going to be, sing its first phrase on "loo" and call on one child to sing it back with words. Or, clap the rhythm of a song known well by the children. Ask one child to name it and sing the first phrase.

The above tasks may seem easy, but they involve learned skills. In a testing program involving more than 400 first- and second-grade children in the schools of San Jose, with no previous musical training, less than 10 percent of them correctly identified the song "Jingle Bells" when it was sung on a neutral syllable. Most knew it when it was sung with words.

In the later part of first grade and in higher grades, when the rhythm symbols ♩, ♫, and 𝄾 are known, memory games may be played with sixteen-beat rhythm patterns on the board, by erasing a measure at a time, while the children continue to clap and say the entire exercise.

INNER HEARING

Of all musical skills, inner hearing is perhaps the most important. One cannot produce a musical sound without first thinking that sound.

It is this process of thinking sound that we refer to as *inner hearing.* Like memory training, it is a skill that can be taught.

While there are many techniques suitable for improving inner hearing in older students (see Chapter 6), the one most useful with younger children is "hiding the song." On a signal from the teacher the children must hide the song in their heads, maintaining a quiet steady beat, i.e., singing inside without making any audible sound. On a second signal they resume singing aloud. If they are in the right place in the song, they have "heard" the song in their heads. Initially, it is best to do this phrasewise. Later the children will become so adept at it that the teacher will have to try to "catch" them in the middle of phrases or even words. If children have difficulty with this process, have them clap the rhythm of the parts of the song they are inner hearing.

LISTENING TO MUSIC

At what point did "listening to music" in the classroom become synonymous with putting a needle down on a record? Whatever happened to the parent or teacher who used to *sing* to children? Singing, not to have them learn the song, but to have them hear it. How much more natural a listening experience this is for both child and teacher. Recordings are cluttered with instrumentation and are invariably too fast for young children.

Begin or end a music period by singing a soft lullaby. Sing a ballad just for the enjoyment of the story it tells. It is possible to stop between verses and discuss the story without worrying about where to put the needle back down.

Learning to listen is one of the most sadly neglected skills in the schools. The child must be taught to listen critically to his own voice, to the voices of classmates, to the voice of the teacher, and to live instruments played by the teacher, other students, or members of the community.

CONCLUSION

If the program outlined here seems ambitious, examine it in terms of one infant song. What different activities might a group of five-year-olds perform while singing "Ring Around the Rosy"? What would be the teaching purpose of each of these activities? It hardly needs to be said that the children's purpose and the teacher's purpose for an activity are not necessarily the same.

Activity	*Teacher's Purpose*
Sing the song, play the game.	To provide relaxation after one period of concentration and before another. To teach circle formation. To help each child perceive a spatial relationship in a game formation and to respect that of the others.
Individual children sing alone.	To give help with in-tune singing.
Sing the song, step the beat—group and individuals.	To assess the children's ability to identify and step the beat; to help those with problems.
Sing the song, clap the way the words go.	To assess the children's ability to identify and perform rhythm.
Sing the song, tap the beat. At a given signal switch to clapping the rhythm.	To assess how well the children distinguish between beat and rhythm.
Sing the song, step the beat, stamp on accented beats.	To prepare for later teaching of meter and measure.
Step the beat; change direction at each phrase ending.	To teach phrase length. To have the children derive the number of phrases in the song; the number of beats in each phrase.
Sing the song phrase by phrase. Choose felt shapes to diagram which phrases are alike, which different.	To prepare for teaching form.
Sing the song softer, louder; faster, slower; as a group, as individuals. Decide how it sounds best.	To assess whether the children understand the terms *softer-louder, faster-slower*. To encourage musical discrimination.
Sing it in higher key placements; lower key placements. Tell which are higher; which lower.	To assess the children's understanding of *higher-lower* in its musical use.
Listen to the last phrase "All fall down." Place three cut-outs on a felt board to show which sound(s) is (are) higher and which lower.	To prepare for later specific intervallic identification (*s-d*).
Sing the song. At a signal "hide the tune in your head." Sing aloud again at a second signal.	To develop musical inner hearing.

If the children were six-year-olds, still other activities might be added:

Clap an ostinato while singing the song.	To develop the ability to hear and perform two different musical ideas at the same time.

Activity	*Teacher's Purpose*
Derive and sing the rhythm in duration syllables (*ta*'s and *ti*'s).	To use the rhythm language of Kodály as an aid to reading and writing musical sounds.
Sing the first three phrases in *solfa* and with hand signs.	To use kinesthethics as an aid to in-tune singing. To give practice with singing in syllables.
Construct the first phrase's rhythm with sticks.	To prepare for later music writing.
Construct the first phrase's melody on felt staves.	To prepare for later music writing.
Given a set of four flash cards in scrambled order, arrange them to show the rhythm of the song.	To give practice with sequencing and independent rhythm recall (memory training).
Still later, in second grade, perhaps:	
Find the lowest note in the song.	To make the new note *do* and its hand sign known to the children.
Sing the song as a canon.	To prepare for later part singing.
Improvise a melodic motif to be sung as an ostinato with the song.	To use the known musical vocabulary to create new patterns.

Surely there are other valid musical activities not mentioned here. The point is that one simple infant song contains within it all the teaching potential one could possibly require for working effectively with young children. Thirty or forty such songs can be the core of a solid music-education program for any nursery school or kindergarten.

A music program for early childhood must contain many of the ingredients of a comprehensive music program for any age level. The subject is the same—music. The skills and concepts involved in comprehensive musicianship can be dealt with at many levels. The early years (three to six) are among the most important ones developmentally. Teachers must take advantage of these years.

SUGGESTED ASSIGNMENT

1. List musical characteristics of young children. Choose a kindergarten or first-grade series song book. Analyze its song material in light of what is known about these characteristics. Evaluate the book as a possible basic song book. List its strengths and weaknesses.

SUGGESTED READING

MARILYN P. ZIMMERMAN, *Musical Characteristics of Children* (Washington, D.C.: Music Educators National Conference, 1971).

GLADYS MOORHEAD and DONALD POND, *Music of Young Children,* vols. 1–4 (Santa Barbara, California: Pillsbury Foundation for Advanced Music Education, 1941–1951). [Reissued in one volume in 1978.]

KATALIN FORRAI, "Music-Teaching in Nursery Schools," in *Musical Education in Hungary,* ed. Frigyes Sándor (London: Boosey & Hawkes Music Publishers Ltd., 1969), pp. 89–106.

H. MOOG, "The Development of Musical Experience in Children of Pre-school Age," *Psychology of Music,* 4, no. 2 (1976), 38–45.

chapter 3

Movement and Dance in Kodály Practice

MOVEMENT IN HUNGARY

László Vikár, Hungarian ethnomusicologist and colleague of Kodály, says that:

Instinctive music is always accompanied by movement.[1]

He goes on to tell that in collecting folk songs, he has found that the country people, from whom he collects, frequently have to stand to sing because they cannot recall words and tunes without the traditional accompanying gestures, dance steps, and turns. He commented that:

The two [song and movement] were welded together so much that [the singers] could not abstract one from the other.

Movement is a part of music education in Hungary from the earliest levels. It is not the so-called creative movement to recorded music or piano practiced in so many American kindergartens—a "creativity" which is usually little more than imitation and response to teacher- or TV-implanted suggestion. It is, rather, movement as a natural accompaniment to singing. It involves, for the youngest children (three-, four- and five-year-olds in the nursery schools and kindergartens), accompanying

---

[1] László Vikár, in a paper "Folk Music and Music Education," delivered at Balatonszéped (Budapest: Hungarian Academy of Sciences, 1969).

songs with such simple actions as walking, running, jumping, hopping, stamping; acting out the words to song-stories and singing games; using body gestures (knee slapping, clapping, tapping, bending) to emphasize the rhythmic quality of a song; performing simple dance steps traditional to particular songs.

As Hungarian children move through the grades of the Singing Primary School, they add movement skills and dance forms needed for songs and singing games appropriate to their developmental levels: partner choosing, arch forming, role playing and changing, circle dances, spiral dances, line dances, partner dances; each is treated and learned through song.

The Czardas, the national dance of Hungary, is taught early. Second and third graders can perform its simple steps quite acceptably. By fourth and fifth grades, in some of the schools fortunate enough to have a fine dancer on their faculty, special folk-dancing classes are offered, separate from the daily music class. The author had opportunity to work in one of these for a period of several months, observing the classes of Eva Karcagi in Szekesfehevar. The artistry of this teacher and these children (fourth to eighth grades) in performing the traditional Hungarian dances was incredible. Recorded music was used, as folk instruments are still used to accompany dancing in Hungarian villages. However, the children never ceased to sing. As the old peasants spoken of by Vikár could not recall words and music without steps, the youngsters in folk-dance classes seem to need words and tune to recall steps.

Is there any pertinence in this to American music education? In America, with its polyglot population and its lack of reverence for the past, is there any "national" American dance comparable to the Czardas in Hungary? Is there any tradition of singing games and movement-oriented songs similar to those found in Hungary? The answer on both counts must be a resounding "Yes!"

THE HISTORIC ROOTS OF DANCE IN AMERICA

No folk tradition in the United States has been as uninterrupted as that of movement and dance. No other folk art is as widely practiced and enjoyed today. There are literally thousands of square dance organizations; no state in the union is without a large number of them. There are, in addition, numerous country-dance societies and countless groups dedicated to the preservation and performance of other specific forms of dance: the contra dance, the reel, the jig. There are ethnic groups performing polkas, mazurkas, schottisches, galops, and jigs.

These groups cut across age and social station. It is not uncommon to see a sixty-year-old dancer with a fourteen-year-old partner; a plumber dancing with a college professor. Proficiency with the dance is a great equalizer.

American folk dancing is descended primarily from two great traditions of dance—the English and the French.

On the English side, its oldest anscestor is probably the Morris Dance, in existence before the fifteenth century. In it, six men, each wearing a leather strip of bells around their calves, danced with vigorous hops and kicks, so that the bells sounded throughout. The patterns through which they moved bear strong resemblance to patterns still existent in American square and contra dances: forward and back, weave the ring, pass through. Music was supplied by a bagpiper.

By the sixteenth century in England, dancing had become a popular pastime, and women were allowed to dance with the men. Circle dances and "longwayes for as many as wille" were danced on the village green to the music of a piper. These dances were the precursors of the present-day contra dance and quadrille. The dancers moved through the figures with light running steps, skips, high leaps, and buoyant walking steps.

It was the longways dance, however, that actually contained the rudiments of almost every square dance pattern. It was the longways country dance that traveled to France and merged there with the French court-dance tradition to produce some of the patterns still performed today in American square dancing: right and left through, ladies chain, Texas star, bend the line, circle, swing, balance, allemande left. The *country dance* of England became the *contredanse* of France. While the English term referred to all dance performed in the "country" (of circle, line, or square formation), the word "contre" in the French referred to the dance formation of line facing line. This came to America as *contra dance*. Contra dances were very much a part of colonial life in America.

The square formation used in earlier times had almost died out by the eighteenth century in England, when it reappeared as an import from France, the *contredanse francaise*. It was not a contredanse in the French sense at all. It was a square dance. The name given to it later by the English was *cotillon*—a word meaning *petticoat,* presumably so named because the women's petticoats showed during the dancing.[2]

Still later, this cotillon became the *quadrille*. Anyone observing a performance of the quadrille today would have difficulty distinguishing it from a modern square dance by its steps performed in a square set of

---

[2] Cotillon became *cotillion* in America, and came to mean an elaborate dance party.

four couples: forward and back, right and left through, balance four, ladies chain, grand right and left. The music, however, was very different: tunes from operas or works of well-known composers of the day, played by orchestras of strings and woodwinds.

By the middle of the nineteenth century the steps of these quadrilles had become so involved that a prompter was needed—someone to remind the dancers what step or formation was coming next—in a word, the ancestor of today's square dance *caller*.

During all of this, what was happening to dance in America?

Many of the dances of England and France came directly to America with the early settlers. Courtly dances were danced by Washington and Jefferson in the ballrooms of Virginia mansions. Country dances accompanied weddings, house raisings, sheep shearings, even religious ordination ceremonies. Dancing masters taught throughout the colonies. If a village was too small for a resident dancing master, it was served by an itinerant one. These "masters" taught the minuet and the quadrille and the popular country dances of the day.

The music they danced to is in itself a capsule of American history: "The Green Mountain Volunteers," "Jefferson and Victory," "Washington's Quick Step," "Hull's Victory," "The Singing Quadrille," all developed during these early days. Instead of dancing to composed European dance music, people began to dance their quadrilles to familiar American folk tunes: "Captain Jinks," "The Girl I Left Behind Me," "Yankee Doodle." And somewhere along the line the country fiddler took the place of the European quadrille orchestra.

As the peoples of America moved westward, their dances moved with them. At various times and in various places in America the Puritan influence was evident. The belief that instrumental music and dancing were the work of the devil was first manifest in New England, although it was short-lived there. It surfaced again in the Midwest with such strength that dance *as dance* was forbidden. Instead of dancing, people went to a "party" on Saturday night, where they "played" games. The American *play-party game* was born; a dance done entirely to the singing of the dancers. Some of these are so ancient in their roots as to be literally untraceable.

With the rising popularity of couple dances in the late 1800s and early 1900s, the contras and quadrilles were pushed to the background and all but forgotten, except in the more remote towns and villages.

The beginning of the tremendous resurgence of dance in twentieth-century America can be directly traced to two people: a Colorado school superintendent, Dr. Lloyd Shaw, and the automobile magnate Henry Ford. Like the ancient Greeks, Shaw believed dancing to be an essential part of the education of the child. He had been using European folk dances with his students, but felt that more characteristically American dances would be preferable. At this time (1925) Mr. and Mrs. Henry Ford, as part of their Dearborn (Michigan) historic re-creation, Greenfield Village, decided to support a study of the American heritage in dance. They hired Benjamin Lovett to teach dance at Greenfield and to research and write on the subject. The result was the book *Good Morning*[3] containing music and dance directions for the early quadrilles, singing squares, circle dances, contra dances—all of the old dances of America except the Western Square. Lloyd Shaw, and many others in the United States, clutched at this small volume, and the American folkdance revival was under way. Shaw, however, was concerned by the omission of the Western Square dance in this work and, to correct this omission, began to collect and write down all that he could find on it. In 1939, he published his *Cowboy Dances*[4] presenting the square dance as he had seen it performed throughout the West. Then, not content with merely writing, Shaw traveled the length and breadth of the country teaching square dancing and training callers.

Today in the United States there are callers' "colleges," journals of folk dance, and state and national folk-dance and square-dance conventions. Millions of Americans are dancing the dances researched and taught by Benjamin Lovett and Lloyd Shaw. American dance has come into its own.

Just what is, or should be, the role of the school in all this? What connection is there, or should there be, between movement as it might be included in the music curriculum for a five-year-old, an eight-year-old, or a twelve-year-old, and this resurgence of folk dancing in America? A great deal more than one might suspect at first glance.

The creative movement of young children, the infant singing games and dances, contain the kernels of adult folk dance. Indeed, a movement curriculum may be arranged so developmentally, so gradually sequentially, that actual dance becomes simply an extension of known and loved games. It is such a developmental sequence that the author would like to suggest in the remainder of this chapter.

MOVEMENT AND THE YOUNG CHILD

Maria Montessori, founder of the *Casa dei Bambini* in Rome (and the Montessori schools everywhere), observed in young children something she referred to as *sensitive periods*—a transient time of special

---

[3] Mr. and Mrs. Henry Ford, *Good Morning* (Dearborn, Michigan: 1926).

[4] Lloyd Shaw, *Cowboy Dances* (Caldwell, Idaho: The Caxton Printers, Ltd., 1939).

sensitivity toward specific skills, limited to the acquisition of *those* skills.[5] If the skill was not acquired during this period the special sensitivity disappeared and any later attempt to acquire the skill required much greater effort. Dr. Montessori found children between the ages of three and six to be particularly sensitive to both movement and singing; she further discovered that body movement contributed to the acquisition of skill in singing.[6]

The importance of beginning early with both singing and movement cannot be too greatly stressed. A number of activities related to both were given in Chapter 2 on early childhood. The author should like to focus on the structure inherent in young children's movement activities. If the child understands the possibilities available, he will be more imaginative, more creative in the ways in which he moves to music. There are only so many different ways of moving, whether that movement is in an infant game or in a formal adult dance. The child needs to become aware of his own body—that he can move arms, legs, head, fingers, hips; that any part can move to the music. He needs to be made aware of the other bodies around him, of the spaces they occupy, and of the space he can occupy in a game or dance. He needs to know how he can move his feet—walk, run, skip, gallop, hop, leap—and be able to determine which kinds of stepping best suit which songs. He needs to know movements that do not require physically changing his place— body movements such as sway, bend, stretch, twist, bounce, that can be done in one spot.

At the earliest levels, activities should be relatively unstructured. The child can move arms, torso, legs, head, hands, or feet *in place* rhythmically as suggested by the character, tune, or words of the song he is singing or rhyme he is chanting. He can rock the baby ("Bye Lo, Baby O"), shoo the rain away ("Rain, Rain Go Away"), see-saw or row the boat ("Bobby Shaftoe"), or stretch high and bend low ("Bounce the Ball to Shiloh").

Free movement in space can follow: walking ("Walk Daniel"), hopping ("Hop Old Squirrel"), tiptoeing ("Hey, Betty Martin"), and various other ways of stepping (gliding, galloping, skipping). Through these songs and others the child should be led to discover the possibilities of the surrounding space—that he can move forward, backward, sideways, higher, and lower. This exploration of body rhythms and external space should precede the teaching of formal game patterns.

---

[5] Elise Braun Barnett, *Movement and Music* (Schocken: 1973).

[6] Strangely enough, in view of the above, instead of using children's singing as the stimulus for movement, most Montessori schools use composed music played on the piano.

The child should, as well, be taught to respond correctly to tempo (faster or slower), to flow (smooth or abrupt), and to weight (heavy or light). He should have opportunity to move alone, with one or two other children, and with the whole group.

All of these kinds of experiences, introduced initially through songs, can be reinforced through traditional singing games. The two most basic formations used in children's singing games are the circle and the facing lines. Each has its own hierarchy of skills, from easy to difficult. Although circle and line games should be intermixed for variety and interest in teaching, they will be separated here in order to make clearer the progression of skills in each.

Circle Games and Dances

The largest number of singing games of very young children are circle games. They can be divided roughly into:

1. Acting-out games
2. Partner-choosing games
3. Chase games
4. Winding games

Of these, the first, the acting-out circle games, are the easiest and require the least dance skill and social maturity. They can usually be performed with some modicum of skill even by three-year-olds. "Oats, Peas, Beans and Barley Grow" and "Here We Go Round the Mulberry Bush" are two well-known examples of this genre; "Little Sally Water" is another.

Acting-out games

Acting-out games are beloved by young children, perhaps because they offer opportunity to mimic adult-life situations. They can involve such simple operations as "wash my face" or "iron the clothes," but they often deal with profound subjects in a light and childlike way. Birth, death, and marriage occur as the subjects of more than one game: "When I Was a Young Girl," "Old Rodger Is Dead," "Jenny Jones."

Partner-choosing games

Partner-choosing games require a higher level of social maturity than acting-out games. Anyone who has ever watched a five- or six-year-old try to "choose a partner" knows how slow and fraught with indecision this process may be. Some beautiful examples of this type of game are "Blue Bird, Blue Bird, Go Through My Window," "Green Grows the Willow Tree," "O Green Fields Roxie," "Go In and Out the Window," "Circle Round the Zero"; there are many others. The easiest of these can be done with very young children, but as a general rule they are better suited to the six- and seven-year-old.

Chase games

Chase games are even more difficult since they involve both choosing someone and then running to get to the "safe" place before being caught by the one chosen. Perhaps best known of these games is "A-Tisket A-Tasket"; some others that children enjoy are "Charlie Over the Ocean," "Little Swallow," "Cut the Cake." Children become wildly excited when playing chase games. There is an element of truly delicious fear involved in them. The "cat" must not catch the "mouse"; the "little bird" must get back to his place in the circle to be "safe."

Of all children's games, chase games are the ones most distorted by teachers. The author has observed classrooms in which the cat and mouse were not allowed to run but had to "walk quietly"; where the watching children in the circle had to be silent rather than give voice to their excitement. Nothing will kill love of singing games more quickly than this sort of misuse. It is natural for children to run; it is desirable for them to voice their excitement. They will come to order quickly enough afterwards; after all, they want to resume the game.

Winding games

No discussion of early childhood circle games would be complete without a mention of winding games. These interesting dance formations exist in many variations, from relatively simple to extremely complex, and are found in many cultures. On the simplest level ("Wind the Bobbin"), one child breaks the circle and starts walking in ever-smaller spirals as the group follows. When the "bobbin" is wound so tightly the children can no longer move, they "break it" and scatter in all directions. More complicated, but still loved by five- and six-year-olds, is the *wind and unwind*, such as in "Snail Snail" and "Stoopin' on the Window." Variants of the winding game, suitable for older children, are "Wind Up the Apple Tree" and "The Alley Alley Oh."

Circle games for kindergarten and primary grades should incorporate all the above.

Double-circle games

For youngsters in grades 4, 5, and 6 there are circle dances based on the movements learned in these earlier circle games. Fourth graders who have had experience with stepping in a circle, with partner choosing, or with arch forming, will have little difficulty with "double-circle" games such as "Turn the Glasses Over," "The Jolly Miller," "Great Big House in New Orleans"; and the double-circle game paves the way for the many circle dances that use square dance patterns: "Shake Them Simmons," "Old Brass Wagon," "Knock the Cymbals." If these are taught in fourth grade, fifth and sixth grades may be spent learning and performing basic square-dance formations.

Up to the point of traditional square dancing, all movement can and should be done to the children's own singing. When square dancing is introduced, the music may still be sung (in keeping with the tradition of singing quadrilles and play-party games), but recorded music may also be used since the American square-dance tradition has been largely one of instrumental accompaniment. However, it would be good for the teacher to choose the recorded material carefully, avoiding some of the more painful adaptations of popular songs and country-westerns. Many fine traditional folk songs still exist in the square dance repertory.

Line Games and Dances

Line games and dances do not exist in the same variety as circle dances. However, children love to perform them, and there is, in line games, a quite clear progression from simple to complex that, if followed, can make the most involved contra dance seem easy for fifth- or sixth-grade youngsters.

Line games should not be introduced until the children are performing easy circle games well. At the beginning level is the single line "follow the leader" type game or the single line "through the arch" game. "London Bridge" is the most ancient example of this genre.

One step beyond this is the game with two lines facing each other— the *confrontation* game. This usually involves question and answer phrases, with each line stepping the beat forward during its own singing and backward during the singing of the facing line; "Lemonade" is an example. A variation of this simple two-line confrontation game has one group form arches through which the facing group rushes at the end of the song: "How Many Miles to Babylon."

These two types of line games are the only ones really suited to the youngest children, the five- and six-year-olds. Seven-year-olds can generally learn to keep their lines straight, to stand directly across from a particular partner, and to step down between the lines to the end of the set: "Here's the Way We Billy Billy." By the age of eight, children can do quite a bit more; they can be taught to swing a partner by the right arm and to make their two lines peel off, meet at the foot of the set and go through an arch: "Amassee," "Paw Paw Patch," "I Wonder Where Maria's Gone."

After the above skills are learned, it is a short step to reel and contra dancing. The nine- or ten-year-old must, in addition to the previously-learned movements, learn to swing the opposite line with the left arm, saving the right for his partner ("Lead Through That Sugar and Tea"), and then to "reel down the set" ("Alabama Gal"). From that point on, there are no new formations to learn; only variations of old ones, such as consecutive arch forming or cater-corner swings.

Other Game Forms

No mention has been made here of singing games for twos or fours. There are many interesting ones, and some should be included in any school music movement curriculum. "The Long-Legged Sailor," "Draw a Bucket of Water," "Four White Horses," "Weavily Wheat" are greatly loved by youngsters.

Such games do not contribute in as direct a way to movement skill development as the circle and line games and dances do, but they may provide a moment of relaxation in the course of a lesson; for this alone they have value.

MOVEMENT AND CREATIVITY

What about movement improvisation? What is its place amid all this structure?

Movement in the singing class does not have to be limited to singing games and dances. However, knowledge of the latter provides a movement vocabulary for children in the same way that knowledge of words makes it possible for them to create stories. With this movement vocabulary, the child is freed to create, and to create something others around him can follow and understand. A child can take a loved song and create a dance to accompany it—a dance for one, for two, or for the entire class. A child can make up a game to accompany a song or step in canon with others. Created movement is not limited by the teaching of traditional games and dances—it is enhanced by it. All the teacher must do is provide opportunity for creativity. He or she will not have to implant ideas; the ideas will evolve from the experiences of the child.

One Possible Skill-Teaching Sequence
in Movements, Singing Games, and Dances

Any sequence for teaching is a problematic thing. A movement skill sequence is even less certain than one in other areas of music. However, the following ordering has evolved over a considerable period of time and has proven successful with numerous groups of children. It interweaves the various types of movement activities and singing games and dances discussed in this chapter.

A Developmental Sequence for Teaching Movement and Dance Via Kodály Principles

Type of Movement	Skills Involved	Age at which this activity might begin
1. Moving in place	Responding with rhythmic accuracy and with motions appropriate to the words, melody, or character of the song or rhyme. Using various parts of the body in rhythmic response.	(3–4–)5–6
2. Free movement in space	Choosing and using the most appropriate form of locomotion for songs and rhymes. Using all the possibilities of movement in space: forward, backward, sideways, higher, lower. Moving accurately to the rhythm and beat of the song or rhyme.	(3–4–)5–6
3. Circle: acting-out games	Correctly forming and maintaining circles. Performing actions identifiably and rhythmically correctly.	5–6
4. Circle: partner-choosing games	Beat-stepping in a circle. Choosing a partner at the right moment and within the time allowed in the game.	6–7
5. Line games of confrontation	Forming two facing lines and keeping them separate. Stepping the beat forward and back.	6–7
6. Circle: chase games	Choosing a "pursuer" at the right moment in the song. Running in the proper direction. Getting back to the space before the other player.	6–7

7. Circle: winding games (one-directional and simple two-directional)	Breaking the circle and moving into a spiral formation.	6–7
8. Line games with arch forming	As in no. 5, with the addition of "going through the window."	7–8
9. Circle games with partner choosing and arch forming	Combining and reinforcing the skills learned in nos. 3, 4, and 8.	7–8
10. Line games (easy)	Forming lines correctly. Facing partners. Stepping down between the lines.	7–8
11. Line games (more complex)	As in no. 10, with the addition of swinging the partner by the right arm.	7–8
12. Double circle games	Moving to the beat in opposite directions in concentric circles. Choosing a partner at exactly the right moment in the song. Changing direction on musical cues.	8–9
13. Line games	As in no. 10, with the addition of swinging someone, other than the partner, with the left arm.	8–9
14. Line games with peeling-off	Leading or following two lines around, through an arch, and back to the head of the set.	8–9
15. Circle games containing square dance patterns	Doing the patterns: circle left, into the center, promenade around, do-si-do, allemande left, grand right and left.	10–12
16. Line dances containing contra dance patterns	Reeling down the set. Making consecutive arches.	10 and up
17. Basic square dance	Doing all the patterns in no. 15, plus as many of the nationally listed "Square Dance Basics" [7] as the teacher is able to teach.	10 and up

[7] Square dance in America has become highly standardized and a specific set of elementary calls and steps has been designated as "Square Dance Basics."

Purposeful movement is often a neglected part of the music curriculum. Teachers have, in the past, tended to underestimate the educational value of traditional singing games and dances. Their inclusion in the music program generates an enthusiasm that can easily carry over into all other areas of musical learning.

The singing games and dances listed in Appendix B are given according to their genre. They were specifically chosen to be used with this chapter. The number after each refers to its place in the suggested teaching sequence shown in the above table.

SUGGESTED ASSIGNMENTS

1. Prepare and teach your classmates one of the dances or games given in this chapter.

2. Find additional games for each category listed.

SUGGESTED READING

RICHARD CHASE, *Singing Games and Playparty Games* (New York: Dover Publishers, Inc., 1967).

RICHARD CHASE, *Old Songs and Singing Games* (New York: Dover Publishers, Inc., 1972).

ALICE B. GOMME, *Children's Singing Games* (New York: Dover Publishers, Inc., 1967).

BETH TOLMAN and RALPH PAGE, *The Country Dance Book* (Brattleboro, Vermont: The Stephen Greene Press, 1976).

SOURCES FOR FURTHER INFORMATION
ON DANCE FORMATIONS, STEPS, AND MUSIC

The Country Dance and Song Society of America, 55 Christopher Street, New York, NY 10014.

The Sets In Order American Square Dance Society, North Robertson Boulevard, Los Angeles, CA 90048.

II

KODÁLY
FOR OLDER
STUDENTS

Introduction
to Part II

Of what should a comprehensive Kodály program for older students, beginning or advanced, consist?

1. Singing.
   a. Unaccompanied:
      i. Folk songs of his own cultural heritage
      ii. Folk songs of other cultures
   b. Accompanied:
      i. Artistic settings of folk songs, such as those of Copland, Britten, Brahms, Kodály, Bartók; art music of known composers.
2. Pitch discrimination. Work on in-tune singing, interval identification, use of absolute pitch terminology, as well as of *solfa* syllables.
3. Work on beat, stressed beat, meter, and rhythm in increasingly sophisticated settings. Use of common rhythm terminology, as well as duration syllables.
4. Recognition and use of various musical forms.
5. Ear training, inner-hearing skills, and musical memory.
6. Listening skills. Development of intelligent focused listening; recognition of period and style through listening to, singing, and analyzing music of recognized composers.
7. Increased skill in part-singing, systematically developed.
8. Discrimination in the application of the expressive elements—dynamics, tempo, timbre—to music being performed.

9. Movement. If dance has begun earlier, it should be continued; if not, it should be begun with simple forms from the adult folk heritage. (This was discussed in Chapter 3.)

10. Improvisation and composition. Experimentation with sound.

All of these (except no. 9) will be considered in the following chapters of Part III.

chapter 4

Beginning a Kodály Program with Older Students

Once in a discussion group, the question was put to Erzsébet Szőnyi, Dean of Music Education at the Franz Liszt Academy of Music in Budapest, "What can we do with older children who have no background in Kodály?" Her answer was simply "We have to start with them at any age at the beginning. . . . We have a responsibility to teach at whatever age and whatever stage we find our children."

Later she told a story about Kodály. "What do you do with your non-singers?" a visitor to Hungary asked him. "We teach them to sing," Kodály answered.

These two statements, one by Szőnyi and the other by Kodály, certainly may be taken as endorsement by the Hungarian founders of the system for beginning instruction in the principles of Kodály at the junior-high level . . . or the fifth-grade level . . . or the college level . . . any level at which musical illiteracy is encountered.

Without question, it would be preferable to begin with three-year-olds (or as Kodály suggested, at 9 months before birth, and then amended to say 9 months before the birth of the mother), but there are students of age 15 who have *no* musical background. There are dedicated music teachers who are trying to teach such students. Surely the principles of Kodály have something to offer these students and teachers.

Of course, the problems involved are manifold. It is often necessary to persuade the teachers of older students that Kodály practice has something to offer them. The idea that Kodály is solely an elementary school method has been prevalent for many years in the United States. In Hungary, the Kodály principles are used throughout the educational system, even at the conservatory and music academy level. The principles and philosophy of the Kodály Concept are as appropriate to older students in the United States as in Hungary. The use of the musical mother-tongue, the folk songs, as the basic teaching material, the pentaton as a starting point, these are as valid with older students as with younger ones. As the five-year-old has a limited range and uncertain pitch, so has the untrained thirteen- to fifteen-year-old, particularly the thirteen- to fifteen-year-old boy. Simple pentatonic folk melodies suit the adolescent voice as well as they suit that of the young child. Hungarian master teacher Erzsébet Hegyi has shown repeatedly in her work with college theory teachers in the United States that even mature musicians may benefit from a firm foundation in pentatony.

However, teachers of older students here will be convinced of the potential of the system for them, only if they are given Kodály techniques that are effective with older students. It may suffice for the three-year-old or six-year-old to work via singing games and infant songs ("Ring Around the Rosy," "Bye, Baby Bunting"), coming to the skill and concept learning via these familiar and loved tunes. But the older student, particularly the adolescent or preadolescent, is unsure of whether he is child or adult. Adolescents are ever wary of being treated like children. A college class, assured of its adult status, may be perfectly happy to learn the skills necessary for creating, writing, and reading music by starting with infant songs ("Bye, Baby Bunting," "Rain, Rain, Go Away"—the so-mi-la songs) so common to our preschool child. At age 20 one may be sure enough of adulthood not to feel threatened by childish things. This is not so for adolescents or older elementary school youngsters. They must constantly be assured that the teacher really considers them "grown up." For this reason, it is important to eliminate infant songs from the musical materials for beginning instruction of older students—socially the so-mi-la songs are unacceptable to them.

If one examines American folk music for its simplest tone sets or scales, it becomes evident that in addition to the group of songs with the three-note so-mi-la tones there is another group of songs with an equally small tone set: mi-re-do. Numerous songs exist with this second tone set, and they are, for the most part, songs from the adult folk heritage, rather than songs of infancy and early childhood.

It would seem logical, then, to begin instruction in musical skills and concepts with older students by using songs in this second tone-set group.

However, no interval tunes the voice of a beginning singer as well as the minor third (so-mi or do-la), and few intervals are as frequently sung flat by untrained singers as the major third from do to mi. The dilemma that arises is that the songs best for teaching good singing are unacceptable to older students for social and developmental reasons, while the songs they will accept and learn from are unlikely to be sung very well.

Because of this, when the schools of the San Jose Unified School District in California initiated a Kodály program beginning simultaneously in fourth, fifth, and sixth grades with students who had no previous music, half the music teachers opted to begin instruction with the *mi-re-do* tone-set songs which they felt would be more acceptable to their youngsters, while the other half decided to begin with *so-mi-la* songs in order to develop better singing.

The conclusions of the two groups at the end of one school year indicated overwhelmingly their preference for the *mi-re-do* approach. Typical of their comments were:

> I taught *so-mi* first, but it really was not successful. The kids were bored with the songs.[1]
>
> The songs were not well received because of their texts. . . . Using hindsight, if I had to do it over again, I would use the *mi-re-do* approach.[2]
>
> We have to start with *mi-re-do*. It offers better song material; but nothing tunes the voices as well as the minor third.[3]

All the teachers agreed that if they had to begin again with an older class without music they would:

1. Use pentatonic rote songs with *s-m* in a strong position for working on the development of in-tune singing.
2. Use songs containing only *m-r-d* for the earliest intervallic teaching.
3. Use wider-range pentatonic songs from which they could extract *m-r-d* phrases for melodic teaching to supplement the songs containing only *m-r-d*.

The melodic learning hierarchy, as it emerged, was:

1. *m-r-d*   (new intervals: major second, major third)
2. *s–m-r-d*   (new intervals: minor third, perfect 4th, perfect 5th)
3. *l-s–m-r-d*   (new interval: major 6th)
4. *l-s–m-r-d–l,-s,* (new interval: octaves)

Past step 4, the melodic sequence is expected to proceed as for students of any age (see Chapter 8, p. 168). These four steps are perceived as two years' work in a situation with music taught twice or three times

---

[1] Kathleen Cain, Kodály teacher, Booksin School.

[2] Richard Nezda, Kodály teacher, Randoll School.

[3] David Cain, Kodály teacher, Reed School.

weekly. No one in San Jose went farther than step 2 (*s–m–r–d*) in the first year. Youngsters who have never sung must first be led to sing and to enjoy singing. This alone can take the first four months of a school year. The time spent in this way is time well spent, since no musical learning at all can take place until the student has a repertory of songs he knows well from which to draw musical learning. Even after the repertory is large and well-established, the importance of moving slowly, making certain that each pattern is thoroughly learned in all its variations before proceeding to a new tone-set, cannot be stressed too much. Older students intellectualize much more readily than young children, but intellectualization and internalization are two different aspects of the learning process. Older students who can tell you what the notes of a song are when seeing them, but cannot sing, read, write, and improvise using those notes, have not internalized their musical learning. What they know is superficial and basically not a musical learning. Internalizing the sound and then relating it to symbol is a much slower process, but it must be achieved by students with each new tone-set before moving on to the next.

Rhythmically also, teaching sequence for older students must differ from the one used with younger children. The pattern most frequently found in early childhood songs and chants—♩ ♩ ♫ ♩ ("Rain, Rain, Go Away," "Blue Bells, Cockle Shells")—is rarely found as the opening motif of adult folk songs, even those of very limited range. More common are the patterns ♩ ♫ ♩ ♩ and ♫ ♫ ♫ ♩ . These, obviously, must be the rhythms with which to begin teaching older children. They are found both in duple and quadruple meter songs indicating the necessity for moving more quickly into more than one meter than one would with young children. In addition, the prevalence of sixteenth notes, dotted rhythms, and syncopation in even some three-note tunes would seem to indicate that these rhythms should be taught earlier than they would be with younger children. Although older students sometimes have more difficulty learning to sing in tune than do younger ones, they have much less difficulty with rhythmic learning. Their physical coordination is better, and usually they have already identified beat in music and can perform it moderately well. There do not appear to be the dangers inherent in compressing the rhythmic teaching sequence that there are in compressing the melodic teaching sequence.

With all the above in mind, then, let us look at one possible first-year plan for older beginning students, drawn from work done some years ago in the Baltimore County Schools in Maryland and recently in the San Jose Unified Schools in California.

One Possible First-Year Skill Teaching-Learning Order
for Older Beginning Students

Stage 1

Learn by rote a core of pentatonic folk songs.
Identify and perform beat accurately.
Work on in-tune singing.
Aurally distinguish between like and unlike phrases.
Aurally distinguish between higher and lower pitches in known songs.
Aurally identify and perform metric accent.

Stage 2

Clap rhythms of known songs.
Distinguish between rhythm and beat.
Inner-hear parts of known songs.

Stage 3

Perform four-beat rhythm patterns drawn from known songs.

Identify: ♩ as quarter note, *ta* ⎫
          ♪ as eighth note, *ti* ⎬ in patterns drawn from known songs.
          𝄽 as quarter rest ⎭

Write rhythms in stem notation.
Read rhythms written in stem notation.
Improvise rhythm patterns and rhythmic ostinati.
Identify binary and ternary song forms (AB and ABA).

Stage 4

Identify the *m-r-d* tone-set and all the intervals and melodic turns con-
    tained in it in familiar songs.
Use the staff for music writing.
Write phrases of known songs with the *m-r-d* tone-set.
Use bar lines, meter signs, and repeats correctly in notating.
Identify known songs in the *m-r-d* tone-set by reading silently, with inner
    hearing, from teacher's hand signs or from a tone ladder.
Read and sing random intervals of *m-r-d* from teacher's hand signs or
    from a tone ladder.
Read new songs with the *m-r-d* tone-set from staff notation.
Improvise using *m-r-d*.

Stage 5

Identify the new note *so* in a *s–m-r-d* tone-set.
Practice all the intervals and melodic turns of the *s–m-r-d* tone-set.
Write phrases of known songs with the *s–m-r-d* tone-set.
Identify known songs in the *s–m-r-d* tone-set by reading silently, with
    inner hearing from teacher's hand signs or from a tone ladder.

Read and sing random intervals of *s–m-r-d* from teacher's hand signs or from a tone ladder.

Read new songs with the *s–m-r-d* tone-set from staff notation.

Improvise using *s–m-r-d*.

Each of the above activities, once begun, would continue for the rest of the year. For example, work on in-tune singing, the third item, presumably included in September lessons should still be part of lesson plans in May.

The first step in implementing the above plan must be to choose a core of songs for teaching, each of which clearly illustrates the musical learning to be presented through it. If we return to the three recommendations by the San Jose group, certain groupings of the song material seem to present themselves:

1. Songs for aiding the development of in-tune singing (in which the minor third occurs frequently or in a position of stress).

2. Songs for teaching beat, accent, meter, and easy rhythm patterns of ♩ , ♫ , and 𝄽 .

3. Songs for intervallic teaching:
   a. *m-r-d* tone-set songs
   b. wider-range pentatonic songs with *m-r-d* phrases
   c. songs for each subsequent tone-set

IN-TUNE SINGING

It is absolutely essential to work with students individually if we hope to achieve truly in-tune singing. Older students, particularly adolescents, tend to be very inhibited in their singing. It is necessary to present them with situations in which singing alone is a natural part of the class activity—something that everyone has done or will do. The following song has been extremely useful in initially encouraging individual singing:

TELEPHONE SONG

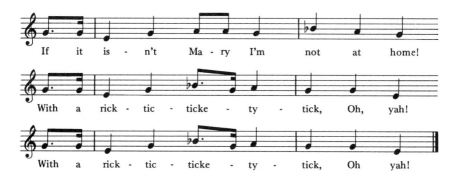

A game based on the *s-m-l* tone-set that appeals to older students, and requires an individual singing response is:

CATEGORIES

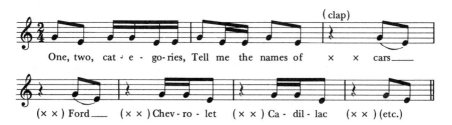

To play this game, the students clap hands and then slap laps to an eighth-note rhythm throughout. The first singer sings the first phrase and states a category such as "food." Each student around the class must then sing the name of a food on *s-m* pitches; for example:

If anyone does not come in immediately on his beat, he must sing the first phrase of the song and name a new category.

Any of the songs listed in Appendix C as being in the *s—m-r-d* or *l-s—m-r-d* tone-sets may also be used effectively for aiding in-tune singing. Once the singers have lost their fear of singing alone, individuals can sing parts of songs while the class sings other parts, or different students may sing each verse, with the whole class singing the refrain.

The possibilities for individual singing are numerous, and the more frequently a student sings alone and hears others sing alone, the more aware that student becomes of pitch and in-tune singing. Two Kodály teachers[4] of older students have reported a high degree of success in the use of a Conn *Strobotuner*[5] for helping older students learn how to produce a correct pitch. A pitch is given. The student attempts to reproduce it. The dial on the *Strobotuner* stops and makes a clear black pattern when the student reaches the exact pitch asked for. The eye helps the ear and voice. In the process, the student becomes aware of what is physically necessary to produce correct pitches. Adolescent love of electronics and gadgetry also probably contributes to the success of this technique.

RHYTHMIC LEARNING

Beat and rhythm may be taught concurrently with preparing for the early melodic teaching, through any of the good pentatonic folk melodies. The pedagogical processes would not differ significantly from those used with younger children, except that the beat is best kept by tapping the lap or desk; adolescent self-consciousness generally makes stepping the beat unacceptable to them.

The order for each new rhythm learning is—as with younger children—hear, sing, clap and sing with rhythm-duration syllables, write, read, and improvise. Many older students will probably be able to find and clap beat from the first music class. When all are able to do so, both in the group and individually, the teacher may move on to the introduction of stressed and unstressed beats. Initially, only simple meters should be focused on. The students may clap the stressed and tap the unstressed beats while singing songs in duple, triple, and quadruple meters. Later, meter and measure will be taught through stressed and unstressed beats.

When students can identify and clap beat and metric accent well, the teacher may focus their attention on rhythm, i.e., "the way the words go." Feeling for the underlying beat or pulse and ability to aurally distinguish among basic beat, metric accent, and rhythm must precede any teaching of notation. Once this learning is established, the teacher may begin attaching symbol (stem notation) to sound.

The Quarter Note

The first rhythmic unit taught should be the quarter note, using phrases in which each word receives one quarter-note beat.

---

[4] Alice Kugler in Missouri and David Garza in Santa Cruz, California.

[5] Registered trademark of the Conn Instrument Co.

Either the first phrase of this Texas song

Rain,   Come   Wet   Me

or the chorus of "Rocky Mountain"

Do,   do,   do,   do

will be easy for students to identify as one sound on one beat. Have the students clap the beat while singing to find where there is one singing sound on one beat. Once aurally identified, the sound can be given a symbol (♩) and a syllable (*ta*). At this time it can also be referred to as a *quarter note*.

The syllables *ta* and *ti* should be used at all times when chanting or reading rhythms but the name in general use by musicians should be used with older students when referring to the notation. In all likelihood, they have heard of quarter notes and eighth notes before, and they will accept *ta*'s and *ti*'s more readily as a way of saying rhythms if they are given a more adult way of referring to note values. The teacher who wishes to have a class do some practice from flash cards, for example, might say: "I am going to show you several patterns of eighth notes and quarter notes. As I show each, clap it and say it in *ta*'s and *ti*'s." *Ta*'s and *ti*'s were never intended as names in any case, even with young children, only as a way of saying durations correctly. It is important that all students eventually be familiar with the common musical vocabulary of American musicians.[6]

The Eighth Note

Eighth notes may be approached through a song with an initial ♩ ♫ ♩ ♩ pattern, such as "Train Is A-Comin' ":

Train   is   a - com - in',   Oh   yes.

[6] Musical vocabulary varies from country to country, even within the English-speaking ones, as witness the use of "quaver," "crotchet," etc.

Focusing the class' attention on the first four beats, the teacher should have the students:

1. sing and tap the beats.
2. sing and clap the rhythm while the teacher maintains an audible beat.
3. answer the questions: "Is there any beat with more than one sound? Which beat? How many sounds do we sing on it?" (There may be repeated singings between the questions above.)

At this point the teacher may show ♩♩, name it *eighth notes*, and say it as *ti*'s in the phrase ♩ ♫ ♩ ♩ . Other songs containing
ta   ti - ti   ta   ta
the same rhythm should then be sung and the rhythm discovered and identified. To cement the learning, the teacher should have students write the rhythm notation of a known song—"I've Been to Haarlem" is a good choice:

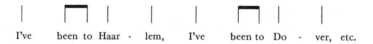

I've   been to Haar - lem,   I've   been to Do - ver, etc.

The above could take place in one class period. It is important to move on quickly in the next lesson to eighth notes in other positions, or the one pattern becomes so fixed that students say it no matter what they hear or see. The generalization they must draw is that there can be two sounds on one beat.

In the next class period, the teacher should present songs that begin with the patterns ♫♫♩ ♩ ("Stoopin' on the Window") and ♫♫♫♩ ("Great Big House in New Orleans"). Students should now be able to generalize that there can be two sounds on more than one beat in a pattern.

After this, the teacher should present all of the four-beat patterns of ♩ and ♫ that occur in the known duple and quadruple meter repertory of the students. Students should be able to sing their known songs with *ta*'s and *ti*'s while clapping the rhythm. They should be able to identify known rhythms clapped by the teacher and to say them back in *ta*'s and *ti*'s. They should be able to read rhythms from stem notation.

The Quarter Rest

The quarter rest may be presented in a similar way, having the students sing a familiar song and focus on the phrases containing rests:

THIS OLD HAMMER

The procedure should be the same as it was for the introduction of eighth notes. The class sings and taps the beat, then sings and claps the rhythm, while the teacher maintains an audible beat. The new questions asked should be: "Is there any beat with no sound? Which beat?" The beat of silence should be labeled *rest* and its symbol ( ) shown.

The musical concepts involved at this point in the teaching process are:

— Music moves to a steady beat or pulse.
— There may be one sound on a beat, two sounds on a beat, or no sound on a beat.

The musical skills involved are:

— The aural skill of hearing how many sounds occur on each beat.
— The oral skill of saying rhythms back correctly in *ta*'s and *ti*'s.
— The writing skill of correctly notating rhythms sung and heard.
— The recognition skill of reading known rhythm components in new musical settings.
— The organizational skill of using known rhythms to create new rhythmic groupings.

When students are doing all the above with ease, it is possible to move into the first melodic teaching.

MELODIC TEACHING

As all rhythmic teaching must be based on the student's ability to distinguish rhythm from beat, all melodic teaching must be based on the student's ability to distinguish higher from lower pitches. From the first class period, the teacher must foster this ability. Among the group of songs learned first, there should be several with very obvious highs and lows in the melody, such as the chorus of "Linin' Track":

LININ' TRACK

Back break - in' work a - lin - in' track.

This song is particularly useful for high and low pitch discrimination because the last phrase begins with the highest note in the song and ends with the lowest note in the song. When students know the song well by rote, they can be asked to raise hands when they sing the highest note and touch the floor for the lowest note. Gradually, the focus should shift to smaller intervals:

the major sixth—"Here's the Way We Billy, Billy"

Here's the way we Bil - ly, Bil - ly,

the perfect fifth—"My Home's in Montana"

My home's in Mon - ta - na

the major and minor thirds—"Rocky Mountain"

Rock-y moun-tain, Rock-y moun-tain, Rock-y moun-tain high

the major second—" 'A' My Name Is Alice"

"A" my name is A - lice, My hus-band's name is And - y,

We come from Ar - i - zon - a with a bas - ket full of ap - ples.

The students are not identifying intervals at this point, only distinguishing which are the higher and which the lower sounds. As they sing, they can move hands or arms to show these higher and lower sounds. It is best to have them close their eyes while doing this to ensure that their motions are based on their own hearing and are not simply a reflection of what someone else is doing. The generalization students must draw is that sounds may move higher or lower or remain on the same pitch. When students can hear and sing pitch changes accurately and can demonstrate this hearing physically, one may begin actual intervallic teaching.

For this, choose a song with no unknown rhythmic elements, i.e., one in simple duple meter, with only quarter notes, eighth notes in pairs, and quarter rests. The song should have been taught by rote earlier and have been sung frequently by the students:

WHO'S THAT YONDER

Who's that yon - der dressed in red?

Must be the child - ren that Mo - ses led.

In making the students consciously aware of the three notes in this song, a number of steps could be taken over a time span of several class periods. Following is an example of such a plan.

Class Period 1

— Have the students sing the song. Then have them derive the rhythm, i.e., sing the song in *ta*'s and *ti*'s while clapping the rhythm.

— Have them write the rhythm in simple stem notation.

Class Period 2

— Have the students sing the song. Then have them sing only the first phrase and move arms to demonstrate the higher and lower pitches.

— Have a student come to the chalkboard and arrange magnetic discs to represent the higher and lower pitches being sung by the class:

— Draw lines across the chalkboard, producing a partial staff:

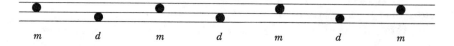

m   *d*   *m*   *d*   *m*   *d*   *m*

— Label the higher note *mi* and the lower note *do*. Give the hand sign for each:

mi   do

— Have the class sing the phrase with the syllables *mi* and *do,* using correct hand signs.

Class Period 3

—Have the students sing the song and arrange discs on the chalkboard, as in the previous lesson.

— Introduce the complete staff by adding two additional lines above the previously drawn ones:

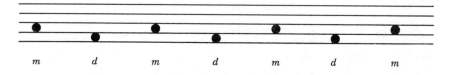

m   *d*   *m*   *d*   *m*   *d*   *m*

— Work with students to achieve facility on staff.[7]

[7] They must understand what is meant by *on a line* and *in a space* in music, and that lines and spaces are counted from the bottom to the top. Individual desk-sized felt staves of the type used in teaching young children (see Lois Choksy, *The Kodály Method* [Englewood Cliffs, N.J.: Prentice-Hall, Inc., 1974], pp. 58–59) are an invaluable aid for initial staff work. Further, it has been the author's experience that beginning students, even at the college level, seem to enjoy working with felt staves and they become familiar with staff notation much more quickly with them than by relying on more traditional printed notation and manuscript paper. Both of these should be used, but later, after students can construct three-note melodic phrases easily on felt staves.

— Have the students construct the first phrase of "Who's That Yonder" in F-*do* on individual staves. Draw the generalization that if *mi* is in a space, *do* will be in the space below.

Class Period 4

— Have students sing the song and construct the first phrase with *do* on G.
— Draw the generalization that if *mi* is on a line, *do* will be on the line below.

After this, one may introduce the note *re* immediately, since there are no complete songs using only *mi* and *do* but quite a few in the *m-r-d* tone-set. *Re* may be introduced through the second phrase of the song used for *mi* and *do*:

If the students aurally perceive which notes are higher and which lower in this melody, they will know the new note lies between *mi* and *do*. The teacher may then label it *re* and give its hand sign: ⟨⟩.

Further Lessons

Students should proceed in subsequent lessons to construct phrases of several other known *m-r-d* songs on felt staves, using only note heads. When they are doing this with ease, it will be possible to introduce music writing on staff and to show how to attach rhythm to pitch notation.

To ensure good writing habits, careful preparation must take place. During the same period that the students were notating *m-r-d* melodies on felt staves they should also have been notating simple rhythms in stem notation (⊓ ⊓ | |) with pencil and paper. The steps for combining the two are as follows. Have students;

1. notate rhythms on staff paper between the second and fourth lines of the staff. This gives practice with correct stem size. At the early stages, ask the students to use a pencil's width between notes. This prevents cramped, closed-in notation:

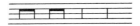

2. notate a known *m-r-d* melody in F-*do,* one with a simple quarter-note rhythm would be best:

3. attach stems to the note heads—stems to the right of the note—being careful that spacing remains good and stems remain as long as they were before:

4. notate phrases of several other known *m-r-d* songs in this same way

5. draw, on a new staff, a red line through the third line. State the rule that above the third line stems must go down, below it they go up; that stems on the third line may go either way; and that a stem going down must be to the left of the note. For this exercise use quarter notes initially. Eighth notes moving higher or lower will require more practice:

Meter and Measure

When students begin writing on staff, meter and measure must be introduced. If students have been clapping metric accents in each class period, there will be little problem in deriving meter. Illustrate for them that a bar line comes before each metric accent. Give them the term *measure* as the distance between metric accents or bar lines. Show the meter sign by the single number that tells how many beats in a measure: 2 or 4. Later, show it as 𝄾 or 𝄾 to indicate that the quarter note is the beat note and, at a still later time, show the traditional meter signs: $\frac{2}{4}$ and $\frac{4}{4}$.

One useful device for determining whether students have grasped the principle of meter and measure is to have them look at a notated example and direct them to "sing the first measure aloud, the second measure silently (internally), the third measure aloud," and so on. Another is to give them the notation of a known song without bar lines or meter sign. Have them sing it, clap the beats and accents, and then mark in the bar lines where their singing and clapping indicate they should do so. After marking the bar lines, they should determine the meter sign and enter it in the correct place.

Reading Music

At this point, actual music reading may begin. To a limited extent, reading has been taking place every time a student has known what song was being shown by the teacher's hand singing, or how to clap a rhythm from stem notation, or how to sing a known song in *solfa*, following note heads on a staff. However, total music reading involves looking at music never seen before, thinking sounds, and then correctly producing those sounds. It is a complicated process. The materials chosen for it must be challenging enough to be interesting, but easy enough to ensure success. For this purpose the Kodály volume *333 Elementary Exercises in Sight-singing* is excellent. It offers extensive practice in each interval, each melodic turn. Numbers 1 to 6 and 9 to 12 use only *do* and *re* and contain only well-known rhythm patterns, while numbers 48 to 55 use all three tones known at this point, *m-r-d,* and also contain only well-known rhythm patterns. However, students will have to have some orientation to D-*do* before using these exercises, since all are written on D, E, and F#. This may be given by having them construct phrases from a few known *m-r-d* songs in D-*do* on felt staves. Erzsébet Hegyi's fine text, *Solfege According to the Kodály Concept,*[8] offers many teaching suggestions for use with these exercises.

We may consider students ready to move on to a new note (*so*) and the various intervals and melodic turns it brings if they can:

1. Sing all their *m-r-d* songs correctly with words, *solfa* syllables, duration syllables, and hand signs.

2. Recognize and identify by inner hearing songs pointed out on a tone ladder on the chalkboard, $\frac{m}{r}$, or shown silently by hand singing.

3. Follow the teacher with hands and voices in hand-singing a random sequence of the known notes (notes sounded consecutively to form intervals).

4. Sing the known notes as the teacher leads two groups in two-hand singing (notes sounded simultaneously to form intervals).

5. Write their known *m-r-d* songs correctly on staff.

6. Read new songs containing known rhythms and the *m-r-d* tone-set.

7. Create original phrases or songs using the known notes.

It is this last point, *create,* that offers the greatest motivation to the adolescent or young adult. When a student knows only the simplest rhythm components, he can use them to create rhythm ostinati. When he has identified like and unlike phrases and the variations of AB form in the songs he sings, he can arrange known rhythms into form to create and perform rhythm compositions. With a knowledge of question and

8 (Kecskémet: Zoltán Kodály Pedagogical Institute of Music, 1975.)

answer phrases, song form, rhythm notation, and a melodic vocabulary of just three notes, *m-r-d*, the student can compose original songs, which can then be duplicated and performed by the rest of the class. If improvisation and creation are a part of the music class from the earliest lessons, composition holds no fear for students. (Chapter 5 will present some specific techniques for developing skill in improvisation and composition.)

This chapter has presented one possible unified approach to the use of Kodály principles by American music teachers of older students. Hopefully, with a sequence of skills and concepts more acceptable to older students and a core of music through which to teach those skills and concepts, music teachers may become less skeptical of using a Kodály approach at the upper elementary school, the junior high school, or the college level. Through Kodály techniques it would be possible to bring musical literacy to many students to whom music would otherwise be a closed book.

SUGGESTED ASSIGNMENTS

1. Find 10 folk songs of wider range that have *s-m* in a strong position, for use with in-tune singing techniques. Describe how you might use each with other students.

2. Perform the role of the teacher and lead the rest of your class through the 7 evaluative steps listed on p. 73. You will have to choose and teach a core of *m-r-d* songs to do this.

SUGGESTED READING

ERZSÉBET SZŐNYI, *Musical Reading and Writing,* vols. I and II (Budapest: Corvina Press, 1974 and 1979). (Available through Boosey & Hawkes, New York.)

ERZSÉBET HEGYI, *Solfege According to the Kodály Concept* (Kecskemét, Hungary: Zoltán Kodály Pedagogical Institute of Music, 1975). (Available through Boosey & Hawkes, New York.)

chapter 5

Understanding Music Through Performing and Creating: A Kodály Approach to Music Listening

Piaget has said, "to understand is to invent." In Kodály practice, this might be paraphrased "to invent is to understand."

A man who can read words or take someone else's words and write them down, but who cannot himself put words together in a way that makes sense, would not be considered literate. Similarly, a musician who can read or take music dictation, but who cannot use musical vocabulary to put together his own musical thoughts, must be considered something less than musically literate.

The educated musician must be performer, listener, and composer. He probably will not excel in all three areas; few musicians do. But he must be able to operate adequately in each, for they are interdependent. Musical understanding depends upon some level of proficiency in all three areas. To perform well, one must understand the work he is performing, i.e., must understand the compositional techniques employed in it. To listen intelligently, one must be able to follow melodic line, form, harmony, rhythm, style, compositional technique. To compose, one must understand all the above, as well as the capabilities of the performers for whom one composes and of the listeners one hopes to attract.

Everyone is potentially, in varying degrees, composer, performer, listener. The Hungarian Singing Schools have recognized this and built upon it. Improvisation and creativity are encouraged from the earliest ages. In the nursery schools, three- and four-year-olds are expected to create and perform rhythm patterns; to improvise tonal answers to the teacher's tonal questions. They are encouraged to create musical dialogues, to act out song-stories, to make up movements to accompany songs.

As Hungarian children move through the 8 years of their lower school education, the creative experiences provided for them are increased in both number and complexity.

In the United States, criticisms have sometimes been leveled at Kodály practice that it inhibits, rather than encourages creativity; that it concentrates on folk music to the exclusion of art music; that it is not relevant to twentieth-century music.

These criticisms have some validity when they refer to the Kodály practices as they often exist within the United States. Many American Kodály practitioners have never progressed beyond the superficial aspects of the method: the *so-mi-la* and *ta-ta-ti-ti-ta* vocabulary of the early grades. However, if one examines existent Hungarian practice, the picture is quite different. Improvisation is a daily experience in the Hungarian Singing School class. Youngsters grow up so comfortable with the language of music that to invent with it is as easy as using words to form sentences. As to the use of folk music to the exclusion of art music, folk music is used extensively (although not exclusively) in the early grades; one does not learn to read and write with the works of Shakespeare. However, by fourth grade the art music of Haydn and Mozart is included, and in sixth, seventh, and eighth grades there is a systematic study of style and period, ranging from Renaissance to the twentieth century.

In the eighth-grade *Ének-Zene (Music Book)*, the text used in the Hungarian Singing Schools, there are 41 songs of known composers, ranging from Palestrina and Monteverdi to Schönberg and Britten. There are 51 notated listening examples for the students to read, sing, analyze, and then hear (14 in the Renaissance and Baroque periods, 11 in the Viennese Classical period, 16 in the Romantic period, and 10 in the Impressionist period), as well as 15 examples of the music of twentieth-century composers: Stravinsky, Hindemith, Schönberg, Berg, Webern, Honegger, Britten, Kabalevsky, Gershwin, Prokofiev, and Shostakovich. In addition, the music of their own national treasures, composers Kodály and Bartók, is illustrated (36 separate notated examples of Bartók's orchestral works and 14 of Kodály's); there are a number of Kodály's songs as well. Hungarian folk music, which predominates the early books, occurs much less frequently at the upper-grade levels; there are only 15 Hungarian folk songs in book 8.

Further, in Hungary there is *one* music text for each grade of the Singing Schools. The teachers must teach the lessons in it. They do not have the option of omitting large parts of the text or of substituting their own musical taste for that of the committee of master teachers who wrote the book and of the Ministry of Education that approved the book.

In the United States, also, there are music texts for the upper grades which suggest good listening material and which offer suggestions for listening lessons. Some of these texts are excellent; however, many assume a level of skill development in youngsters in sixth, seventh, and eighth grades that the material in the same publisher's early books has done little to develop. Placing an orchestral score before a youngster who cannot yet read a melody line is surely an absurdity. It is not easy to make music intelligible to illiterates. It would seem to make better sense to produce literacy, if not first, at least concurrently.

In Hungary, improvising, creating, performing, and listening are all part of the same whole: musicianship. They are practiced daily as a part of every music period. Skills in each are developed sequentially and concurrently with the skills in the others.

This chapter will examine improvisation and composition as one path to understanding and enjoying music.

IMPROVISATION

How may students be led to create? A teacher who feels secure when teaching a singing class, an instrumental lesson, a listening lesson, or a choir period, may experience some anxieties when told to help students *create*. The teacher's own training may have omitted this aspect of musicality. Lack of experience with improvisation and composition should not inhibit experimentation—the teacher can learn with the students.

It is not important that first efforts be of high musical quality. An acceptant atmosphere, with class and teacher looking at the activity and the results as fun, will help students acquire the skills necessary to more advanced compositional techniques as time goes on and melodic and rhythmic vocabularies increase.

At the lowest level, if little or no musical notational knowledge exists, students may improvise "by ear." The teacher may clap a pattern; the student must clap it back, changing it in some way: making it longer, shorter, louder, softer, faster, slower, a different rhythm, etc. Or the teacher may sing a pitched question to which the student answers on pitches. In these exercises there can be no "incorrect" response, since no criteria for response have been given. Any answer is a correct one.

As soon as the first rhythm notation (♩   ♫ 𝄾) and three *solfa* notes (*s-m-l* or *d-r-m*) have been presented, criteria can begin to be established. For example, the teacher might specify:

for a rhythmic   {The response must be 4 (or 8) beats long.
improvisation   {It must include ♫   (or ⅄) (or both).

or

for a melodic   {It must be sung on these pitches (*s-m* for younger and
improvisation   {*m-r-d* for older students).

Some Ways to Encourage Rhythmic Improvisation

There are a number of ways to encourage rhythmic improvisation on an easy level.

    1. A cumulative game may be played improvising four-beat rhythms as follows. The teacher claps four quarter notes ♩ ♩ ♩ ♩ and then maintains an audible steady beat. Without losing a beat, each student in turn claps the pattern of the preceding student, altering it by changing one quarter note to two eighth notes anywhere in the measure. The patterns might emerge like this:

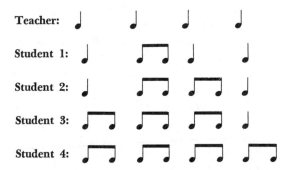

Student 5 must then find some other way to alter the rhythm (by changing one ♫ to ⅄). For example,

Student 5: ♫ ⅄ ♫ ♫ ,

and so on. The students should say these patterns in duration syllables as they clap them. If anyone "loses" the beat, he is temporarily out of the game. Later this can be done with eight-beat rhythm phrases.

2. Put a sixteen-beat rhythm exercise on the chalkboard. Leave one measure blank:

Have the whole class clap and say the measures given; have individual students supply the missing measure. This must be done on the spot, orally, and with no change in tempo or loss of beat.

3. Have individual students improvise and perform four-beat rhythm ostinati to accompany favorite folk songs.

4. Have two students notate (in stem notation) and perform a four-phrase rhythm composition in AABA form and in simple duple meter. One would be responsible for the *A* phrases and the other for the *B* phrase. Their composition could be performed by a group on rhythm instruments, choosing instruments of different timbres for the *A* and *B* phrases.

5. Put a sixteen-beat rhythm statement on the chalkboard. Have the class clap and say it. Consider the statement as *A* in a rondo form and ask individual students to improvise additional sixteen-beat rhythm patterns as the *B, C, D, E,* statements. After each improvisation, have the entire class repeat the *A.*

All the above can be done by students with only the most rudimentary notational skills. However, they each involve the student as composer, performer, and listener.

Some Ways to Encourage Melodic Improvisation

It was suggested earlier that students sing melodic answers to the teacher's melodic questions. This should be done at first without restriction, except that the answer must be on a singing pitch. For example:

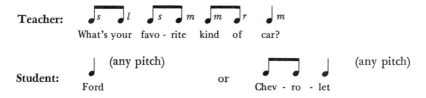

Later, criteria may be placed on the answer: that they be of a specific length (four beats) and on certain relative pitches (*m-r-d* or *l-s-m*).

Teacher:

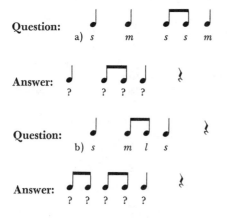

| What | do you | like to | eat? |

Student:

I   like   piz   za.

When the concept of balance in this sort of melodic question–answer seems to be established, words should be eliminated. The teacher may sing a question in *solfa*; the student must answer on a given rhythm, using the same notes in a different arrangement:

Question:

a) *s*   *m*   *s s*   *m*

Answer:

?   ? ?   ?

Question:

b) *s*   *m l*   *s*

Answer:

? ?   ? ?   ?

When *do* is learned, the student will perceive that it gives a feeling of completion to the tonal answer. The teacher should sing musical questions to which the answer sung by the student must end on *do*.

Question:

s   *m l*   *s*

Possible answer:

s   *m s*   *d*

With the basic pentatonic notes (*l-s–m-r-d*) known, melodic improvisation and composition may begin to take more specific form. The simplest complete musical thought at this level is still in question-and-answer form. Initially, the teacher should carefully choose examples in which only one alteration is necessary to turn the question into the answer. The teacher's phrase should end on *re, mi,* or *so;* the student's response should end on *do:*

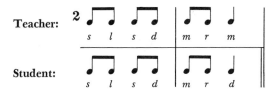

or a longer example:

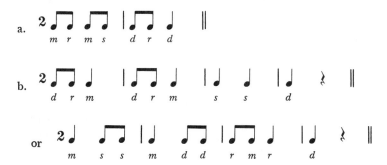

Later, students should be encouraged to give answers that are tonally or rhythmically different from the question. Using the above questions, alternate answers might be:

a.
```
2 ♩♩ ♩♩ | ♩♩ ♩ ‖
  m r m s   d r d
```

b.
```
2 ♩♩ ♩ | ♩♩ ♩ | ♩ ♩ | ♩ ♪ ‖
  d r m   d r m   s s   d
```

or
```
2 ♩ ♩♩ | ♩ ♩♩ ♩ | ♩♩ ♩ | ♩ ♪ ‖
  m s s m   d d r m r   d
```

When students can do the above well, the teacher might sing the first three phrases of a folk song not known to the students, giving them only the words to the last phrase. Individual students improvise rhythm and melody. Then, all compare the improvisations to the original melody. Example:

GOIN' DOWN TO NEW ORLEANS

I'll take my knap-sack on my back, my ri - fle on my shoul - der,

And march right down to New Or - leans, to be a re - bel sol - dier.

Traditional Ending of Folk Song:

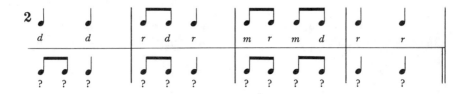

To be a re - bel sol - dier.

Or take one exercise from Kodály's *333 Elementary Exercises* and put the rhythm and half of the melody on the chalkboard.

Have individual students improvise a melody for the second phrase. Then, have the class look at the original and sing the second phrase as composed by Kodály.

At a more advanced level, question–answer examples may be used from music literature. The students should see the notation for the question phrase, sing it in *solfa*, memorize it, and then improvise vocally the missing measures of the answer phrase. They should then see, hear, and sing the solution given by the composer.

W. A. Mozart

Solution given by Mozart:

!

In the above example from *Eine Kleine Nachtmusik* by Mozart, the answer phrase is a repeat of the question phrase with only the last two bars changed to produce the *do* ending. While in the following Haydn example, the answer phrase is in the character of the question, but is melodically different.

Allegro con brio   Haydn—C Maj. Sonata

?

Solution given by Haydn:

!

Numerous examples may be found in the music of the Classical and Romantic periods. For example, from the choral movement of Beethoven's *9th Symphony:*

Beethoven

?

or from Beethoven's *Violin Concerto:*

Beethoven

?

!

Solution given by Beethoven:

Students should have experience with improvising answers in minor keys as well:

Tambourin   Rameau

Solution given by Rameau:

Allegro from *The Moldau*   Smetana

Solution given by Smetana:

Hearing the composer's solution should not be viewed as listening to the "right" answer, after all the "wrong" answers supplied by the students. The students' solutions must be valued, and evaluated on their own merits. The teaching purpose of such improvisational exercises is to provide for creative experience within form and in the context of fine music.

All the above exercises require that the student think music without the aid of pencil and paper; they are vocal improvisations, improvisations within a given structure, but improvisations nevertheless.

Development of Compositional Skills

The terms *improvise* and *compose,* as used here, have different meanings. Both are means of organizing musical sounds. Both are steps toward musical creativity. However, *improvise* is used to mean immediate oral response in a structured situation. *Compose* refers to the process of thinking through music and writing down one's musical thoughts. Improvisation is viewed as an oral and aural skill; composition as an inner-hearing and writing skill.

Composition involves so many musical skills and understandings that, at the beginning, it is best to separate these skills and deal with them one at a time. Melody, harmony, form, rhythm, meter, words, these present too many decisions for the beginner. If the teacher supplies some of them, the task becomes less formidable. For example, supply the melody of a folk song not known to the students ("Good-bye, Ol' Paint"):

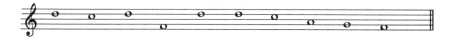

Individual students may organize the melody into rhythm and meter and perform their work for the class. Then, all should look at and sing the original folk song. In the initial singing of the melody, it is important that each note be sung evenly, that no hint of the original rhythm be present.

The same activity may be done with a motif from composed art music (Dvořák: *Symphony in E minor* (New World), Op. 95):

Again, have individual students add rhythm and meter to the given melody and perform their arrangements. Then, listen to the original composition on a recording and compare it with the various student compositions.

Alternatively, meter, rhythm, and words could be given and the students asked to supply a melody within a specified tone-set; or words alone could be given and the students asked to decide rhythm and meter.

In each instance it is important that perimeters be established. To say to a beginning student, "compose a song," may cause much frustration. To say, "compose a song using the notes, *l, s, m, r, d* and this poem; put it in simple duple meter and in ABA form," is to set a performable task. As proficiency develops, less guidance will be needed.

There will come a time when the student can choose or write a poem and set it to music, making his own decisions as to tone-set, meter, rhythm, melody, and form.

LISTENING TO MUSIC

Listening is among the most private of all sensory activities. The fact that sound (or music) is present does not necessarily mean that one is *listening* to it. That one is listening to and *appreciating* it is even more difficult to determine. The child who is sitting at a classroom listening station, earphones on, with rapt expression, may be thinking of last night's television program.

The United States is bathed in unwanted sound. The grocery store, the shopping center, the elevator, the bus, there is seemingly nowhere one may go to escape what passes in today's society for music. The refuge of the adult is simply not to hear. Children, too, learn very quickly not to hear. They may, however, be less selective in what they filter out than the educated adult.

How can the teacher be sure that a student:

1. is really listening?
2. is understanding what is heard?
3. is appreciating (liking) what is heard?

In the old-fashioned approach to music appreciation, students learned about the lives of composers (e.g., Bach had two wives and 22 children); they heard supposedly interesting or amusing stories about particular composition (e.g., . . . and when the loud chord came, was the Prince *Surprised!*). Then they listened to the music. A year later, or even a week later, what the student remembered is that Bach had 22 children and that the Prince was surprised.

This approach answered none of the above questions. How can the teacher ensure that students are listening, understanding, appreciating, liking the music they hear?

Looking at the last two qualities first, there is no way the teacher can ensure appreciation and liking; he can only hope for them. What the teacher can ensure is response. If a student is not really listening, that student will have no response to the music. If the student is listening, he may like or dislike what is heard, but he will have some response to it. It should not be necessary, in any case, for the student to like every listening example the teacher selects. Knowledgeable dislike is preferable to bland acceptance. Appreciation for music, if and when it occurs, is an outgrowth of the other two aspects of the listening task: first, focused listening (not simply being in the room with the sound), and then understanding what is being heard.

Skill in listening is not necessarily best developed in the lower grades by listening to records. Skill in listening is involved even in simple person-to-person speech communication. The teacher says, "Open your books to page 78." How many children hear the direction? How many look at someone else's book to see what page was said? Does the teacher have to repeat the direction? In such an instance, the children are practicing selective listening. They are expressing (in a nonverbal way) an opinion on the importance of what the teacher has said. If children have difficulty listening to and correctly interpreting speech, how can the teacher expect intelligent listening to and interpretation of recorded music, a much less concrete communication form?

For this reason the foci of the earliest levels of music listening in a Kodály classroom are:

1. Listening to the teacher sing.
2. Listening to classmates sing alone.
3. Listening to and evaluating one's own singing.

The earliest nonvocal music-listening experiences are live ones. The teacher may bring an instrument in to accompany a favorite song. An older student may play the flute, the violin, or the trumpet for the children. A musician or group of musicians from the community may perform for the class. Live musicians, with instruments children can see and touch, precede recorded music in the classroom.

It is not until fourth grade in the Hungarian Singing Schools that music on records is used to any great extent; although it must be pointed out that, in a small country with four major symphony orchestras in its capital city and innumerable others, professional and amateur, throughout the towns and country, this does not imply that children have not been exposed to good music. Concerts are cheap, frequent, and well-attended. There are special performances for children, usually sold out. What this does mean is that the study of art music is delayed until students have the prerequisite skills for understanding what they hear.

By fourth grade, Hungarian students are performing, reading, writing, and improvising easily in the major and minor diatonic systems and are conversant with modes. They have an extensive rhythmic vocabulary and can analyze song forms. They have a beginning knowledge of harmony. They are ready to begin analytic focused listening.

In American schools, too, this is time enough to begin to include music listening in lessons. American youngsters will seldom possess the skills of their Hungarian counterparts; but if they have received Kodály training from first grade, they will probably know the tones of the diatonic major and minor tonal systems and, if they are not this advanced, they can begin with pentatonic themes from art music.

It is not so much the music used as the way of approaching it that differs from the old-fashioned "music appreciation" class method.

As with all facets of the Kodály approach, listening begins with singing. In Hungary, the earliest recorded listening example is likely to be of a Kodály or Bartók setting of a folk song the children know and love. A correlative in American music might be hearing "Simple Gifts" in the Copland setting (*Appalachian Spring*) of this Shaker tune, or Ives' treatment of patriotic tunes: the "Fourth of July" section of his *Holidays Symphony*.

As a general rule the children do not listen to music until it has first been seen in notation and sung in *solfa*. The order of presentation may vary:

— The notation may be shown by the teacher and read by the student.
— The teacher may teach the theme by rote and have the *solfa* derived by the class and then notated on staff from memory.
— The theme may be given as a melodic dictation example and sung after being written.

Whichever of these approaches is used, the theme is sung and memorized before it is heard on recording. At later levels, partial scores are shown in the school texts, and voice movement and harmonic structure are analyzed by the students as well, before hearing recordings.

When the recorded listening experience is provided, the student is not listening to see how the tune goes, he is listening to hear how Bach or Brahms or Bartók treated the melody (or rhythm or harmony or form).

The teacher, to guide listening, might ask some of the following questions.

1. How did the composer alter the melody? What did the composer do to make it more interesting? Some possible student answers might be:
   a. Changed it from major to minor.
   b. Added extra notes to it (ornamented it).
   c. Turned it upside down (inverted it).
   d. Used little pieces of it (fragmented it).
2. How did the composer use rhythm to create interest? Possible answers:
   a. Used sustained notes in one part against moving notes in another.

      b. Altered the basic rhythm from smooth to jagged.

      c. Changed the meter.

      d. Augmented (or diminished) the rhythm.

3. How did the composer harmonize the theme? What did the composer do with the other voice parts? Possible answers:

      a. Had the theme repeated by lower and higher voiced instruments. There was a countermelody. It was like a canon.

      b. Put chords under the melody.

      c. Used broken chords to accompany the melody.

      d. Seemed to be using two (or more) keys at the same time.

4. What instrumentation did the composer use? Possible answers:

      a. Whole orchestra with solo violin.

      b. String quartet.

      c. Voice and piano.

      d. Harpsichord.

5. How did the composer organize the theme within the composition? Possible response:

      The students would listen to identify the form used.

6. How and where in the composition did the composer use dynamic changes to create interest? Tempo changes?

    Later, after students have listened to numerous examples of music from various periods, the teacher may draw from them the characteristics of each style. Have the students compare one period with another. Guide questions should be asked about melody, rhythm, form, harmonization, dynamics, tempo, instrumentation. The students will probably suggest some of the following:

Renaissance: steady beat, steady rhythms, little change in dynamics, thin sound, few instruments, melodies against other melodies.

Baroque: more instruments, bigger sound, much repetition, steady beat, even rhythms, form easy to follow, more than one melody at a time.

Classical: strong and regular beat, melody easy to follow, one melody at a time with chord or broken-chord accompaniment, neither very loud nor very soft, larger sounding orchestra, feeling of balance, simplicity.

Romantic: much larger orchestra sound, more contrasts in dynamics and tempo, more brass and percussion sound, much rhythmic variety, usually one melody at a time with accompaniment.

Impressionist: the beat has a weak shifting feeling, rhythm patterns are complex, the phrases are long and flowing, small and frequent tempo changes, longer melodic lines, the tonal center is not always clear, large orchestra.

Twentieth Century: two or more keys sounding at a time (bitonality and polytonality), sometimes there is no feeling at all of tonal center (atonality).

These responses are simplistic, admittedly, but each is characteristic of the period nonetheless and each is a characteristic fifth, sixth, or seventh graders can hear and identify.

Only one of the above aspects (melody, harmony, form, etc.) should be considered in one listening. Each repeated listening should be for a specific purpose. At the earlier grade levels, guide questions should be drawn from the class and placed on the board before the selection is played.

Repeated listenings are not only desirable but necessary if the student is to become familiar enough with a work to form any valid value judgement. Each listening should have a new purpose and new guide questions. It would be preferable for students to hear 5 works in depth, rather than 25 superficially.

Such listening experiences feed back into the improvisational and compositional aspects of the music lesson. The class may experiment with known songs, applying to them the compositional techniques learned by singing themes and listening to recorded works of great composers. For example, how might "Are You Sleeping, Brother John?" be dealt with by a composer? The original melody is:

BROTHER JOHN

The composer might:

1. Rhythmically augment it:

2. Rhythmically diminish it:

3. Do it in minor:

4. Do it in a mode:

(Dorian)

5. Try it in a different meter:

6. Ornament it:

7. Alter the rhythm:
   a. by substituting jagged rhythm for smooth:

   b. by using repeated notes:

   c. by doing it staccato:

8. Invert the melody:

9. Try it backwards (retrograde):

10. Try the canon at intervals other than the unison and/or at distances other than two measures:

or

11. Harmonize it with broken chords:

12. Place one voice on F-*do*, the other simultaneously on G-*do* (thus producing bitonality):

13. Construct the melody on a whole-tone scale:

14. Add notes between the melody notes (chromaticism):

15. Use a dissonant chordal accompaniment:

These and other suggestions should come from the students as a result of their listening experiences. Each should be tried vocally and evaluated by the class when it is suggested.

In "Brother John," the melodic repeat is exact:

Youngsters will discover, through singing and listening, that a repeat may sometimes occur:

1. higher or lower, creating sequence:

Flies in the but-ter milk, shoo, fly, shoo,   Flies in the but-ter milk, shoo, fly, shoo.

2. as a repeat with modification:

O   beau - ti - ful, for   spa-cious skies

3. as a sequence with modification:

My coun-try 'tis of thee, Sweet land of li - ber-ty

These techniques, too, should be tried with other songs, used in vocal improvisation and in composition.

Simply singing a theme is better preparation for hearing it than being told the story of the composer's life. However, singing it and anticipating what a composer might do with it is even better preparation.

To return to the original premise of this chapter, "to invent is to understand," youngsters who use the musical techniques of composers will both understand and appreciate the music of those composers more than students who simply listen to that music. Listening may be passive—simply allowing sound to wash over one while the mind is otherwise engaged—or it may be a conscious activity. In the world outside, particularly in the United States, passive listening is unavoidable and continual. In the music lesson it is imperative that listening be focused and active.

Selecting Music for Listening Experiences

Music selected by teachers for student-listening experiences should vary widely in period, style, and instrumentation. Within a given style and period, the music selected should be the very best available. One does not learn to love the best music by hearing that which is second rate.

What is the best? Surely no musician doubts that the music of a Beethoven is more enduring than that of an Offenbach; that the music of Debussy has greater artistic merit than that of Dukas. This being so, why do so many listening experiences suggested for youngsters consist of of "Danse Macabre," "The Sorcerer's Apprentice," "Carnival of Animals," and similar potboilers? Probably because they have stories that the teacher believes will make the music more palatable to children. The teacher who does this underestimates children's capacities to appreciate and enjoy truly good music.

Who are the two or three true giants of each musical period? What is a characteristic work of each of these composers that can be made understandable to the student in fifth, sixth, or seventh grade? Two teachers may have quite different answers to these questions, but using the questions to guide choices will result in better choices than might otherwise be made.

Following is one sample long-range plan for a series of listening lessons using some of the techniques discussed in this chapter.

A Series of Listening Experiences Using Bach's "The Little Fugue in G minor"

FUGUE IN G MINOR, "THE LITTLE FUGUE"

Bach

First exposure

1. Teacher plays the theme on piano. Students notate it. (Or, teacher gives the theme by hand signs and students sing and notate it.)
2. Students sing back in *solfa* what they have notated.
3. Students memorize the theme and sing it in *solfa* from memory.
4. Teacher draws ideas for theme development from the students: How can we make this tune more interesting? What can we do with it? Some possible student suggestions may be:
   a. Do it in major.
   b. Try it in higher and lower places.
   c. Put it on top of itself (canon at unison, fifth).
   d. Sing root tones against it. Decide where the tonic *(la)*, the subdominant *(re)* and the dominant *(mi)* sound best (harmonize it).
   e. Sing short running notes against longer ones; make another tune go with it (add counterpoint).
   f. Add notes at the end to make the theme longer (extend it); use little pieces of the melody (fragment it); repeat parts of the melody a step higher or lower (sequence it).
   g. Make it fancy by adding notes between the notes already there (ornament it).
5. Students listen to recording (use as written for organ, not an orchestral transcription) to see which of the compositional techniques they suggested was used by Bach; what others he used.

Second exposure (at the next class period)

1. Sing the theme in *solfa*.
2. Listen to the recording to hear:
   a. how many times the complete theme occurs as originally stated;
   b. how many times it occurs altered or fragmented;
   c. in which voice the theme occurs at each statement (bass, soprano, alto or high, middle, low).

Third exposure (a month later)

1. Sing the theme in *solfa.*
2. Listen to the recording. This time focus on the accompaniment to the theme.
3. Discuss the characteristics of the accompaniment at each new statement of the theme, such as: scalewise (up or down), wide leaps, chords, dissonance, dynamic levels.

Fourth exposure (in the next school year)

1. Sing the theme in *solfa.*
2. Listen to a portion of the recording for organ.
3. Listen to an orchestral transcription of the work.
4. Identify which instruments play the theme at each statement.
5. Discuss what makes the two recordings sound so different.

Fifth exposure (later)

1. Sing the theme in *solfa.*
2. Listen to the orchestral transcription of the work.
3. Listen to a section of a previously-studied work of the Viennese Classical School (Mozart: *Symphony #40 in G minor,* first movement, for example).
4. Compare the two works. What seems to be the characteristics of each period? List them. (After hearing and studying other works from the same periods these apparent characteristics can be added to, altered, refined, re-evaluated.)

A worksheet, such as the one following, may be prepared for students as an aid to focused listening. Such worksheets are not used in Hungarian schools; they are unnecessary since their students' books contain many pages for guided listening. The author has found this form to be useful with American students in the absence of a student listening text. The form must be varied somewhat by the teacher, depending upon the work being studied. It would be kept from one listening lesson to the next, and only those portions of it pertinent to that lesson would be filled in during the lesson.

SUGGESTED ASSIGNMENTS

1. Choose two composers from each period whom you consider to be giants of that period. Choose one work (or part of one work) of each that you believe could be made understandable for and enjoyable to children.
2. Construct a long-range listening strategy, such as the one given in this chapter, for one of your choices.

Work: _____ Composer: _____

Instrumentation: _____ Period: _____

Theme (notated by student):

No.	No. of times theme is stated. List each occurrence and list voice (or instrumentation).				Accompaniment		Dynamics and Tempo	Other characteristics (Rhythm, Form, Style, Timbre, etc.)
	Complete	Fragmented	Voice		Characteristics	Voice		

chapter 6

Applying Kodály Principles in the Training of Choral Groups

THE SINGERS

> *There is not any Musicke of Instruments whatsoever, comparable to that which is made of the voyces of Men, where the voyces are good, and the same well sorted and ordered.*
>
> WILLIAM BYRD, Psalmes, Sonets, & Songs of Sadnes and Pietie (1588).

One of the real joys of teaching music to children lies in the beautiful choral sounds that may be achieved. There is a purity and clarity when children sing well that surpasses that of any instrument. It is unique.

It is a task of the music teacher to help children sing well; to initiate them to the very real pleasure of blending their voices with other voices around them to create sounds one voice alone cannot. This is what choral singing is all about. Few situations offer as rich a teaching potential as the children's choir.

To reap the greatest benefit from time spent with children in a choral situation, it is necessary to have a clear mental image of the three facets of the choral teaching task:

    the *singers* — the choosing, organizing, planning, rehearsing, and performing.

the *singing* — the technical aspects involved in producing good choral sound.

the *sung*   — the song material, concert and other, through which we teach musical concepts and skills to the choir.

The first of these—the singers—involves the tasks of:

auditioning
organizing
rehearsing
performing

Auditioning

Choosing the singers

What does one really need to know about each potential singer to place him correctly in a choral situation?

1. His voice range (both easy and extreme ranges)
2. His rhythmic ability
3. The level of his sightsinging skill
4. The keenness of his ear
5. The quickness and correctness of his musical memory

The teacher who has taught the same children since first grade may already possess much of this information about them before choir tryouts. However, the tryout can give more specific information in each of the above areas. The tryout can also pinpoint specific instances, such as the hoarse voice that may indicate nodes, or the exceptionally talented child, the one with the beautiful voice, who may do some solo work. How may one test, quickly and efficiently, the five areas listed above?

Voice range

Fifth and sixth graders' most favorable tessitura lies between D and D', and the range usually extends up to high G and down to B♭ or A below middle C. The majority of voices tested will lie in this range. When testing, the teacher should be careful that the child's voice quality remains easy. If the child's voice has a harsh ugly sound, he is pushing.

In the testing procedure, it is important to create an atmosphere of acceptance. The child who fears criticism and rejection is not going to audition well. If the children appear to be tense, it may prove helpful to audition three or four together. To hear them individually have them drop out one at a time until one is left singing alone.

To test for range, it is preferable to use a phrase of a song the children know well, rather than an isolated scale or vocal exercise. The first phrase of "Joy to the World," for example, is a descending diatonic major scale. However, because it is familiar and because it is set to a rhythm, it is much easier for the child to reproduce vocally than a diatonic major scale played or sung in quarter notes.

The tune chosen to start the testing should have a descending rather than an ascending line. The former is easier to sing and will warm the voice for the ascending patterns.

One possible procedure for voice testing follows:

1. The teacher sings the line first (or plays it or plays and sings it) from D' to D on a neutral syllable *(la)*. **Example:**

The student repeats it after the teacher *without the piano*. This is the middle register; most youngsters will sing it with ease.

2. The teacher repeats the phrase, this time from A' to A below middle C. **Example:**

The student repeats the phrase, unaccompanied. Students who sing the notes below middle C clearly and without strain may be strong altos.

3. Invert the melody; use the inversion of the familiar rather than a scale. Perform it on F to F' and G to G'. **Example:**

The children who sing these with ease will be good first sopranos.

Rhythmic ability

To test for rhythmic ability have the student face away from the teacher, so that there is no visual help, and clap back a series of eight-beat patterns ranging from easy to more difficult:

Stop at the pattern with which the student has difficulty. Do not give pattern *c* if *b* was performed incorrectly.

Sightsinging

To test sightsinging skill:

1. Give the notation, without words or identification, of a song the student knows well. Allow him a few moments to "sing it softly" to himself. Ask him to identify and sing it. This is sightsinging, but at an easier level than *prima vista*.
2. If he did the above well, have him sing at sight an unknown melody such as those in Kodály's *333 Elementary Exercises*. If the student had difficulty with task 1, omit task 2.

Ear ability

To test the keenness of his ear, have the student close his eyes and sing back, on a neutral syllable, what he hears. The teacher sings or plays on the piano (in order of increasing difficulty):

Musical memory

The two preceding tests are tests of musical memory as well. No additional test is really necessary. However, if a further test of memory is desired, play *a* and *b* above with only a brief pause between the two. Ask the student to sing back only *a*.

To review, the complete audition could consist of: for *range*—two descending and two ascending scale patterns; for *rhythmic ability*—four short exercises repeated after the teacher; for *sightsinging*—one song to recognize and, possibly, one short exercise to read; for *musical ear* and *memory*—four short melodic lines to repeat after the teacher.

In each area, the testing should continue only as long as the child is successful. When he begins to experience difficulty, the remaining tests in that group should be skipped. All the above tests can be performed in less than five minutes.

Audition techniques

Consider testing without piano—the results are much more accurate. In any case, do not play piano with the child's voice while testing.

Tape the auditions, if possible, to be able to consider them later under less pressure. If they are not taped, be sure to have a scoring sheet prepared in advance with each child's name and a box for each test. Use a numbering system that means something to the teacher but not to the child who is watching. It is useful to classify the child according to height on the same form. This can be an aid later when arranging seating order.

The boy–girl ratio in children's choirs is often very much out of balance. Music should not become a "girl's subject." Weight auditions in favor of boys. Boy sopranos have a beautiful voice quality, quite unlike that of girls at the same age. It is not good or necessary to have fewer boys than girls in a choir; in a group of 60, 30 or more should be boys. If they want to sing and can carry a tune, the director should take the boys who try out. Musicianship, reading, and part singing can be taught. Almost invariably, the girls at this age are musically (and academically, for that matter) more advanced than boys. This is no excuse for the choir composed of 55 girls and 5 boys—and that is what happens if auditions are not slanted somewhat in favor of boys.

When auditioning children for admission to choir the examiner tests:

1. Their musicality—but that is something a teacher can use the choir experience to refine
2. Their voice quality—a teacher can use the choir period to develop that
3. Their music reading skills—a teacher can improve these through choral music

What then is really pertinent to the selection of choir members? Of course, one must know a child's range for correct placement; but aside from that, the single most important factor is the child's desire to sing.

He must want to be in choir. This, along with reliability and responsibility, makes a good choir member. Other skills can be taught; his attitude he brings with him.

Zoltán Kodály, writing in 1929 on children's choirs, said:

> Below the age of 15 everybody is more talented than above it; only exceptional geniuses continue to develop. It is a crime to miss that talented age. If we do not organize children's choirs properly, our adult choirs will increase neither in number nor in quality. A grown-up person will in any case sing differently if he has the opportunity to preserve the fervent enthusiasm of singing from his childhood. And the child will remember and understand that without conscientious work there are no results.

Kodály believed in music for all children. In the Singing Schools of Hungary all upper-grade children have 2 hours a week of choral experience. Should the American music teacher really *select* children for elementary school choir? The author is not at all convinced so. When a teacher chooses 60 children out of a possible 200, he automatically denies 140 children the experience of rehearsal and performance. Of course, one cannot easily manage a choir of 200 voices. As an alternative, consider having more than one choir, so that all who wish to perform may. At one elementary school the author had four choirs: a fourth-grade choir (every child in grade 4), a fifth-grade choir (every child in grade 5), a sixth-grade choir (every child in grade 6). There were three classes in each grade. The groups numbered between 80 and 90 children. Each class met for two 40-minute lessons, and each grade for an additional hour a week of choir. Each performed once during the year.

In addition, a small selected group of 30 children met at the noon recess three times weekly. These were the youngsters who sang most beautifully, who read music fluently. The choral sound admittedly was much better in the selected group than in the unselected ones, but in this manner all had the experience of rehearsal and performance.

The cambiata voice

If the choir includes seventh graders, one may very well encounter some changing voices among the boys. Even some sixth-grade boys may be beginning voice change. It is important that the teacher recognize the changing voice and alter the voice testing accordingly. The easy range for a changing voice is less than an octave—from about A below middle C to about the G above. The total range may be from F below middle C to C above; but this range is sung with considerable difficulty. Unison work in a choir with unchanged and changing voices is obviously impossible. To include such voices in a choir necessitates finding two-part music with a very small range for the lower voice.

The procedure for testing the changing voice is the same as for the unchanged voice, but a smaller-range song should be used: "Deck the Halls" (five tones). Begin on G above middle C, go down to E, go up to C:

If the teacher is uncertain whether a particular boy's voice is actually changing or whether he is simply singing incorrectly, there are certain physical guidelines to adolescence that may help. As the boy matures:

> his nose bridge changes
> his lips become thicker
> his complexion becomes paler
> his Adam's apple appears
> his limbs become longer in proportion to his body
> his facial hair begins to appear
> his coordination becomes less good

If none of the above physical characteristics are in evidence, the likelihood is that the youngster is simply singing incorrectly. Peer influence often induces twelve- and thirteen-year-old boys to lower their voices before there is any physical necessity. A boy whose voice is on the brink of change may be a very fine addition to a treble-voice choir; a brilliant upper register comes just before voice change.[1] Praise and encourage such a voice.

Whether or not boys with changing voices should be encouraged to continue singing or allowed to "rest" for 2 years or so during the voice

[1] Arpad Darazs, presently Professor of Music at the University of South Carolina and formerly Director of the Columbus Boys' Choir, says that a slow-changing voice makes promise of a tenor, while a quick one will probably be a baritone or a bass.

change is an issue that has been much discussed in the literature. It is an unfortunate fact that if we drive the adolescent boy from choir, he may never return. There is no medical evidence that any physical damage results from continuing to sing during voice change. The only reason for excluding changing voices from the choir is the difficulty of finding appropriate materials.[2]

Dr. David Woods, Professor of Music at Iowa State University, conducted a 10-year experiment with cambiata voices. In the context of an all-male secondary school choir, he met with the changing voices separately during the first several months of each school year. The boys sang small-range folk songs, chorales, and other relatively simple works. Gradually he lowered the range of the materials used, asking the boys not to force the sound but to sing lightly and with ease. The result was a pure mellow quality coming from the bottom of the cambiata range, without strain. After two months he introduced standard choral literature with high first-tenor parts. The boys sang these lines in their developing bottom range cambiata. If the part became too low, they were to drop out, inner-hearing the part and resuming singing when the part returned to their comfortable range. The few low notes were also covered by selected voices from the second tenor and baritone sections as needed.

There were two significant results from this 10-year experiment. In Dr. Woods' words:

1. "The first-tenor line was performed with good musicianship, and with a warm, mellow quality (unlike those in neighboring schools using forced voices for the high tenor part). The 30 to 35 cambiata tenors balanced the male chorus into a rich blend of 4 'equal' voice types."

2. "The cambiata voices were kept singing. When their voices had lowered into other areas of voice placement, they naturally took on another part. Their voices had a great deal of musical quality and their understanding of music had increased. There was not a sudden confusion or embarrassment which sometimes occurs when there is a 'nonsinging period' between boy voice and changed voice. The cambiatas were not injured in any way because they were not forced. They were kept singing lower and lower without strain until they experienced their natural singing voices."

Organizing

The smoothness with which choir periods run all year can be established or completely undermined in the first choir period.

[2] This is no longer the problem it once was. Much music for the cambiata voice is being published. For example, see the list put out by The Cambiata Press, c/o Dr. Don Collins, Conway, Arkansas.

First of all, one should consider the seating arrangement. Seats should be assigned and changed only by the teacher. If the teacher has made a note of the child's height on the audition form, preliminary seating can be established before the first choir period and name tags may be placed on the chairs. This is also the time to anticipate and avoid discipline problems by seating students in a way that will reduce the temptation to misbehave. If the choir teacher does not know the children, he should ask the classroom teachers to suggest which youngsters should or should not be seated together. In addition, the children should be arranged so that it will be easy for the director to see every child and for every child to see the director. The arrangement should, if possible, be the same one used for concerts. If risers are available, use them for rehearsals, not just for performances. If not, arrange the singers by height. Singers must be able to see the conductor and hear the piano when one is used. Seat the strongest singers toward the back. They will lend support to the whole group from there. Put soft sure voices in the front row.

The arrangement for part-singing, when there are only two parts, is a matter of no consequence—altos here, sopranos there. However, for three-voice singing there are very real advantages to placing first sopranos in the center with altos and second sopranos on either side of them.[3] The second sopranos have the most difficult part to sing. This way they have only one other note immediately in their ears. Since they are often singing in thirds and sixths with the first sopranos, their closeness to that section makes musical sense. This arrangement also puts the outside notes of the harmony together—the altos and the first sopranos—making it easier for the altos to hear their part in relation to the whole. And, in this arrangement the two other voices are heard equally clearly by the section with the easiest voice parts—the first sopranos. The arrangement looks like this:

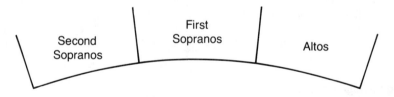

There is an implication here of equal-sized sections, which may not always be practicable with a children's choir. Many three-part treble selections are actually two parts with a high-voice descant part. The high

[3] This technique, suggested by Paul F. Roe (*Choral Music Education*) for adult choral groups, has been found by the author to be very effective with the three-voice children's choir.

voices in such instances can be fewer, while melody and alto voices should be evenly divided and greater in number for a balanced sound. Balance is dependent also upon voice quality and the range in which the voices are singing. There is a tendency in many children's groups toward large alto sections, perhaps with the idea that 60 voices will carry the part more securely than 25. The resultant sound is often coarse and strident. For most three-part music the numbers in each section should be approximately equal, with flexibility to add to or subtract from a voice part according to the demands of the music.

Routines

Use choir children to help with the routines that are a necessary part of every choir rehearsal. Children can take responsibility for numbering and giving out new music and checking roll. It should not be necessary to give out and collect music each period. Instead, assign a number to each choir member and number all octavo correspondingly. Music, once given out, may then be kept in a numbered pocket folder in the student's possession as long as the choir is working on it. This procedure has the advantage that the member can work on music outside the choir period and that little time has to be spent during choir period giving out and collecting it.

Student accompanists

Children should be used to accompany the school choir whenever and wherever possible. Of course, the teacher must work with these children outside the choir period if they are to play well, although private piano teachers are often happy to have their students acquire accompanying experience and are willing to help them prepare for it.

Rehearsing

What can be accomplished in choir in a year? What are reasonable long-range goals; short-range objectives?

"To get ready for the Christmas program" is not a worthy objective for a teacher; it may be a motivating factor for the children, but it should not be the motivating force for the teachers. Teachers are hired to teach, not to entertain. Entertainment may be a by-product of the teaching, but it should not become the teaching purpose.

What kinds of objectives should a teacher have for a choir, then? Hopefully, as a result of choir experience children will:

1. sing beautifully in-tune, in unison, and in parts; correctly hear and adjust their singing to fit that of other voice parts and/or the accompaniment;

2. interpret musical scores with intelligence (music reading);

3. develop a keen sense of inner hearing;

4. learn to memorize music quickly and accurately;

5. follow a director;

6. use good vocal technique when singing;

7. enunciate words more clearly than before, with more awareness of correct consonant and vowel sounds.

It is on such goals as these that the choir director must focus attention, while working on the Christmas or spring program.

In order to accomplish these seven goals it will be necessary to work on them in each choir period.

In-tune singing

In his *Let Us Sing Correctly,* Kodály stated:

Those who always sing in unison never learn to sing in correct pitch. Correct unison singing can, paradoxically, be learned only by singing in two parts: the voices adjust and balance each other.

Some exercises designed to promote in-tune singing must be a part of each choir period. Two-hand singing is perhaps the best way to work on such exercises. The students are free of paper and books, they are focused only on the director and the sound they are producing. The style of such exercises should be legato. Rhythm is unimportant in them. Complete attention should be given to the intervallic sounds being produced. Director and choir listen intently to these sounds, adjusting each interval until it has a pure, clean sound.

Only the director uses both hands. The choir is divided, with one group following the director's right hand, the other his left. The teacher who is insecure with two-hand singing should begin with extremely simple exercises. For example, use the left hand to lead the choir through a pentatonic tone-set. Then pause on *so* and bring the right hand to the *so* position also. Keep the right hand on *so* while the left moves to *do* and back to *so*. Then move the right to *do* and back to *so* while the left sustains *so*. This is enough for the choir as an initial two-hand singing experience. As the choir develops more skill in singing from hand signs, the director will develop more skill in using two hands to indicate intervals.

Music reading

Hopefully, the children are already reading music by the time they come to choir. If so, the director should build on that skill. If not, he is certainly remiss if he does nothing to help them. One of the most important tasks facing music educators is that of making students musically independent—giving them the tools with which to discover music for themselves. Some part of every choir period should be spent to this end.

Simple folk-song material lends itself well to a beginning sightsinging approach with choir. There are a number of songs with only a three-note (*m-r-d*) tone-set, and many with simple duple-meter rhythms and groupings of quarter notes, eighth notes, and rests (see Chapter 4). Using these to warm up with early in the choir period—clapping and identifying their rhythms, singing *solfa* as a second verse—can help to build a useful level of sightsinging fairly quickly. As soon as the children can sing the three tones *m-r-d* in *solfa* and can identify and perform quarter-note and eighth-note patterns, the Kodály volume *Pentatonic Music*, vol. 1, may be used as an exercise book, working on only one new exercise in a rehearsal period. As the children progress, their reading and exercise material should be pulled directly from the concert music in preparation. In this way, rhythmic or melodic difficulties can be anticipated and overcome before they arise.

For example, place the following rhythms (from "Strawberry Fair" [4]) on the board:

Have the choir read the rhythms from the board, using duration syllables, practicing them until they are fluent. Then have them look at the octavo and read the first page, on which these phrases occur. Or, to help them with a melodic line that may give difficulty, approach it through hand singing. For example, page 2 of Aaron Copland's "Simple Gifts" [5] contains a broken tonic chord [*m-d-m-s-d'*] followed by a broken subdominant [*f-l-d*]. If first sung as chords following hand signs, they become much easier for children. There are very real values to be derived from using the Kodály techniques of *solfa*, hand singing, and rhythm duration

4 Arrangement by Christopher Brown. Copyright 1974 by Oxford University Press.

5 Copyright 1950, Boosey & Hawkes Inc., New York.

syllables with a choir, whether or not these techniques are used with the students in their classroom music.

Solfa is valuable because it provides pure vowel sounds and clean consonant sounds that seem psychologically to promote in-tune singing. Although the syllables were arrived at almost accidentally by Guido d'Arezzo in the eleventh century, they would certainly not have persisted so long had they not provided for more beautiful singing than any of the many other systems that have come and gone in the meantime.

Hand signs are used because relative pitches, once securely fastened to specific hand signs, become much more secure than they are without the addition of this kinesthetic dimension.

Rhythm duration syllables are helpful because they reduce rhythmic problems to easily voiced patterns.

Solfa, hand singing, and rhythm duration syllables are all aids to helping children interpret musical scores with intelligence. Only a small part of the choir period, perhaps 5 minutes, should be spent in activities directly related to the improvement of music reading. However, whenever the eye helps the voice, music reading is taking place. Throughout the choir period the teacher can help the eye help the voice, by using *solfa,* stem notation, and hand singing.

Inner hearing

Inner hearing is that ability that allows one to "think" music. It does not happen accidentally, it must be taught. (See p. 35 of Chapter 2.)

On the simplest level, it involves having children sing a song aloud, then on a signal put the tune inside their heads, and on a second signal resume singing aloud at the correct place in the music.

Other, more advanced, inner-hearing exercises might include (in order of increasing difficulty):

1. Give the beginning pitch and show the hand signs for a song known to the group. The group identifies the song and sings it back with words.
2. Place a tone ladder on the chalkboard:

		d'
		t
l		*l*
s		*s*
	or	*f*
m		*m*
r		*r*
d		*d*

(Be sure that the spacings visually represent the whole step—half step musical relationships.) Point out known songs on the tone ladder while the group thinks the tune. After the pointing, the choir identifies and sings the songs with words.

3. Give the beginning pitch and show the hand signs for a song known to and identified by the group. Make deliberate mistakes in several places. Show the wrong hand sign. The children must sing the correct *solfa* and show the correct hand sign whenever the teacher makes a "mistake." Youngsters thoroughly enjoy doing this and quickly become facile with it.

4. Choose a favorite folk song or an exercise from Kodály's *333 Elementary Exercises.* Have the group sing it in *solfa,* leaving out all the *mi*'s or the *so*'s, only thinking those sounds.

5. Put an unfamiliar melody, 4 bars long, on the board. Allow the class to study it for a few moments. Erase it. Have the group sing it back.

It is this ability to look at notation and think sound, not place on an instrument, that truly separates musicians from nonmusicians. It is not a talent. It is a skill that can be taught.

Memory training

One of the biggest problems facing any elementary-school choir director is children's seeming inability to memorize their words and music. Memory, like inner hearing, is a learned skill. It can and must be taught. The choir director must guide memorization. For example, using Kodály's *Pentatonic Music,* vol. 1, have the group: look at No. 1; sing it correctly aloud; then read the first four measures silently; close the books and sing the exercise again aloud from memory; then look at the books to find where mistakes were made; correct them. There is value to using short and easy examples at the beginning for memory work. In this way, one may establish behaviors for memorizing. Later, use the concert music itself in the same way; focus on one section at a time. Be sure the children know by what date a particular piece of music is to be completely committed to memory; and stagger the due dates so that choir members are not faced with memorizing twelve pieces of music during the week before the concert.

Following the director

How may the director help children to understand and respond correctly to conducting motions? First, by being consistent in conducting techniques, simplifying them, always using certain motions for cutoffs, and others to indicate crescendos, decrescendos. Second, by teaching children how to conduct at least the basic simple meters: 2, 3, and 4. Actually, one seldom needs more than these to conduct anyway.

| | is sufficient for | 2 & 2   6 |
| | | 4   2   8 |

| is sufficient for | 3   9 adagio $<$ 3 |
| | 4   8   8 |

| is sufficient for | 4   12 |
| | 4   8 |

Combinations of the above may be used for $\frac{5}{8}$ and $\frac{7}{8}$. Children can learn to perform these gestures for beating time. They can, in addition, learn to recognize and respond appropriately to specific gestures for entrances, attacks, releases, and other special emphases such as crescendos, decrescendos, ritards, fermata.

Signals can be worked out to remind the choir to focus on a vowel sound, to sharpen a pitch, to watch a rushing or lagging tempo.

A word here about clean attacks and endings. Most conductors worry about attacks and so achieve them cleanly. Clean endings are another matter. The dropping of final notes is one of the most common errors in both classroom singing and elementary choirs. Cutoffs should be conducted with a clearly identifiable sign at the beginning of the beat following the note duration; for example, in ♩ ♩ ♩ 𝄽 , the cutoff should be given at the beginning of the fourth beat.

For attacks, the director should breathe obviously with the children and form the first word noticeably. The whole body should prepare them for an entrance, not just the conducting arm.

The folk-singing portion of the choir period can be used as one opportunity for individual students to conduct. The entire choir should evaluate the conducting of each student-conductor with respect to accuracy in beating time, tempo, dynamics, etc.

The last two goals, *vocal technique* and *enunciation,* are functions of the second facet of the choral teaching task: the singing.

THE SINGING

Vocal technique and enunciation

Faulty intonation is a problem that plagues choir directors the world over. A children's choir singing simple unaccompanied unison numbers well in tune is vastly to be preferred to one that can sing involved three-part music, always a little flat. Yet, one hears much more of the latter than the former. What can be done to develop good intonation in children's choirs?

It is a mistake to be too technical when talking to children. Teachers must understand the techniques involved in the production of good vocal tones, i.e., good singing posture, loose jaw, open throat, good vowel and consonant sounds, and proper breathing, and then translate that understanding into child behaviors, so that they become singing habits. It is not necessary to "explain" them to children—in fact, to do so may actually deter rather than aid in their mastery. Far more can be accomplished by demonstrating rather than explaining—far more through imagery than through telling. Diagrams of the throat, tongue, larynx, etc. may mean a great deal to serious voice students, but it is doubtful that they ever helped a child to produce a good tone. How then should one deal with voice production?

Good singing is dependent upon several factors:

1. Accurate inner hearing.
2. Good singing posture.
3. Proper breathing.
4. Loose jaw, open throat, and properly placed tongue.
5. Good vowel and consonant sounds.

Inner hearing

A child must have the correct pitch in mind before singing it. Under choir rehearsal techniques (p. 110), five inner-hearing exercises are suggested to aid in the development of children's ability to think sound. Here the concern is for the quality of that sound, the correctness of the pitch.

The average person can hear minute pitch deviations. Unfortunately, ability to match pitch lags far behind. One must train the younger singer first to hear the pitch as it should be produced, and then to match it. To accomplish this, models must be provided—and it is at this point that the whole procedure is undermined with most choirs. The model usually provided is the piano, an instrument that contributes to, rather than corrects, pitch problems. The piano is tuned (if it is tuned) to an equal-tempered scale. Voices should not be. If one investigates the choral training of any really fine children's choir, one will probably find they are rehearsed without piano via the Pythagorean intervallic principles, based on the overtone system, in which:

— the third of the major scale is always sung higher than C to E on the keyboard sounds;
— the third of the IV and V chords is sung high (in *solfa, mi, la,* and *ti* are sung higher);

— the fifth scale degree *(so)* is sung high, but comparatively less so than the *mi, la,* and *ti.*

It is this tonal system of the Greek philosopher and mathematician Pythagoras that is used by all Hungarian children's choirs. It results in a bright very in-tune sound.[6] To use these principles with children simply involves thinking and singing a bit higher or more intensely on *mi, so, la,* and *ti.* The sounds actually produced are the ones heard as overtones when singing in a very live room.

To help the choir arrive at the correct pitches, have it sing the following exercises. Each section should sing each voice part:

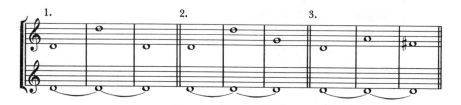

The octave, if sung intensely, causes the correct fifth sound to ring in the ears. The fifth sound, if sung in tune, produces the third. These exercises and the ones like them in the Kodály volume *Let Us Sing Correctly,* when practiced regularly, enormously aid in developing good choral intonation.

The hum, too, is an invaluable tool for helping singers to hear their own pitches. A singer hears his voice principally through the bone and muscle tissue in his head, rather than through his ears. Closing the lips— humming—intensifies the singer's pitch sensitivity. To hum correctly, choose a vowel sound, sing it, then close the lips lightly, still singing the vowel inside. If doing *a cappella* singing, give the pitch as a hummed sound. In vocalizing, use a hummed consonant "m" or "n" to precede the vowel sound as an aid to more accurate hearing.

Singing posture

A second behavior important to in-tune choral singing is good posture. Good posture is the first step toward correct breathing. It is important to establish and insist upon a comfortable but correct singing position to be used always, not just for performances. Children should

---

[6] For anyone who would like a more technical explanation of it, the Hungarian music educator Laszlo Dobsoy has written an excellent mathematical analysis of it, and in the United States, Paul F. Roe, in his book *Choral Music Education,* has discussed it quite fully and has shown a specific note-by-note comparison with the tempered piano scale.

sit forward, on the front third of their chairs—any other position leads to slumping, rounded backs, concave diaphragms.

Feet must be placed in a way that promotes good posture. Make sure the chairs in the rehearsal room are of the right size. Folding chairs induce improper posture. It is impossible for fourth and fifth graders, whose feet do not even touch the floor, to sit correctly in the usual auditorium chair. "Feet flat on the floor" is both uncomfortable and incorrect. Feet slightly back of the body, with only the toes touching the floor, will automatically throw the body forward into a better singing posture.

Do not tell children to "sit up" or "stand up straight." This almost always results in a forced and unnatural raising of the shoulders. The shoulders should be felt as pulling down—"your hands are heavy, let them fall loosely at your sides. You are a puppet, there is a string fastened to the middle of your chest; your chest is high, your shoulders low." To the teacher looking at the children, their shoulders and hips should appear to be in line and their backs straight, not arched.

Show the students how to hold their music. Then be consistent and have it held that way at all times. Have them place one hand under it to support it, the other over it to turn pages. It should be held at chest level so that the director is visible by merely shifting the eyes.

Breathing

Kodály said, about breathing for singing:

> With us it is scarcely every twentieth person who uses his speech and breathing organs correctly. This, too, should be learned during the singing lesson. The discipline of rhythm, the training of throat and lungs set singing right besides gymnastics. Both of them, no less than food, are needed daily.

Breath is to singing what wind is to a sailboat: the power that keeps it moving. When the wind dies down, the sail flutters to a stop and the boat ceases to move. When air pressure (or breath) stops in singing, sound fades away or stops, and as air pressure fades, tones go flat. One actually sings on air *pressure,* not on air. Children should be helped to concentrate on releasing as little air as possible when singing. "Take a breath, hiss, keep your ribs out, use the smallest amount of air possible, raise your hand when you run out." Time this; aim initially for 25 seconds. It can be built up to 50. Later, go from the "hiss" to an "ah" sound.

Music teachers know that the diaphragm is the breath-controlling muscle; the abdomen, the power. The waistline expands when a singer inhales. The ribs must be held out from the time he begins until he finishes. Students can be helped to feel this in any one of several ways: To feel deep breathing—

1. Put hands at waistline. Yawn. Feel the expansion.
2. Take a deep breath. Blow out all candles on the birthday cake at once.
3. Lie on the floor. Put a book on your stomach. Make the book move up when air is inhaled; down when air is exhaled. (It is almost impossible to breathe incorrectly when lying flat on the back.)
4. Pant or laugh on pitch.

Actually, correct breathing results almost automatically if posture is good, shoulders down and relaxed, and throat open. However, air must be held back at the ribs and diaphragm, not in the throat. If the latter occurs, throat tension and a breathy tone result.

Sometimes, a note that is in tune at the attack is not in tune at the end of its duration. This is particularly true of sustained notes and phrase endings. Children tend to hit and fade on sustained notes. They run out of breath before they run out of note. Good singing for a children's choir is legato singing. "Make a ribbon of sound—an unbroken ribbon of sound." To do this as a choir, it is necessary that the children learn how to stagger breathing, i.e., to become softer just before taking a breath, to breathe in quickly, to return softly singing the same vowel, and to swell to normal volume. This can be practiced very effectively with the Kodály *Let Us Sing Correctly* exercises, all of which are performed in a sustained legato style.

Jaw, throat, tongue

It is pointless to keep telling children to "Open your mouths." They think they have them open. The fingers-in-the mouth technique is equally faulty. Who can sing with a mouth full of fingers! A technique that works—all the time—is to have the children find "the hole in front of the ear." When the hole is there, the jaw is dropped and in a relaxed position correct for singing. It will not be there if the jaw is jutted forward or to one side or is not open wide enough. What they are feeling is a synovial cavity—although it is certainly not necessary for the children to know that. The opening produced in this way is too wide for the lower register, but excellent for high notes. Practice with finding the opening and using it to make better sounds on high notes also helps children keep a more correct throat and jaw position throughout their singing. They learn to modify the openness to the demands of the music. Do watch that children do not duck their heads for low notes or raise their heads for high notes.

Vowel and consonant sounds

If posture is good, jaws loose, throat relaxed, inner hearing good, and breathing done from the diaphragm, the sounds produced may still be poor if there is not specific work with vowel and consonant sounds. In Hungarian choirs, no time need be spent on pronunciation; each letter in the Hungarian alphabet has but one sound, the vowels are pure vowels. English vowels are not pure sounds, but diphthongs:

a is actually a–ee

i is actually i–ee

o is actually o–oo

In correct singing, one of these sounds must be sung and the other barely touched on. Much bad choral singing comes from singing on the wrong part of the diphthong. Generally, the added sound must be the extreme endpoint of the duration being sung. For example: in "I'm going to pray when the spirit says pray" the two vowel sounds in the word "pray" are *eh* and *ee*. The *eh* should be the singing vowel; the *ee* should be sounded at the very endpoint of the duration. Also:

i—ah-ee: "The Water is Wide." In "wide" the *ah* should be the singing vowel; the *ee* should be sounded at the very end of the duration.

o—oh-oo: "Let us Walk Through the White Snow." In "snow" the *oh* should be the singing vowel; the *oo* should be sounded at the very end of the duration.

In this same general vowel class are:

ow—ah-oo, as in "hour," "now," "round": "Round and Round, Old Joe Clark." In "round" the *ah* is the singing vowel; the *oo* must be sung very quickly at the end of the duration.

oi—o-ee, as in "joy": "Joy to the World." In "joy" the *o* is the singing vowel; the *ee* must be barely touched, just before the next note.

The last sounds in these diphthongs are referred to by choral experts as *vanishing sounds*. Unfortunately, in children's choirs all too often they are anything but vanishing.

In addition to diphthongs in which the second sound must become a vanishing one, there are diphthongs in which the first of the two sounds must be barely touched on, the second sound becoming the singing vowel:

u—ee-oo: "Like Morning Dew." In "dew" the *oo* must be sung; the *ee* must be taken lightly and quickly.

There are, as well, a few other vowel-production related problems: "a" as in "ask," "had," "man," and "an" as in "dance" are ugly singing sounds. A broader sound is both more beautiful and easier to understand. Have the children take the dropped-jaw formation they use for vocalizing on *ah* when singing these sounds. They will sound better.

The *ar* as in "farm" also is often a problem. There is a tendency to sing the "r" as a vowel. Again, sing with the mouth in the *ah* position and simply eliminate the "r." The author has occasionally spelled out the word on the board without the "r" and had the children say it that way before singing: f–ah–m. The singing sound is better and the audience's ear supplies the missing "r."

A vowel must be sustained unchanged for the duration of the note. It is common for the lip and mouth position gradually to change in anticipation of the coming consonant sound. This produces ugly vowel sounds. The vanishing vowel or the closing consonant must be produced in the fraction of the moment that is the end of that note's duration.

To practice this, the British award-winning choir director and Kodály specialist, Margaret Holden, has children sing entire songs only on their vowel sounds, eliminating the consonants. It is not easy to do, but can be a useful technique to develop. When doing this, one may hear on which vowel sound of the diphthong the children are singing, and correct it if necessary. In "rose" are they singing on the *oh* or on the *oo* sound? In "I" are they singing on the *ah* or on the *ee*?

Another useful technique is to have children sing the song through on one pure vowel sound, *ah, o,* or *oo,* concentrating on open relaxed jaw and good tone.

Tongue position is also important for correct vowel production. "Tip of the tongue, tip of the teeth," says Margaret Holden, meaning that the tip of the tongue must always be at the fleshy ridge at the base of the lower front teeth on vowel sounds. Children are not accustomed to doing this. The teacher will have to remind them many times; but eventually it becomes habit. With the tip of the tongue in this position, the rest of the tongue moves naturally into the various correct positions according to the vowel being sounded—from the highest front position (*ee*) to the lowest back position (*aw*). This need not be discussed with the children; it will happen if they feel "tip of the tongue, tip of the teeth."

Turning to consonants, these must be sounded as quickly as possible, so that the tongue may return to its correct vowel position. The choir must sound consonants cleanly and identifiably. If they are initial consonants, the children must learn to get through them quickly and on to the vowel sound. Children enjoy and benefit from tongue-twisting consonant exercises such as those devised by Margaret Holden:

T: Try teaching to tax temper.

V: Vain Vernon vowed vengeance.

R: Round rough rocks ragged rascals ran.

W: Wise women won't whine.

Ch: Church chaps chirp chants cheerfully.

Students delight in making up their own exercises like these. The thing to remember about consonants is that children should not sing on them, even if they are consonants on which pitch can be sustained (m, n, ng, l, r). Pitch should be sustained only on vowels. The "ing" is a case in point. Indeed, some pop groups sing on such voiced consonants as a matter of style. It is not good singing practice, however, and should be avoided. With "ing" words, have the children hold the *ee* sound, adding the *ng* at the very end: *see—ng* ("sing").

As a general rule, avoid regional speech sounds. For vocalizing, use pure Italian vowel sounds. Also be sure that *solfa* sounds are pure vowels and not diphthongs. Children imitate their teachers. If the teacher sings *solfa* with pure vowel sounds, the choir will.

The teacher may work long and hard on all the above aspects of good singing and still occasionally find the choir has problems with intonation. Sometimes the reason can be very simple: it's a rainy, depressing day; the room is stuffy; the children are tired; the acoustics of the room are poor. None of these are permanent conditions. Correct them if possible and move on.

Most often, however:

flatting is caused by	*correct flatting by*
Not opening the jaw enough.	Finding the synovial cavity. Use it to get the jaws open.
Not using pure vowel sounds.	Singing the song in *solfa*, concentrating on pure vowel sounds; then singing it only on its vowels, leaving out all consonants.
Singing too loudly.	Reducing the volume; lightening the tone quality.
Poor posture.	Standing, one foot before the other in a position of presentation.
Shallow breathing.	Placing hands on diaphragm; feeling the expansion.

Encourage critical listening and self-evaluation. The children should ask themselves: "Were we in tune?" "Where was the problem?" "What do we need to do to correct it?" Accurate self-evaluation is the beginning of learning.

Once the long-range goals have been established (seven are given in this chapter) and the techniques decided on through which to accomplish them, the choir director is ready to begin selecting musical materials and planning for sets of individual rehearsals. This introduces the third facet of the choral teaching task: the sung.

THE SUNG

If the teacher plans for about six rehearsals at a time, they will hold together better than if he plans just one at a time. In order to achieve continuity and variety, it is easier to look at a somewhat longer time span than one rehearsal or one week.

The author, working with a fifth- and sixth-grade choir, developed the chart given here. The headings are related to the seven goals to be accomplished. Under each are listed specific musical materials and activities intended to aid in the accomplishment of that goal. These do not give the individual rehearsal order. They are a long-range plan of action for achieving musical goals. Once these are in hand, it is necessary to write out each rehearsal order from them. A sample rehearsal order based on the second part of the chart is also given.

A single rehearsal order for the lesson given here might be (55-minute rehearsal):

Folk songs to warm up; conducting. (10 minutes)

1. Open with hand singing—lead into "I've Been to Haarlem." Sing the song with words, then with *solfa*; do an inner-hearing game—leave out all low *la*'s, *mi*'s—think them while singing the rest of the song on *solfa*.

2. "Shady Grove." Have this conducted by a student who was given it as an assignment at the previous rehearsal. Class evaluates tempo, dynamics, attacks, and cutoffs.

Singing technique; intonation. (5 minutes)

3. Vocal exercises for intonation. *Let Us Sing Correctly:* No. 6 and No. 8—work on singing the major third (*m-d*) wide. Relate the exercise to "Ladybird" in which the opening *m-r-d* tends to be sung flat.

Work on the most difficult piece early in the rehearsal. (10 minutes)

4. "Ladybird." Examine and describe the movement of the voice parts. Work on the two outside voices (p. 3).

Materials		Music Reading	In-Tune Singing	Inner Hearing	Memory Training	Conducting	Vocal Technique and Enunciation
Concert	Other						

I. What would be included during the year:

Materials		Music Reading	In-Tune Singing	Inner Hearing	Memory Training	Conducting	Vocal Technique and Enunciation
The year's concert material (chosen before the first rehearsal)	Folk songs Vocalizes Kodály: *Elementary Exercises* and *Pentatonic Music,* vol. 1	Ear training, interval drills, reading from hand singing and tone-sets Kodály: *Elementary Exercises* and *Pentatonic Music,* vol. 1	Scale singing Root singing Chord singing Exercises from Kodály: *Let Us Sing Correctly*	The five techniques given earlier, sequenced from easy to difficult through the year	Work on one section of one piece each rehearsal for memorization Establish deadlines for completion of memorization of each concert piece	All students have opportunity to conduct during the year	Breath control Vowel production Treatment of consonants Attack, release of tone Voice blending Phrasing Use of tongue, jaw in singing Posture

II. What might be listed for one rehearsal period:

Materials		Music Reading	In-Tune Singing	Inner Hearing	Memory Training	Conducting	Vocal Technique and Enunciation
"Ladybird" "New Year's Carol" "Strawberry Fair" "Simple Gifts"	"I've Been to Haarlem" "Shady Grove" No. 6 and No. 8 from Kodály: *Let Us Sing Correctly*	Rhythm: "Strawberry Fair" Tone-set: s, d r m f s Hand singing Set: A-do with fingers Read a section of "Strawberry Fair"	No. 6 and No. 8 of Kodály: *Let Us Sing Correctly* m-d interval Relate to "Ladybird"	"I've Been to Haarlem" (leave out low *la*'s and *mi*'s)	"New Year's Carol" (chorus *with* dynamics)	Student conducts "Shady Grove" Class evaluates for tempo, attacks, cut-offs	"Simple Gifts" (breathing for full phrases; watch releases)

Polish a more familiar piece. Work on memorization. (10 minutes)

5. "New Year's Carol." Work on vowel sounds; sing the song through on *mah* first, then with words. Memorize the chorus. Pay special attention to the crescendo and decrescendo while memorizing. Note the difference on the third singing: *mf* to *pp*.

Music reading. New piece introduced. (10 minutes)

6. Read these rhythms from the board:

Practice tone-set *s, d r m f s* with hand singing. Use open fingers as a staff to prepare the choir for reading in A-*do*. Look at the octavo: "Strawberry Fair." Find the familiar patterns. Read the first statement of the melody in *solfa* (p. 1).

Close with well-known, well-loved piece. (5 minutes)

7. "Simple Gifts." Draw attention to final durations and to cutoff points before singing. Emphasize breathing for long phrases. Perform with accompaniment.

Budget your time

Know how long each activity should take and, within reason, stick to it. If you must run over on one activity (usually by getting stuck on some difficulty), be sure to provide a balance by going to something easier after it and not plunging into another potential problem area. Students need periods of concentration, broken by periods of relaxation, to learn effectively.

Performance

A song, such as one of those mentioned in the sample rehearsal plan, takes about 3 minutes to perform. A set might have five or six such numbers, or might consist of some simpler music—folk songs the children have been singing, mixed in among the more difficult octavo pieces. Two such sets are certainly enough for young voices to sing—30 to 40 minutes of actual singing time.

Arrange the material so that the choir begins with something light and easy—to warm the voices; then do the more difficult music while the children are still fresh, and close with lighter, more relaxing material.

Repeat some numbers from year to year, for the sake of both the choir and the audience. Many people do not care for Benjamin Britten's "Ceremony of Carols" or Kodály's "Evening Song" the first time they sing or hear it. Almost without exception, they do the third or fourth time. A youngster who sings the relatively easy soprano line of Kodály's "Christmas Dance of the Shepherds" when in fourth grade will be aurally familiar with the alto part and able to perform it well in sixth grade. Do make certain that the numbers repeated from year to year are of musical worth.

Do not attempt to make youngsters sound like adults. Here lies vocal strain. Remember that loud and soft are comparative concepts. If their "soft" is soft enough, the choir need never sing too loudly; the contrast will make a *mezzo-forte* seem loud.

A solo performance here and there in the program lends variety and gives the talented or exceptionally musical child an extra boost.

Hold the final rehearsal in the performance hall if possible and be sure everything is lined up to run without pause. Delays lose audiences.

Selecting Music for Choir

Kodály said, "Only the best music is good enough for children." He spent a major part of his creative life composing for children. He considered the development of taste in music—an ability to discriminate the good from the bad, the fine and enduring from the cheap and transitory—to be the major goal of music education. Even music literacy, which he also held to be very important, did not occupy as large a place in his speaking and writing as this development of musical taste; indeed, he believed it to be the single most important aspect of music literacy. He wrote in an article on children's choirs:

> Bad taste spreads by leaps and bounds. In art this is not so innocent a thing as in, say, clothes. Someone who dresses in bad taste does not endanger his health, but bad taste in art is a veritable sickness of the soul. . . .
>
> In grown-ups this sickness is in most cases incurable. Only prevention can help. It should be the task of the school to administer immunization.[7]

When Kodály said that we should use "only the best" music with children he had two kinds of music in mind:

1. authentic folk music
2. fine art or composed music

[7] *The Selected Writings of Zoltán Kodály* (London–New York: Boosey & Hawkes Music Publishers Ltd., 1964), p. 120.

At whatever ability level a choir is, there are beautiful folk songs and lovely art music they can perform.

However, it is important that a teacher gauge accurately where in the hierarchy of part-singing his children are, if he is not to frustrate them with music too difficult or bore them with music too easy.

Part-singing is a developmental skill. It does not suddenly bloom full-grown at the fifth or sixth grade. It must be prepared step by step from kindergarten. If this is not possible—if the choir director does not also teach the younger children—then the choir must be taken through a learning hierarchy in part-singing until the director finds their level of competence, and new learnings can start from that point.

Types of musical experiences appropriate to child-developmental stages in part-singing may be arranged from easiest to most difficult as follows:

1. Ostinati—first, rhythmic; then melodic.
2. Descants.
3. Two-hand singing of known intervals.
4. Canons—first, rhythmic; then melodic at the unison; later, melodic at other intervals or with rhythmic variation (augmentation, diminution).
5. Root singing of the I, IV, and V chords as a second part.
6. Two-part singing in which the voices are in contrary motion or are imitative of each other. Each part has a "tune."
7. Three-part singing of music in which there are canonic or descant-like parts.
8. Two-part singing based on thirds and sixths harmony.
9. Vocal chording—as accompaniment to songs and through hand singing.
10. Three-part singing with the upper voices in thirds and sixths harmony and the lower voice singing the root of the chord.
11. Part songs (two or three parts) in which the parts create unusual or dissonant harmonies.

If the director comes into a choir situation in which there has been little or no music instruction previously, he will need to begin at the very first of these steps toward part-singing and move through them systematically, going on to the next step only when the students are comfortably performing at the previous level. Of course, none of these should be discontinued; after each begins, it continues throughout the choir experience. A group performing at competency level 11 would have in their continuing repertory music using descants, canons, ostinati, chording.

However, the group that cannot perform a canon well should not be pushed into singing two-part songs with thirds and sixths harmonies. Some teaching techniques and materials for each step of the hierarchy are suggested below.

Ostinati

Ostinato, in this context, is a repeated motif, rhythmic or melodic, used as an accompaniment for a song.

Rhythmic ostinati. On the simplest level the choir might sing a nursery song, "Ring Around the Rosy," while clapping ‖: ♩ ♩ ♫ ♩ :‖ . As easy as this seems, students sometimes have difficulty doing this if they have never clapped an ostinato before. Once they are able to perform the given ostinato with one short simple melody, the teacher should transfer the same ostinato to a longer, more involved tune, perhaps, a folk song the group knows. When they can perform the same ostinato well in several different musical contexts, the teacher may then present a new ostinato: ♩ ♫ ♩ ♩ or ♫ ♩ ♫ ♩ ♩ . After several four-beat ostinati are being performed well, longer ones (eight beats) may be attempted. This experience with producing simultaneous musical sounds in an extremely simple setting is a good foundation for later part-singing.

Melodic ostinati. Repeated pentatonic or wide-range motifs may be used to accompany small-range songs:

M. E. Allen

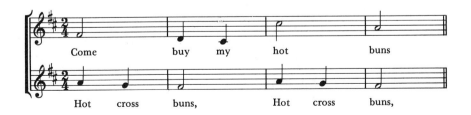

Small-range motifs may be used to accompany pentatonic songs:

Tell it on the moun - tain, Tell it on the moun - tain

Go tell it on the moun - tain

Some other ostinati that work well with pentatonic songs are:

The teacher will have to experiment with these and others to discover which ostinati provide the best accompaniments to which songs. Children can create their own ostinati with a little practice. The rhythms should, of course, be altered to suit the word context and to create some contrast with the song rhythm, i.e., sustained notes against moving ones, moving notes against sustained ones.

In presenting an ostinato (rhythmic or melodic) for the first time, there are a series of steps which will ensure that the students have success with it:

1. The group sings the song softly while the teacher performs the ostinato for them to hear.
2. The group claps or sings the ostinato softly while the teacher sings the song.
3. Half the group sings or claps the ostinato while the other half sings the song.
4. The two groups switch parts.
5. The entire group claps the ostinato while singing the song. (With rhythmic ostinati only.)

When students experience difficulty with an ostinato it is generally because one or more of the above steps has been omitted.

Descants

A descant is an (independent) countermelody sung along with the melody, related to the melody; it is usually decorative in character.

There are numerous collections of descants for young choirs. Among the best known and most musical of these are those by Beatrice and Max Krone.[8] In addition, many school-music series texts contain songs with descants in the fourth-, fifth-, and sixth-grade books. These are often interesting enough to be used as concert selections for children's choir. Sometimes several descants may be layered with the same song to create interesting harmonic effects. The following descants by Betty Bertaux, Director of the Children's Chorus of Maryland, are examples:

WHAT SHALL WE DO WITH A DRUNKEN SAILOR

Arr. B. Bertaux

[8] Several books of descants for children (Park Ridge, Illinois: Neil A. Kjos Music Co.)

There are two additional descants for this tune in the published octavo.[9]

Two-hand singing

Kodály says:

> The simultaneous sound is the guarantee of correct attack, not the method of stepwise climbing up the scales; for, when we reach the fifth or sixth note, the first will have been forgotten; . . . (*Let Us Sing Correctly*)

Two-hand singing involves the use of Kodály hand signs by the teacher to guide the choir through simultaneous interval sounds. Half the group follows the left hand, the other half, the right. Exercises should be short, and performed in legato style. No more than two such exercises should be done during one choir period, and each choir section should in turn sing both the lower and upper voice parts. The intervals worked on should, if possible, be related to choral music being studied.

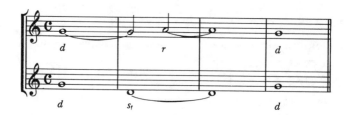

The *do* to *re* major second is often sung flat. In the above exercise, hearing *re* with low *so,* the perfect fifth, causes it to be sung higher and more in tune.

Canons

In canons, the second (and other) voices imitate the first voice and follow at a distance. They commonly end one voice following the other, as they begin; however, the later voice parts may be altered so that all parts end together. The voices may be imitation at the unison or at other intervals. Rounds are a type of canon at the unison.

Few musical experiences prepare children's ears for part-singing as well as canons sung in tune. The young choir cannot sing too many of them.

The variety and number of available canons is seemingly limitless. They exist at every level of complexity, in many musical styles, and from

---

[9] This and other excellent arrangements by Bertaux for children's choir are available through C. T. Wagner Music Publishers, 3303 18th Street N.W., Washington, DC 20010.

many musical periods. There are simple nursery tunes that may be sung
in canon:

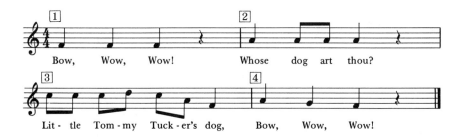

Bow, Wow, Wow! Whose dog art thou?
Lit - tle Tom - my Tuck - er's dog, Bow, Wow, Wow!

Easy folk tunes may often be performed in canon effectively:

I got a let- ter this morn - ing, Oh, yes;
I got a let - ter this morn - ing, Oh, yes.

Canons at the unison are the most usual and the easiest to sing;
however, there are also canons at other intervals, simple enough for
performance by children:

FLY, LITTLE SWALLOW

Josquin Des Pres
1450–1521

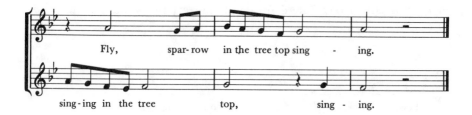

or

E. Szőnyi

Bicinia Americana, Boosey &
Hawkes [in press].

Canons sometimes work well in rhythmic augmentation or diminution. One beautiful example of this can be found in Britten's *Friday
Afternoons:* [10]

OLD ABRAM BROWN

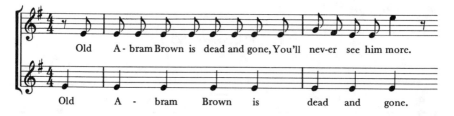

Rhythmic augmentation of this sort may be done with many canons; the
choir will enjoy experimenting to see with which it sounds euphonious
and with which it creates dissonance.

Root singing of the I, IV, and V chords as an accompaniment to songs

This is a type of ostinato performance, since it involves using a
simple repeated melodic motif as accompaniment to a song. However,
the choir at this point should be made aware of the degree of the scale

[10] Copyright 1936 by Boosey & Co. Ltd. Published by: Boosey & Hawkes,
New York.

on which the motif is being sung. The foundation for later understanding of harmonic structure can be established here; later, vocal chording may be built over the root tones.

To introduce the root of the tonic chord (*do* in major, *la* in minor) as an accompaniment, have the choir sing a song with *do* as a drone. Use hand signs to guide the first singing of the second voice part and have the group sing it in *solfa*. Later, substitute words.

Drone:

Sing:

LONDON'S BURNING

Canon

The minor modes should not be neglected when working on this easiest level of harmonic understanding. For example, with the song "I Got a Letter" (see notation under canons above) the choir could sing on *la*:

as an accompaniment to the canon. This use of the tonic root as a drone is one of the simplest of all part-singing experiences. However, it should not be overdone since, by its very nature, it tends to lead to flatting. It should be an occasional activity for fun, rather than a rehearsed one for performance.

When the root of the dominant (V) chord (in *solfa*, *so* in major, *mi* in minor) is added, many more songs are useable and the problems with flatting become less.

SKIP TO MY LOU

or

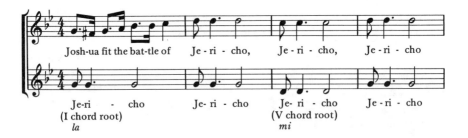

Very few American folk songs can be harmonized correctly with a IV chord. There are some.

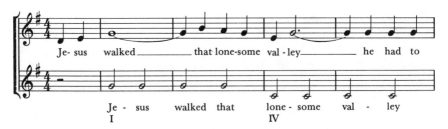

However, so many are pentatonic in character that it may be easier to find examples from composed music:

ALLELUIA

Mozart

As the youngsters become proficient in root singing, the director should stop giving hand-singing cues for changes from *do* to *fa* and *so* or *la* to *mi*. The group should be able to determine aurally and to anticipate where the changes occur.

One caution about root singing as a second voice part to folk songs more modal in character than built on classical harmonies: most of these should be harmonized with the chord built on the flatted seventh rather than on the fourth and fifth steps. In *solfa*, the roots of the harmonization would be *la*, and *so*, for modes of minor character (Dorian, Phrygian):

SCARBOROUGH FAIR

Dorian modal character

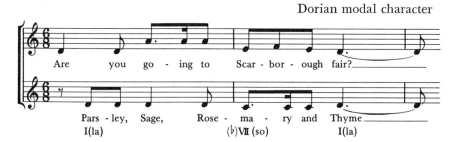

and do, and ta, for modes major in character (Mixolydian, Lydian):

with

GOOD MORNING, MY PRETTY LITTLE MISS

Mixolydian modal character
Appalachian

She an - swered "I'm___ too young,"

Two-part singing in contrary motion or imitative

A level of difficulty above canons and root singing are two-part songs in which the voices are somewhat imitative but not completely so. In such pieces, the voices may begin canonically, but then frequently are in contrary motion, or one voice is sustained while the other moves. Kodály composed many such choruses for treble voices. Examples can be found throughout his *Bicinia Hungarica*, as well as in his octavo pieces such as "Christmas Dance of the Shepherds." [11] Unfortunately, a number of his lovely simple two-voice children's songs, found in Hungary in the volume *Gyermek-És Nőikarok (Children's and Women's Choruses)*,[12] are as yet untranslated and unpublished in the United States.

The style referred to here was not invented by Kodály, however. Other examples may be found throughout the literature in composed music and in arrangements of folk music. Of American folk songs arranged in this way, among the best are Erzsébet Szőnyi's *Bicinia Americana*[13] and Mark Williams' *Two-part American Songs*.[14] From the latter:

WHAT'LL WE DO WITH THE BABY?

Arr. Mark Williams

What'll we do with the ba - by?

What'll we do with the ba - by?   What'll we do with the

The director should not overlook choral music of great composers as a materials source for two-part songs of this type. The soprano–alto

---

[11] Copyright 1938 by Universal Editions (Bryn Mawr, Pennsylvania: Theodore Presser Co.).

[12] Zoltán Kodály, *Gyermek-És Nőikarok* (Budapest: Editio Musica Budapest, 1972).

[13] Erzsébet Szőnyi, *Bicinia Americana* (Oceanside, New York: Boosey & Hawkes, Inc. [in press]).

[14] Mark Williams, *Two-part American Songs* (San Antonio, Texas: Southern Music Co., 1977).

duets from Bach chorales, selected portions of full choruses by Brahms, Haydn, and Mozart may be performed by treble voices. What better way to encourage the love of great choral music than by singing it.

Often, very little arranging is necessary; as for example in the following adaptation of "He Watching Over Israel" from *Elijah* by Mendelssohn. The chorus has been transposed a major second lower and only the first 18 measures are suggested for performance. However, this is enough to provide students an experience with truly great music.

HE WATCHING OVER ISRAEL

Mendelssohn

Three-part singing of music in which there are canonic and descant-like parts

There are, unfortunately, all too few examples of this genre in arrangements of American folk songs and in composed English-language music for young choirs. It is the easiest kind of three-part singing possible. Every choir should have some experience with it.

Many of the Kodály choruses are constructed in this way. In his "Ladybird," [15] for example, the alto states the melody, the second sopranos repeat it in canon at an octave, and the sopranos sing a countermelody, a descant. There is nothing unfamiliar in structure, no difficult voice leaps, no unexpected or unmelodic turns for any voice part. This piece is a model for the kind of initial three-part singing a treble voice choir should have.

[15] Copyright 1967 by Boosey & Hawkes Music Publishers Ltd.

LADYBIRD

Kodály

This type of three-part song is actually easier for youngsters to sing than more chordally constructed two-part songs.

**Two-part singing that is harmonic in character
(singing largely in thirds and sixths)**

The choir may be prepared for this kind of harmonic experience through exercises in the warm-up period. When singing scales, the altos could begin on *do* when the sopranos reach *mi*. They should sing in a legato style, taking time to hear the major and minor thirds sounded in this way.

For hearing sixths, the sopranos may begin on *mi* and move step-wise to high *do*, while the altos sing stepwise from low *so* to *mi*.

Experience with singing simple thirds and sixths harmonies by ear should precede the use of octavo based on these harmonies. Many Christmas carols may be harmonized in this way, as well as a number of folk songs. Cowboy songs, particularly, lend themselves to this sort of easy harmonization.

Chording with folk songs

Students can be led to discover that they can build chords by singing any note of the scale and the third and fifth degrees over it. Then, using the root-singing technique learned earlier, they can perform chordal accompaniments to songs. Students should determine, by singing them, which inversions lead most easily from the I to the V chord. Chords can often be pulled directly from the melodic line of previously-taught songs.

a.

b.

I'm goin' to   leave_____old__Tex - as   now_____
s,   d   m   s   (l) s   m   d   m

c.

I's   the   b'y   That   builds   the   boat
m   m   m   m   r   t   s

SURPRISE SYMPHONY

Haydn

d.

d   d   m   m   s   s   m

f   f   r   r   t,   t,   s,

The teacher can indicate chord changes by showing the root position with hand signs. Later, students should be involved in deciding
where chords should change and to which chords they should change.
For chording, it is easiest initially to use songs to which the choir has
already done root singing. Example: "Skip to My Lou" (do and so
chords):

Skip to my lou,   Skip to my lou,   Skip to my lou,   Skip to my lou.

Encourage them to invent interesting rhythms to which they can
sing their chords. This use of chords as an harmonic ostinato is good
preparation for the next step.

Three-part harmonic singing

The easiest examples of this contain two voices in thirds and sixths
harmony and one voice root singing. Music of the eighteenth century
abounds with such examples.

AIR FROM THE MAGIC FLUTE

Mozart

Sweet__ mu-sic is ring-ing fall-ing soft on the ear

It is a small step from this to three-voice chorales. The ear helps the eye.

Part songs with unusual or dissonant harmonies

More dissonant choral music may follow. Some contemporary sounds should be a part of any choral experience. At the simplest level, those sounds could be provided by a Bartók or a Copland accompaniment to a unison song. However, the treble-voice choir that has progressed through the 10 steps outlined here and has learned to read music, at least to some extent, can also sing some of the more interesting contemporary choral literature. Bartók's lovely two-voice Lydian mode chorus "Don't Leave Me" and John Coates' interesting arrangement of "Parsley, Sage, Rosemary and Thyme" are examples of contemporary sounds which appeal to young singers.

In each of the above categories, one can find music, ranging from easy to difficult, suitable for the young choir. Hopefully, in the course of a year in choir the children will have experienced some music from each.

Unison singing

Unison singing has not yet been mentioned. Some of the most beautiful music available for treble-voice choirs is unison music. It should be a part of every repertory. However, it is a mistaken notion that the choir that cannot sing well in parts should just perform unison numbers. If children cannot perform two-voice numbers well in tune, they certainly will not be in tune when they sing in unison. The first involves concurrent intervals, the second, successive intervals, and it is far easier to sing a fifth in tune as a two-voice interval than to sing *do* to *so* in tune with no support other than one's inner hearing of what the *do–so* fifth should sound like.

Unison numbers, like part songs, should be practiced unaccompanied. Only when they are being quite perfectly performed should the accompaniment, if there is one, be added.

Searching for New Music

What should the choir director look for when searching for new music? First and foremost, quality music. He is going to be working on it with students for many months, in all probability. He should be sure that it is worth the time. If it is good music—a beautifully arranged folk song or a composed piece by a known and respected composer—the director should examine it with his particular group in mind. He should ask himself:

1. What are the ranges of the voice parts?
2. Is the difficulty level right for my choir? Where does this piece fall in the hierarchy of part-singing skills?
3. How will the second sopranos and altos find the pitches for each new entrance? Is it in another voice part?
4. Is the accompaniment, if any, an artistic addition or is it simply a crutch for the voice parts?

If the director finds satisfactory answers to these questions, he is ready to purchase the music and prepare it for teaching. The all-too-pervasive behavior of buying one copy for the director and one for the accompanist and of dittoing-off words for the choir is an appalling one; and the practice of buying one copy for each two choir members, not much better. If they are to learn anything about music, students must have music in front of them. To learn effectively, there must be one copy for each choir member. Vocal music reading involves reading of words, pitches, rhythms, and dynamic levels, and while doing all of this the student must also be watching the conductor, thinking about breathing, and blending his voice with others—a task made impossible if the student does not have his own music in front of him.

The mathematics or reading teacher would not try to teach without books or materials; no more should the music teacher.

If lack of money for octavo is the problem, consider establishing a central choral library in the school district, from which all schools may borrow sets of octavo. Choices of what music should be included in such a library could be made by a committee of music teachers, with suggestions coming from any other music teachers who cared to make them.

Once the choices for the year's choral work have been made (some unison numbers, some descants and canons, some two- and three-part work) and the sources are all available to place in students' hands (song sheets with the notation written out for folk songs, for example, series books for certain rounds, octavo for other selections), how should one study each piece of new music in order to present it well to the choir? It goes without saying that the director must know a piece well before attempting to teach it, even if the choir members read music fluently. How well should the director know it? The director should ask:

1. Can I sing all the voice lines without piano?
2. Have I made decisions as to tempo and dynamics?
3. Have I found ways to help each voice part find its beginning note at each entrance?
4. Have I isolated potential rhythmic and melodic problems and decided on solutions to them?

If the director can answer "yes" to these four questions, he is ready to put the music in the hands of the choir.

When the choir looks at new music for the first time the director should go through the following steps:

1. Before giving out the music, prepare by vocalizing on the tone-set used in the song, using *solfa* and hand signs.
2. Give out the music. Have the choir look through the first statement of the melody to determine whether there are any melodic or rhythmic problems. If so, help them solve these problems.
3. Have the choir sing the first statement of the melody in *solfa*. Insist that they keep going. In later choir periods, if it is a part song, have each part examined and sung by all.
4. Have them read the words and discuss them, noting, particularly, the relationship of words to dynamic markings.
5. Have them sing the melody again, this time with words, observing dynamics.

This is usually enough work for the choir's first time with a new piece. At later rehearsals they will:

1. Follow the melody through the piece to see what happens to it. (For example: "Here the melody is in the soprano, there in the alto voice.")
2. All read in *solfa* through all voice parts. To sing his own part well, each choir member must hear the other voice parts.

Not until the music is together and being sung well should the accompaniment, if there is one, be added.

Sometimes, at this point, it may encourage the choir to hear a fine recording of the piece they are studying. (For example, there are recordings of Benjamin Britten's "Friday Afternoons" and of Kodály and Bartók choruses, beautifully sung by children's groups.)

Children should never be directed in a rehearsal to "sing it again" without a specific focus. Repetition without reason accomplishes nothing. Either the director or the students can make suggestions as to what is needed: "What happened to our pitch on the passage?", "What can we do to correct it?" or "Did our tempo continue as we started it?" "What must we do?" If every member in the choir is evaluating as he sings, flatting is less likely to occur, tempo more likely to remain stable. Awareness can be developed by asking questions of the students. The questions should be directed, however; not just "What happened?", but "What is the dynamic marking on the top of page 3?" or "How should we have sung that phrase?"

Students will also perform choral music better if they have some understanding of the compositional techniques involved. If they can identify the sequence structure in "Waters of Babylon," the augmentation in "Old Abram Brown," the canon at an octave in "Ladybird," they are more likely to perform these works correctly.

The director should look on the choir period as one more opportunity for teaching—a marvelous opportunity, because he is working usually with children selected for their musicality and motivated by performance. If he does not use this opportunity to help students come to a love of good music, supported by intelligent concepts about music and by skills in music, the loss is his and theirs.

SUGGESTED ASSIGNMENTS

1. Find one musical example for each of the levels listed in the part-singing hierarchy on page 124.

2. Choose a two- or three-part treble-voice octavo selection. Analyze it in terms of the four criteria given on page 140.

3. Plot out one choir rehearsal, using the form given on page 121. Then write a plan for rehearsal, such as the one on pages 120 and 122.

4. Choose materials for a Christmas program. Plan for variety by including examples of unison numbers, canons, part songs, and solos. Arrange the numbers in performance order. Explain why they have been ordered in this way.

SUGGESTED READING

Music for Children's Choirs—A Selected and Graded Listing, compiled under the direction of the Boy and Children's Choirs Standing Committee of the American Choral Directors Association; Donald W. Roach, Project Coordinator (Reston, VA: Music Educators National Conference, 1977).

HELGA SZABÓ, *The Kodály Concept of Music Education* [textbook with three LP records] (London: Boosey & Hawkes Music Publishers Ltd., 1969).

III

PLANNING FOR
MUSICAL LEARNING

Introduction
to Part III

In Hungary, what Americans call "The Kodály Method" is a national system for music education. It is endorsed by the Ministry of Education and is the basis for all Hungarian school music texts. Teacher-training in Hungary is directed toward enabling teachers to work within the framework of this method.

In the United States, there is no national agency which establishes the way teaching is to be performed or which concerns itself with the sequencing of concepts for musical learning or with the selection of materials for use in each grade. It is unlikely that the United States will ever experience the uniformity of approach that exists in Hungary.

However, the very diversity of music education in America has led to the development of curriculum-construction processes which this author considers to be among the best in the world. Since there is no national agency dictating how to teach or taking responsibility for determining what to teach or when to teach it, curriculum construction has evolved at the grass roots level—within the individual school and school system. Even state guides, where they exist, are so general, they allow great latitude at the local level. It is at this local level that the most meaningful curriculum work is being done in American school systems, and it is being done largely by committees of teachers.

For this reason, teachers who wish to see Kodály philosophy and pedagogy in their school systems would do well to become acquainted with American curriculum-writing techniques. One capable teacher with knowledge of both Kodály principles and practice *and* basic principles of

American curriculum construction can influence music teaching for years to come in his or her district.

It is to aid in the wedding of these two highly compatible approaches—American curriculum construction methods and Kodály principles, methodology, and sequence—that the next three chapters are offered.

One final word of caution: in their zeal to effect change, Kodály teachers may go into curriculum committee work determined to make of every teacher a Kodály teacher. Nothing could be more off-putting. Much more can be accomplished if labels are left behind. Good teaching practice *is* good teaching practice. It does not have to be labeled "Kodály" and, indeed, may meet far less opposition if it is not. One should never lose sight of the fact that the subject of good curriculum writing is not Kodály but *music*.

chapter 7

Constructing Curriculum via Kodály Principles

Over the years, the author has served on countless curriculum committees and has been involved in the writing of numerous curriculum guides. It seems to be a favorite pastime of school districts—writing curriculum guides in every subject, to be passed down to teachers who then have to decipher and teach from them. Gradually, within a year or so, the guides get pushed to the back of the shelf where they gather dust until the next committee produces the next curriculum guide to end all curriculum guides—and it follows the same path. Most frequently, the only people who learn anything from curriculum guides are the people who write them. For them it can be a real learning process.

In Kodály practice, curriculum decisions should, one would think, be easily made. After all, Kodály is a system with a well-defined philosophy and with specific hierarchies of skills. However, when Kodály teachers meet to make curriculum decisions, all too often the topic of heated discussion is whether sixteenth notes should be called "tiri-tiri" or "tifi-tifi"; whether half notes should be "taa" or "too"; or whether ♩. ♪ should be taught before or after ♪ ♩ ♪; decisions of great moment! Many teachers who claim to be devoted to the philosophical goals of Kodály, in actual teaching practice seem simply to move from one rhythm pattern to the next, from one melodic turn to the next, with, perhaps, a nod to form along the way, in a sequence somewhat arbitrarily arrived at. Teachers who themselves have no understanding of the basic concepts and goals necessary for understanding music surely cannot do much to help children understand music. If teachers cannot identify, agree upon, and state a core of basic ideas about music, how can they possibly hope to teach music to children?

What really is the purpose of curriculum construction? It is three-fold:

1. To effect change for the better in the teaching process (teachers).
2. To facilitate learning (learners).
3. To determine what body of ideas about the subject should be taught (content).

Of these the last is frequently the only one actually dealt with by curriculum committees, although, surely, the first and second are equally important.

What is the purpose of evaluation? It, too, is threefold:

1. To see whether that change in teaching has really taken place (teachers).
2. To see whether the students have achieved what the new curriculum says it wants them to achieve (learners).
3. To assess the validity of the "new" curriculum (content).

Of these three evaluation areas the second—assessing the students' learning—is frequently the only one considered. The first is as important; the third—assessing the validity of the curriculum—is surely the most important.

To examine the process of curriculum construction, look first at these beginning and ending points: purpose and evaluation; it is in these areas that the key to valid curriculum construction lies.

THE TEACHER: CHANGING TEACHING BEHAVIOR

With respect to the first point under both purpose and evaluation—to effect change and to assess the change in the teaching process—people tend to teach as they were taught, not as they were taught to teach. It has been the author's experience that summer-school students—people with good teaching backgrounds—often write beautiful lesson plans and exhibit good intellectual understanding of the Kodály philosophy. When these same students stay on for a full year's program, and must assume responsibility for one class of children for the year, the initial reaction is frequently to fall back on what they knew about teaching before, on what they did before, which in itself is usually based on what their teachers did to them. Changing one's own teaching behavior is a difficult thing to do; no words in a book, no curriculum guide alone, can effect such a change. Such documents can at best only outline possible ways of changing the teaching. To ensure that such changes take place, a number of other actions are necessary—evaluative actions:

1. Frequent supervision (not of the punitive rating variety): analytical and critical of the teaching process, while acceptant of the teacher.
2. Self-evaluation: listening to cassette recordings of one's own lessons or parts of lessons, with specific questions in mind; viewing video tapes of one's own teaching to observe how closely a procedure was followed, how well the children really perceived what was being presented.
3. Evaluation by one's peers: interschool visits, cassette tapes, video tapes of other teachers involved in the same process. Again it is important that the focus always be on the teaching process and not on the teacher. It is both possible and essential to separate the two for purposes of evaluation; otherwise the teacher feels so threatened that no change in teaching behavior, good or bad, occurs.
4. Also effective are group discussions, group planning sessions, in-service days, and meetings centered around some particular curriculum-building activity. For example:
   a. working out an order for presenting music writing skills, with uniform manuscript papers acceptable to the whole group; or
   b. deciding on a core of high-quality musical materials for use with older children in a beginning Kodály program.

All the above are ways of both influencing change and then evaluating that change in teaching behavior, and as such are one essential element of the curriculum planning process.

THE LEARNER: FACILITATING THE LEARNING PROCESS AND EVALUATING WHETHER STUDENTS HAVE LEARNED WHAT THE CURRICULUM ESTABLISHED FOR THEM TO LEARN

Facilitating the learning process is totally a function of the teaching process. If teaching patterns are altered for the better, learning automatically becomes easier.

To determine whether the students have learned, it is essential that the instructional objectives of the curriculum be stated simply and in terms of specific learning behaviors. If they are, then evaluation becomes simply a matter of repeating the same task in a new musical setting. Instructional objectives are the desired outcomes of each learning situation, stated in terms of musical behaviors. They consist of those objectives we can see and hear carried out in children's performance. They may be stated using such behavioral verbs as:

The children will:	*Example of use of the verb:*
sing	their *l-s-m* songs in tune.
clap	patterns of ♩ , ♫ , and 𝄽 accurately.
step	the beat while singing.
identify	a song by its clapped rhythm.
distinguish	between higher and lower sounds in a two-note song (*s-m*).
write	the rhythm of a familiar song.
construct	rhythm patterns with sticks, tonal patterns on felt.
improvise	an answer-phrase to teacher's question-phrase within a known tone-set.

Each of these verbs requires an observable action on the part of the children. In writing instructional objectives, it is pointless to use such verbs as "understand" or "appreciate" or such phrases as "develop an awareness of." The former behavioral verbs imply their own evaluation. The teacher can hear the child sing in tune (or out of tune), can see the child step the beat accurately. The teacher cannot see the child "understand" or hear the child "appreciate." Through singing, stepping, clapping, identifying, constructing, and improvising one hopes the student will also understand and appreciate, but understandings and appreciations are not observable or measurable. They may be stated as eventual desirable results of the educative process, but they have no place in specific instructional objectives.

THE CONTENT

The last of the three stated purposes of both curriculum writing and of evaluation is determining what body of ideas about the subject should be taught, and then assessing the validity of those ideas as they are used by teachers and with children.

What must teachers who follow the principles of Kodály teach? Bunches of sounds in certain orders? | | ⊓ | followed by | ⊓ | | followed by ⊓ ⊓ | | , *ad infinitum?* Should not Kodály practitioners be helping children to form concepts, to make generalizations about music: "music moves in longer and shorter sounds and silences over the beat"; "a beat can have one sound over it, two sounds (or more) over it, or no sound over it"; "pitches may move higher or lower or may stay the same"? There are an infinite number of facts about music; one can never hope to cover them all. There are a finite number of basic musical concepts. If the teacher is aware of what they are, he can make choices among them and then work toward making his choices conscious knowledge to children. Such generalizations and concepts can be the key for unlocking further musical doors long after the children have left the music room or the school.

It is important to concentrate curriculum work on ways of teaching and on concepts to be taught; such things as what to call dotted eighth notes or where in the sequence a particular melodic turn falls may be left to the individual teacher or group of teachers who certainly know the musical materials best suited to the children they teach. Sequence, materials, and vocabulary will and should be different for Hispano-American children in San Jose, Anglo-American children in Baltimore, and Black-American children in Chicago. Musical concepts will not.[1]

Numerous statements of basic musical concepts and generalizations exist.[2,3] Any of them certainly can be examined and choices made concerning content, in the light of Kodály philosophy and pedagogy.

Deciding on curriculum content is not a particularly difficult task. Assessing the effectiveness of curriculum content, once it has been decided on and put into practice for a period of time long enough to assure results of some sort, is more difficult. How can one know whether a particular curriculum is good or bad? Or whether it is actually achieving the results it set out to achieve?

One can tell, if the original statements of goals and instructional objectives were written to say what teachers meant to say, and not simply to sound good. Many goal statements are so general as to be virtually useless. The long-range effectiveness of any curriculum is directly related to how clearly the teachers (the curriculum writers) see what it is they wish to achieve as end results; in other words, their statement of goals.

If a desirable outcome of music education is love of music, supported by knowledge about music, then some goals appropriate to Kodály

---

[1] One possible skill and concept sequence appears in the next chapter (Chapter 8). It is the one used by the author with teachers in the San Jose Pilot Project.

[2] *Instructional Objectives In Music* (Reston, Virginia: Music Educators National Conference, 1977).

[3] S. Edelstein, L. Choksy, P. Lehman, N. Sigurdsson, and D. Woods, *Creating Curriculum In Music* (Reading, Mass.: Addison-Wesley Publishing Co., 1980).

programs might be to develop the ability of all children to:

1. Sing, play, and dance from memory a large number of traditional singing games, chants, and folk songs, drawn first from the children's own
   heritages and later expanded to include music of other cultures.
2. Perform, listen to, and analyze the great art music of the world.
3. Achieve mastery of musical skills, such as musical reading and writing,
   analysis of musical forms, inner hearing and memorization, and singing
   and part-singing.
4. Improvise and compose, using their known musical vocabulary at each
   developmental level.

These four goals, while intended to be comprehensive, are not
meant to be exclusive of other possibilities. Goals should be established
by the people who must achieve them, not be superimposed by some
authority with no knowledge of situation, children, or cultural surrounding in which they are to be achieved.

However, there must be goals—and they must be thought through
and clearly stated if the educational process is to have focus.

With goals agreed upon, instructional objectives become easier to
determine, since they are directly related to goals. For example, looking
at the goal "achieve mastery of musical skills," some possible instructional objectives, in order of increasing complexity, might be the following. For rhythmic learning, the child will:

— maintain an audible steady beat while performing (step, clap, tap, etc.)
  known songs.
— identify and perform metric accent correctly.
— maintain a steady beat internally while performing music.
— clap rhythms of known songs while singing.
— distinguish between beat and rhythm when performing music.
— identify familiar songs by their clapped rhythms.
— clap and sing or say the rhythms of known songs.
— write or otherwise notate the rhythm motives of known songs.
— read rhythm phrases from flash cards, clapping and speaking duration
  syllables.
— read the rhythms of familiar songs, using duration syllables.
— read new songs in which the only unknown element is the new rhythm
  pattern being studied.
— improvise or create, using the new rhythmic learning.

Instructional objectives for each new melodic learning might include the following. The child will:

— sing in tune many songs in which the only new element is the new note being prepared.

— sing the above songs correctly, using *solfa* and hand signs.

— follow the teacher in random hand singing of the new note in combination with notes learned earlier (consecutive intervals).

— follow the teacher in two-hand singing of simultaneous intervals formed by the new note within known tone-sets.

— place familiar songs, containing only the known notes, on staff (on chalkboard, magnetic board, felt, manuscript paper).

— read familiar songs from staff notation.

— read new songs from staff notation.

— create or improvise, using the new note in familiar tone-sets.

These are completely provable objectives.[4] Children either will or will not achieve them. If they do not, something is wrong with either the teaching process or the content, and both should be re-examined. If the objectives are achieved, that part of the curriculum is validated.

Thus far this chapter has dealt with only the beginning and ending points of the curriculum process: purpose (goals and objectives) and evaluation. At this point it might help to summarize and place them into the perspective of an overall curriculum-construction outline. The actual terms used may vary from one guide to another, but all complete curriculum guides for any subject (not just music) must include:

A. *Goals*—what the teacher hopes to see as broad final results of the teaching.

B. *Concept Statements*—what is to be taught about the subject; broad generalizations about important ideas.

C. *Instructional Objectives*—desired outcomes of each educational process, usually stated in terms of specific behaviors (in music, these are related to skills in performing, analyzing, and organizing sound).

D. *Procedures*—the teaching process; the teachers' "how to."

E. *Evaluation*—the on-going process of determining whether the Instructional Objectives (C) and the Goals (A) are being achieved.

Looking at the whole curriculum process from another aspect, how might the teaching of one new rhythmic figure or melodic turn be planned? The following outline is one way of organizing the teaching of

---

[4] Skill hierarchies, easily translatable into objectives, have been suggested elsewhere in this book for part-singing, inner hearing, understanding musical form, and moving to music.

rhythmic and melodic elements; it includes the last four of the five points listed above, and relates directly to the goals stated earlier.

A LONG-RANGE TEACHING PLAN
FOR MAKING CHILDREN CONSCIOUSLY AWARE
OF A NEW MELODIC OR RHYTHMIC ELEMENT

    I. Statement of the concept.

    II. Musical experience through which the concept will be learned.

    III. Objectives:
- a. Objectives dealing with conscious knowledge (i.e., aurally identify, name, sing in *solfa,* clap, etc.).
- b. Objectives dealing with construction and writing.
- c. Objectives dealing with recognition of the new pattern.
- d. Objectives dealing with reading (generalization of the knowledge to new situations).
- e. Objectives dealing with improvisation and composition.

    IV. Readiness—what the child must be able to do before dealing with the new learning.

    V. Procedure to be used in the "make conscious" lesson or lessons (step by step how to and with which songs).

    VI. Reinforcement (how to and with which songs).

    VII. Assessment (how to and with which songs).

    VIII. Song list—categorized by melodic turn (for new melodic element) or by rhythm pattern (for new rhythmic learning).

A sample plan, following this outline, for teaching ♪♩ ♪ to a third-grade class is given below. It should take about 6 weeks to accomplish after a core of preparation songs have been taught.

I. Statement of the concepts involved

1. There may be even or uneven rhythmic arrangements of longer and shorter sounds over beats.
2. Three sounds that are aurally perceived as a rhythmic unit may take two beats to perform.
3. Short–long–short over two beats may be sounded as either "ti-ta-ti" or "syn-co-pa" and is notated ♪ ♩ ♪.

II. Musical experience through which the concepts will be learned

The class will sing by rote many duple and quadruple meter songs in which the only rhythm pattern not known to them is ♪ ♩ ♪. These are the songs through which ♪ ♩ ♪ will be prepared and made conscious knowledge. The students should perform this repertory of songs:

1. expressively (with appropriate dynamics, in appropriate tempo, with enjoyment of text and sensitivity to the character of the song, with movement where appropriate).
2. accurately (in tune, in a steady tempo, rhythmically correctly).

III. Objectives

The students will:

1. Aurally identify the three sounds, short–long–short, on two beats as ♪ ♩ ♪ ; say the pattern in correct rhythm as "ti-ta-ti" or "syn-co-pa"; sing patterns of ♪♩ ♪ in familiar songs (conscious knowledge).[5]
2. Notate known songs and/or phrases of known songs containing ♪ ♩ ♪; notate dictated rhythm patterns containing ♪♩ ♪ (construction and writing).
3. Aurally identify known songs containing ♪♩ ♪ after hearing only their clapped rhythms; aurally identify and say back in rhythm syllables random patterns clapped by the teacher, incorporating ♪ ♩ ♪; visually identify ♪♩ ♪ in the notation of known songs; visually identify and say in rhythm syllables ♪♩ ♪ patterns shown on flash cards (recognition).
4. Read the rhythm of new songs containing ♪ ♩ ♪ (reading-generalization).
5. Use ♪♩ ♪ in improvisation and composition (improvisation).

IV. Readiness

Before learning ♪ ♩ ♪ the students must be able to:

1. perform beat accurately,
2. perform rhythm accurately,
3. distinguish between beat and rhythm,
4. perform rhythmic ostinati with ease while singing.

[5] Such characterizations were suggested by Scott McCormick, one of the group of young Americans who went to Hungary under the leadership of Dr. Alexander Ringer to study the Kodály system.

In their known rhythmic vocabulary, the students must have:

1.

2. meter, measure, bar line in duple and quadruple,
3. the tie as a way of extending duration.

V. Procedure for making 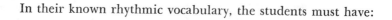 conscious
knowledge to the students

1. Class sings several songs containing the ♪♩ ♪ figure: "Alabama
Gal," "This Train," "I Got A Letter," "Zion's Children." On each they:
   a. *tap* the beat,
   b. *clap* the rhythm.
2. From "Zion's Children," the class derives and sings, in duration syllables, the rhythm of the last phrase "Talk about the judgement day"
((4 ♫♫♩ ♩ ♩|♩.)).
3. The teacher places this on the board, using separated eighth notes:
4 ♪♪♪♪♩ ♩ |♩.·
4. The class then sings "Alabama Gal," using the ♪♪♪♪♩ ♩
as a clapped ostinato while singing.
5. Concentrating on the phrase "Ain't I rock candy" (♪♩ ♪♩ ♩), the
teacher asks the students to listen carefully while singing to determine:
"Is our singing rhythm the same as our ostinato?" (Clap the singing
rhythm; clap the ostinato; are they the same?) "How could we change
the notation of our ostinato so that it will sound the same as our singing rhythm? Where do we need a longer sound? How much longer?"
If the students understand the use of ties to extend duration, as they
should from previous lessons on ♩ , ♩., and ○ , they will suggest:

Ain't I____ rock can - dy

They may also suggest that two *ti*'s are equal to a *ta*: ♪♪ = ♩ . If
not, the teacher can draw this from them.

6. The pattern may then be shown as ♪♩ ♪ and sung as "ti-ta-ti"
wherever it occurs throughout the song. The students sing the entire
verse in rhythm syllables. Later, the word "syn-co-pa" may be given,
since it suggests one unit of related sound across two beats rather than

three unrelated durations. However, ♪ ♩ ♪ *ti- ta- ti* should be used when the last eighth note is felt, because of word stress, as an upbeat: for example,

ti - ta - ti

Go - in' up the riv - er, from Cat - tles - burg to Pike;

and "syn-co-pa" should be used when ♪ ♩ ♪ is felt as a rhythmic unit; for example,

syn - co   pa

This train   is bound for glo - ry

VI. Reinforcement

The class should perform again all songs learned by rote to prepare for ♪ ♩ ♪ and

a) derive the rhythm of each, singing it with "ti-ta-ti" or "syn-co-pa,"
b) notate these rhythms in manuscript books.

The teacher should give flash card practice with ♪ ♩ ♪ in all positions in which it occurs in known songs.

Present new songs by rote, from which the class derives the rhythm before seeing the song in notation.

Dictate clapped rhythm patterns incorporating ♪ ♩ ♪, which the students must aurally identify and say back in rhythm syllables.

VII. Assessment

The class reads, at first sight, a song with no previously unknown elements other than ♪ ♩ ♪. (Example: "Don't Let Your Watch Run Down")

Individual students improvise the B, C, and D eight-beat phrases using ♪ ♩ ♪ in a rhythm rondo, the rest of the class performs a given A section.

VIII. Song list (categorized by the
position of ♪♩ ♪ in the pattern)

♪♩ ♪♩ ♩ : "Alabama Gal" (make conscious song), "Don't Let Your
Watch Run Down" (assessment [reading] song), "How Long the Train
Been Gone," "Hop Up, My Ladies" (+) [6]

♪♩ ♪♩ : "Zion's Children," "Don't Let the Wind," "I Saw the Light,"
"Lil' Liza Jane," "Riding in a Buggy," "Land of the Silver Birch" (+).

♪♩ ♪♩ ♫ : "Sometimes I Feel Like a Mournin' Dove" (+), "New
River Train" (+).

♪♩ ♪♫ ♫ : "This Train," "Captain, Go Side Track Your
Train" (assessment song).

♪♩ ♪♫♩ : "I Got a Letter" (+).

♪♩ ♪♪♩ ♪ : "Do Lord," "Goin' Home on a Cloud."

The approach demonstrated in this long-range plan is based on
child learning behaviors and has been known for some time now; yet
when teachers try to incorporate it in daily teaching they sometimes have
difficulty. Why is this? If there is no basic fallacy in the statement of the
concepts or of the musical outcomes, the problem may lie in the teaching
process itself. Musicians and teachers see the enormity of the subject—
music—and the infinitesimal amount of time so often allotted to teach
it, and they frequently take one of two equally dead-end roads: either
they rush through musical skills and concepts so fast that children acquire a vocabulary of surface facts about music but do not develop
actual musical skills and understandings (these take time) or they say "I
haven't enough time to teach musical concepts. I'll just teach children
to enjoy music." The latter approach is an impossibility—one only truly
enjoys and appreciates things one understands. Love of music, if it is to
be a genuine love, must be supported by knowledge about and understanding of music.

As to the former approach, that of rushing through skill after skill
and concept after concept in rapid-fire order, teachers must stop trying
to cover the enormous subject of music and begin to uncover it a little

[6] The songs marked (+) may be found in the author's book *The Kodály
Method* (Englewood Cliffs, New Jersey: Prentice-Hall, 1974); all others are
notated in Appendix D.

bit at a time. This uncovering process involves four steps: prepare, make conscious, reinforce and assess; four steps that must be applied over and over again to every new rhythm pattern, every new melodic turn, every concept about musical form.

Prepare refers to the rote performance of a new rhythm or tonal pattern in many musical settings. The children sing the new interval or the new rhythm in songs without seeing it, i.e., by the old-fashioned rote process. This step may take weeks or months to accomplish. The next step, *make conscious,* must not be taken until the children are performing the new interval or rhythm quite perfectly. This is the way in which children learn their native language—they speak before they write or read; they have extensive aural and oral experience before they encounter symbolization. This natural order is as true in music as in speech: sound must come before sight.

When the rote performance of the new note (or of the melodic turn through which the new note is being taught) or of the new rhythm pattern has been mastered, the children are ready to move to the *make conscious* stage. This is the point at which the teacher names and fastens a symbol to the sound (or interval or rhythm pattern) he has been preparing. During this stage the children learn the *solfa* or rhythm duration syllables for the new skill, they are shown what it looks like, they derive its place on the staff or its specific duration, they are given the new hand sign, and they construct on felt or write with pencil and paper a song phrase containing the new tonal or rhythmic pattern. They do not read it at this point. Practice must come first if reading is to be a successful experience.

The third step in this teaching sequence, *reinforce,* involves going back to all the songs used in the *prepare* stage, singing them again to find and identify the new note or rhythm, and learning new songs by the rote–note process, deriving the *solfa* or rhythm. This may take several weeks.

Assess refers to reading the new note or rhythm in totally new songs and to improvising or creating phrases and whole songs using the new interval or rhythm in combination with other known patterns. This last step is in reality an evaluation of the whole process; it is this that tells the teacher whether he has really accomplished what he set out to accomplish.

There are still other aspects to consider. The song materials to be used in each step must be extremely carefully chosen. The song or songs through which the concept or skill is made conscious must not contain anything new other than the specific new element (tonal or rhythmic) being taught. It is most important that the child find only one unknown in the entire example. Only through this technique can the teacher properly focus the child's attention on the new learning.

The assessment songs—those to be read—must be chosen equally carefully. They must be made up of well-known melodic turns and rhythms with only the one new element, i.e., the learning to be assessed.

Ideally, even the preparation songs and the reinforcement songs should follow this prescription. In actual practice, while it is desirable, it is not always possible. As more folk music is collected and analyzed for teaching purposes, hopefully, enough material will become available. At the present, however, if there are extraneous elements in the preparation songs, they should be insignificant ones—a descending scale line, for example, at the end of a song preparing the *s-m-l* turn, or a half note in a song preparing *re*. The song(s) would prepare the ear and the singing of *re* but could not be used in notation until after the half note has been taught.

In selecting the songs to prepare, make conscious, reinforce, and assess new tonal or rhythmic learning the teacher must also keep in mind:

1. the frequency with which the new pattern occurs and
2. its position in the song.

A pattern that occurs in the first phrase of a song is generally better for teaching purposes than one that occurs only in the middle or at the end. A song with a pattern that occurs three times is a better teaching example than one in which the pattern occurs just once.

This four-stage process must be gone through over and over for each new rhythmic learning, each new melodic learning. Melodic and rhythmic elements must be overlapped, so that when a rhythmic concept is being reinforced a melodic one is being prepared and made conscious. When done in this manner, concepts are learned, they are internalized, they become a part of the learner and not just a surface fact to be forgotten tomorrow.

Of course, this kind of teaching takes time, time both in the classroom as well as out of the classroom, preparing and finding the right song materials. No children's school music text has yet been put together that is much help in achieving this kind of teaching. The work falls on the shoulders of the individual teacher who really wants to teach, not simply entertain children.

SUGGESTED ASSIGNMENT

1. Following the format given in this chapter, construct a long-range plan for teaching either a new melodic turn or a new rhythmic figure.

SUGGESTED READING

R. W. TYLER, *Basic Principles of Curriculum and Instruction* (Chicago: University of Chicago Press, 1949).

R. F. MAGER, *Preparing Instructional Objectives* (Palo Alto, California: Fearon Publishers, 1962).

S. EDELSTEIN, L. CHOKSY, P. LEHMAN, N. SIGURDSSON, and D. WOODS, *Creating Curriculum In Music* (Reading, Mass.: Addison-Wesley Publ. Co., 1980).

chapter 8

Planning and Sequencing for Musical Learning— Long-Range to Individual Lesson

Planning for musical learning involves knowing exactly what one wishes to teach about melody, rhythm, form, harmony, the expressive elements; finding the best musical materials through which to teach; and arranging the whole into some kind of integrated teaching order.

None of these tasks is easy. The Hungarians have sequenced musical learning perhaps better than anyone in the world, but it has not worked well simply to take the Hungarian teaching sequence and superimpose it on American children and American songs. Instead, it is necessary to find a skill sequence inherent in American folk song and, combining that with knowledge of which skills are developmentally appropriate to what age American student, to design an American musical-skill hierarchy. It is this that the author has attempted to do in the last eight years, working first with school children in Maryland, then with teachers and children in the San Jose Project and in the two pilot schools associated with Holy Names College in California.

The result is a skill and concept sequence which appears to be valid for the children in these latter situations, at least, and one that may have validity over a far larger geographic area, since the folk material on which it is based has been drawn primarily from the two largest ethnic heritages in the United States—the Anglo-American and the Black.

At the earliest levels, it differs little from the Hungarian prototype: the minor third and major second are, after all, the earliest identifiable intervals sung by young children[1] and a child's walking tempo is the most natural rhythm with which to begin in the United States as well as in Hungary. However, once past the infant materials, there are numerous instances where the order does not follow the specific order of the Hungarian model. It is taken instead from the frequency with which a particular melodic turn or rhythmic figure occurs in the collected American folk music being used for teaching. Sixteenth notes, as an example, occur sooner in this list than they do in the Hungarian one; they occur infrequently in Hungarian folk music, but with great frequency in American folk music. It is necessary to deal with them earlier with American children.

One other factor should be considered when examining this particular sequence. Teaching order is changing even as it is being written down. As the San Jose Project teachers use it, they alter it if a problem is perceived. It is not meant to be a rigidly observed order, but merely a guide from which to decide on the ordering. Almost every year some aspect of it has had to be changed. The placements of some items ($\frac{6}{8}$ and $\frac{3}{4}$, for example) are still very much in question.[2]

When the author first constructed this sequence it was in four lists, categorized under rhythm, melody, form and part-singing. While this arrangement facilitated one's understanding of how skills in each area are hierarchical in nature, it was not found to be a very helpful ordering for teaching. The problem encountered over and over again was the meshing of concepts and skills across these and other areas:

Should ♩ be taught before or after *re*?

Should the *l,-s,* turn be taught before or after ♪ ♩ ♪ ?

At what point should canon singing begin?

When should youngsters be asked to discriminate like from unlike phrases?

It is to provide one possible answer for these and other questions like them that the following skill and concept hierarchy is offered.

----

[1] There is some evidence that Black children's infant songs tend to be built on the *d-l,-s,* melodic turn rather than on the *l-s-m* melodic turn of the Anglo-American tradition; nevertheless, in both instances the intervals are minor third–major second.

[2] See Chapter 9 for treatment of the $\frac{6}{8}$ and $\frac{3}{4}$ problems.

ONE POSSIBLE ORDER FOR TEACHING
MUSICAL CONCEPTS AND SKILLS

1. Distinguishing between *faster* and *slower* in tempi and *louder* and *softer* in dynamics, and using each appropriately in performing songs and rhymes.

2. Identifying and performing *beat* in simple duple meter (tapping, clapping, stepping).

3. Distinguishing between *louder* and *softer beats* (accented and unaccented beats, to prepare for later understanding of meter, measure, and bar line).

4. Distinguishing *higher* from *lower pitches* to prepare for first melodic notational learning.

5. Physically exhibiting a *feeling for phrase* [form] (with arm motions or by phrase turning).

6. *Identifying rhythm* as "the way the words go."

7. *Distinguishing rhythm* from beat.

8. Improvising free *melodic answers* to teacher's *question phrases*.

9. Identifying *one sound on a beat* in duple meter songs and rhymes as ♩ ("ta"). Identifying *two sounds on a beat* in duple meter songs and rhymes as ♫ ("ti-ti") and progressing through all four-beat patterns of ♩ and ♫ found in songs.

10. Using sticks to construct phrases from known songs using ♫ and ♩ symbols.

11. Distinguishing *like* from *unlike phrases*.

12. Using the *repeat sign* (:||) where possible in rhythm writing and construction.

13. Observing the ||: :|| correctly when reading from stem notation.

14. Identifying the *rest* (𝄽) as a beat of silence.

15. Analyzing known songs to *aurally identify* patterns of like and unlike phrases [form (simple binary and ternary)].

16. Performing *rhythmic ostinati* as accompaniment to known songs.

17. Identifying by *stressed beats* where bar lines should be placed. (Meter, measure, and bar line in duple meter as a function of accent.)

18. Identifying the *minor third (descending)* as *s-m*. Singing it correctly in tune with syllables. Performing its hand signs correctly.

19. Constructing phrases of *s-m* songs in F-, C-, and G-*do* on staff. (Introduction of musical staff.)

20. Aurally identifying *la* in the *s-l* turn as higher than *so*. Singing it correctly in tune with syllables. Performing its hand sign correctly. Constructing phrases of *s-l-s* songs in F-, C-, and G-*do* on staff.

21. Identifying *la* in the *m-l* turn. Singing it correctly in tune with syllables. Constructing it on staff in F-, C-, and G-*do*.

22. Correctly singing *l-s-m* pitches following the teacher's hand signs shown in random order.

23. Improvising short phrases using *l-s-m* pitches.

24. Aurally identifying *do* in *s-d* pattern. Singing with syllables and showing hand signs.

25. Aurally identifying *do* in *s-m-d* and *d-m-s* patterns. Singing with syllables and showing hand signs. Constructing on staff in F- and G-*do*.

26. Clapping *simple rhythm canons*.

27. Singing *simple melodic ostinati*.

28. Identifying *re* in the *m-r-d*, *s-m-r-d* and *l-s-m-r-d* tone-sets. Singing with syllables and hand signs. Constructing on staff in F-, C-, and G-*do*.

29. Improvising using the notes of the basic pentagon *l-s–m-r–d* and rhythm figures with ♩ ,   ♫ , and 𝄽 .

30. Following the teacher in *two-hand singing* of known intervals.

31. Writing music on manuscript paper (begun here at the latest if felt staves and sticks have been used exclusively before).

32. Taking *aural rhythm dictation* of eight-beat patterns.

33. Singing *two-voice melodic canons*.

34. Improvising question and answer phrases using the *l-s–m-r-d* tone-set.

35. Singing the intervals of the *do*-pentaton when they are shown in random order in a variety of visual ways:
    a. child xylophone (children representing the pitches)
    b. tone ladders on board: *l*

      s

      m
      r
      d

    c. staff notation (following a "flying note" moving randomly with the pentaton in F-, C-, or G-*do*)

36. Using *ties* (♩ ♩) in simple duple meter to extend duration.

37. Identifying the half note ♩ as equal to ♩ ♩

38. Conducting simple duple meter.

39. Identifying four beats in a measure as $\frac{4}{4}$ meter (secondary accent).

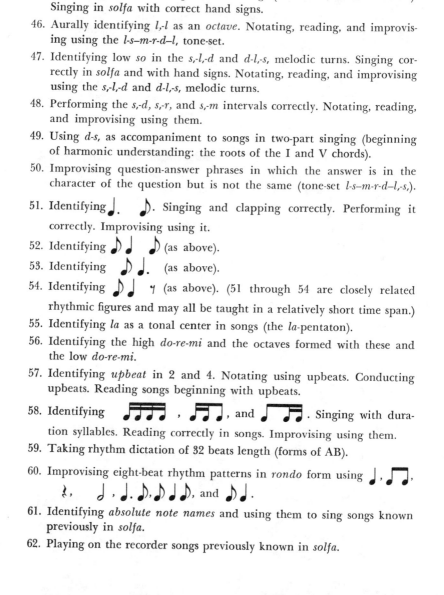

40. Identifying ♩. and 𝅝 as equal to ♩ ♩ ♩ and ♩ ♩ ♩ ♩.

41. Taking aural rhythm dictation of sixteen-beat patterns.

42. Conducting $\frac{4}{4}$ meter.

43. Identifying separated eighth-notes ♪ ♪ as an alternate way of writing ♫.

44. Aurally identifying, reading, and correctly performing *re* in the *s-r* and *r-s* intervals in songs.

45. Identifying low *la* in *do*-pentatonic songs (in the *d-l,-d* melodic turn). Singing in *solfa* with correct hand signs.

46. Aurally identifying *l,-l* as an *octave*. Notating, reading, and improvising using the *l-s–m-r-d–l,* tone-set.

47. Identifying low *so* in the *s,-l,-d* and *d-l,-s,* melodic turns. Singing correctly in *solfa* and with hand signs. Notating, reading, and improvising using the *s,-l,-d* and *d-l,-s,* melodic turns.

48. Performing the *s,-d*, *s,-r*, and *s,-m* intervals correctly. Notating, reading, and improvising using them.

49. Using *d-s,* as accompaniment to songs in two-part singing (beginning of harmonic understanding: the roots of the I and V chords).

50. Improvising question-answer phrases in which the answer is in the character of the question but is not the same (tone-set *l-s–m-r-d–l,-s,*).

51. Identifying ♩. ♪. Singing and clapping correctly. Performing it correctly. Improvising using it.

52. Identifying ♪ ♩ ♪ (as above).

53. Identifying ♪ ♩. (as above).

54. Identifying ♪ ♩ 𝄾 (as above). (51 through 54 are closely related rhythmic figures and may all be taught in a relatively short time span.)

55. Identifying *la* as a tonal center in songs (the *la*-pentaton).

56. Identifying the high *do-re-mi* and the octaves formed with these and the low *do-re-mi*.

57. Identifying *upbeat* in 2 and 4. Notating using upbeats. Conducting upbeats. Reading songs beginning with upbeats.

58. Identifying ♬♬ , ♬♩, and ♩♬ . Singing with duration syllables. Reading correctly in songs. Improvising using them.

59. Taking rhythm dictation of 32 beats length (forms of AB).

60. Improvising eight-beat rhythm patterns in *rondo* form using ♩ , ♫ , 𝄾 , 𝅗𝅥 , ♩. ♪, ♪ ♩ ♪, and ♪ ♩ .

61. Identifying *absolute note names* and using them to sing songs known previously in *solfa*.

62. Playing on the recorder songs previously known in *solfa*.

63. Identifying *so* and *re* as tonal centers in some songs (the *so*-pentaton and the *re*-pentaton).

64. Singing *easy two-part songs* in which the parts are *canonic* or in *contrary motion.*

65. Identifying *fa-mi* as a smaller-sounding interval than any sung before (all scale steps to this point have been major seconds and minor thirds).

66. Singing, writing, and reading *fa* in G- and C-*do* placements.

67. *Root Singing* as a melodic ostinato, now using *fa* $\left(\begin{smallmatrix} d & f, & s, \\ \text{I} & \text{IV} & \text{V} \end{smallmatrix} \text{chord roots}\right)$.

68. Perceiving the need for a lowered tone to produce the correct scale sound of *fa* in F-*do*. (Function of the flat; whole-step, half-step scale progression.) $\left.\begin{matrix} do\text{-pentachord} \\ do\text{-hexachord} \end{matrix}\right\}$ tone-sets.

69. Identifying *ti* in F- and C-*do* [*do* scale (major) first, *la* scale (minor) later].

70. Perceiving the need for a raised tone to produce the correct scale sound of *ti* in G-*do*. (Function of the sharp; whole-step, half-step scale progression.) $\left.\begin{matrix} la\text{-pentachord} \\ la\text{-hexachord} \end{matrix}\right\}$ tone-sets.

71. Identifying $\frac{6}{8}$ meter. (See Chapter 9 for a discussion of the compound meter problem.)

72. Incorporating *thirds* and *sixths harmonies* in two-part singing.

73. Singing and analyzing *diatonic major* and *minor* scale construction with whole steps and half steps (the *do* scale and the *la* scale).

74. Singing *three-part songs* in which two voices are canonic and one voice is performing a descant or ostinato.

75. Vocal chording with known songs, using the I, IV, and V chords and their inversions as accompaniment to the songs.

76. Identifying ♪. ♪ and ♪♪. .

77. Extending reading and writing to keys with *two sharps, two flats.*

78. Identifying, conducting, and performing *cut time.*

79. Identifying, conducting, and performing the *triple meters* $\frac{3}{4}$, $\frac{3}{8}$, and $\frac{9}{8}$.

80. Extending reading and writing to keys with *three sharps, three flats.*

81. Identifying songs as being of *mixolydian* or *dorian* modal character according to characteristic tone-sets and melodic turns: the *la* scale with *fi* or the *re* to *re* scale as dorian; the *do* scale with *ta* or the *so* to *so* scale as mixolydian. *Ta* as the flatted seventh in a *do* scale; *fi* as the raised sixth in a *la* scale.

82. Identifying *si, ma,* and other altered notes as they occur in music.

83. Performing, analyzing, and improvising in *mixed meters* and *unusual meters* ($\frac{3}{4} + \frac{2}{4}$; $\frac{7}{8}$ or $\frac{5}{8}$; etc.).

84. Extending reading and writing to all keys.

Once a sequencing of skills and concepts, such as the preceding one, has been tentatively agreed upon, it is necessary to decide just how much is likely to be accomplishable in each school year. For example, in the San Jose schools numbers 1 to 23 are considered to be the work of grade one, 24 to 38, of grade two, and 39 to 62, of grade three. The program is presently in its third year and so the divisions into grades four, five, and six are arbitrary and as yet to be tested: numbers 63 to 71 for grade four, 72 to 78 for grade five, and 79 to 84 for grade six.

These will differ from school to school and, perhaps, from class to class within one school, but making some decision is a necessary step in planning. Once such a decision is made the teacher may begin to block out the year's teaching. The following chart is a sample yearly plan for third grade.

When this has been mapped out for each grade the teacher should select song material through which to teach each of the new learnings listed in the Make Conscious column, and then write the long-range plans for teaching each new learning (such as the one given for ♪ ♩ ♪ in Chapter 7).

For grade three, as shown above, five such long-range plans must be constructed (the *la*-pentaton can be included in the overall plan for teaching low *la*).

With this new material in hand, the teacher is ready to begin constructing individual lessons. Many aspects of the musical experience must be considered in the planning of any one music lesson.

PLANNING FOR MUSICAL LEARNING

Variety, according to the old saying, is the spice of life. It is also the spice of the music lesson. Through it one may achieve the small miracle of keeping thirty youngsters interested from beginning to end of a 30- or 45-minute music period. Educational psychologists have found that children learn best if periods of concentration are short, frequent, and intense, and are followed by periods of relaxation and play. It may be difficult for the teacher of mathematics or reading to act upon this, but the teacher of music has a made-to-order situation. By its very nature, music can produce great variation in levels of concentration and tension-release within one class period. The teacher must plan with this variety and balance in mind if he is to use it effectively.

Each music lesson should in some sense provide a microcosm of all that is to be learned about melody, rhythm, harmony, form, and style. Each must foster skill in singing, moving, musical memory, inner hearing, reading, writing, and improvising.

<table>
<tr><th>September</th><th>October</th><th>November</th><th>December</th></tr>
<tr>
<td>Prepare: low *la* (through *do*-pentatonic songs)

Reinforce: aural rhythm dictation up to 16 beats using ♩ ♪ | ; ⁴₄ meter; half note; canon singing; question-answer improvising; ties to extend duration</td>
<td>Prepare: low *la*–low *so* turn; s,-d, s,-r and s,-m intervals

Make Conscious: low *la*

Reinforce: question-answer; ties; 𝄐 as ♪ ♪ ♪</td>
<td>Prepare: ♩. ♪

Make Conscious: low *la*–low *so* turn and the s, to d, r, m intervals

Reinforce: low *la*; use of ties; ♪ ♪ ♩ as ♪ ♪ 𝄐</td>
<td>Prepare: ♪ ♩ ♪

Make Conscious: low *la*; the l,-s, melodic turn

Reinforce: low *la*; the l,-s, melodic turn

Assess: low *la*–low *so*</td>
</tr>
<tr><th>January</th><th>February</th><th>March</th><th>April</th><th>May</th></tr>
<tr>
<td>Prepare: ♪ ♩ ♪

Make Conscious: (none—review will be needed here)

Reinforce: ♩. ♪ ; low *la*–low *so* singing; use of *d-s,* as a second part; use of ties</td>
<td>Prepare: ♪ ♩. ;

Make Conscious: ♪ ♩ ♪

Reinforce: ♩. ♪ ♩ ♪ ; s,-d, s,-r and s,-m intervals</td>
<td>Prepare: the *la*-pentaton (*la* as tonal center)

Make Conscious: ♩. ; ♩ ♪ 𝄼

Reinforce: ♩ ♪ ♪ ♩

Assess:</td>
<td>Prepare: the *la*-pentaton

Make Conscious: the *la*-pentaton

Reinforce: ♪ ♩. ;

Assess: ♪ ♪ ♩. ; ♩ ♪ 𝄼</td>
<td>Prepare: for next Fall's tonal and rhythmic learning; songs with *fa* and *ti*; . . . .

Make Conscious: (nothing new)

Reinforce: all the new learnings of the year

Assess: all the new learnings of the year</td>
</tr>
</table>

Outline for a 30-Minute Music Lesson

    I. Greeting (2 minutes)
Sung by teacher on the tone-set most recently learned.
Replied to tonally with words first, then in *solfa*, by the class and next by individuals, with attention to pitch accuracy and correct hand signs.

    II. Opening Song (one the children know well in the tone-set just practiced) (3 minutes)
Attention to beautiful singing, phrasing, dynamics, general musicality. A rhythm or melodic ostinato may be added if it suits the character of the song.

   III. New Rote Song (to prepare for a new tonal or rhythmic learning that will take place in a later "make conscious" lesson) (5 minutes)
Taught by the process given in Chapter 2.
Derivation of the form of the song (through phrase turning, inner hearing, etc.).
Memorization of the song.

   IV. Rhythm Skill Activity (this may or may not involve a song) (3 minutes)
Aural-oral dictation, or
Flash-card patterns to be clapped and said, or
Derivation of the rhythm of a known song, or
Rhythm improvisation games, etc.

    V. Movement, Singing Game or Dance (5 minutes)
Can be a wider-range tone-set or a different tonal center to provide melodic variety.

   VI. Melodic Skill Activity (song using the tone-set in I and II) (7 minutes)
Deriving, through *solfa* and hand singing, the notation of a familiar song and constructing the first phrase on felt staves (first grade) or writing a part of the song on staff in manuscript books (fourth grade); or
Reading a new song from printed staff notation or stem and *solfa*

    notation (♩ ♩ ♫ ♩); or
           s   m   r m d

Improvising in the known tone-set.

  VII. Familiar Song with (2 minutes)
Inner-hearing exercise (see Chapter 2, p. 35), or
Part work (ostinato, descant, canon).

 VIII. Movement or Dance to a familiar song, or A Song for Listening, sung by the teacher (ballad, lullaby, etc.) (3 minutes)

With so much to accomplish, it is clear that to be effective the music lesson must be as tightly and carefully planned as choreography. To aid in this planning it is helpful initially to follow some basic lesson outline. The author has used the one on page 172.

The times shown are, of course, approximate. They will vary, among other things, with the length of the songs. The fourteen verses of "Frog Went A-Courtin' " obviously take longer to sing than the one verse of "All the Little Horses." However, the times given do imply weight. The most involved skill, melodic reading and derivation, requires more time than the singing of a known song. The timing is indicated so that teachers will not spend too much time on the less complex aspects of the lesson and fail to get to the skill work or, equally a problem, spend so much time on skill teaching that there is no time left for singing loved familiar songs or for performing singing games and dances. A balance must exist between concentration activities (I, III, IV, VI) and relaxation activities (II, V, VII, VIII). (Even the so-called relaxation activities involve some musical thought.) A total of six or seven songs is suggested for a half-hour lesson. These should be selected with musical variety in mind, some slower, some faster, some, perhaps humorous, others beautiful. The largest number of songs used should be in the tone-set consciously known to the children, with some songs containing the next rhythmic figure or melodic turn to be taught, and at least one song of wider-range to stretch voices and ear ability. For an older class, fourth, fifth, or sixth grade, the lesson outline should be expanded to include more improvisation, analytical music listening, and part-singing. The period length suggested for older students is 45 minutes, in order to accommodate the additional skill work.

The outline as given is not designed for lessons in which new musical learnings occur. It is not a "make-conscious" lesson. The procedure for making students consciously aware of a new melodic turn or rhythm figure is a time-consuming one and generally occupies the space given to III, IV, V, and VI in the above outline.[3]

There are probably six or more lessons such as the one above for every single make-conscious lesson. The outline relates to lessons in which known skills and concepts are being reinforced and new skills and concepts are being prepared.

It may occur to the reader that no time has been allowed in the lesson outline for teacher explanations, for passing out and collecting materials, for general discussion. This is a quite deliberate omission. In general, music teachers talk too much. Explaining is much less effective than demonstrating. And comments such as "Now let's see how well we

[3] See Chapter 7, p. 158, for a "make-conscious" procedure.

can do our flash cards" or "I have a nice new song for you today" add absolutely nothing to children's learning. The teacher who can move without pointless verbalizing from one musical activity to the next can usually rivet the children's attention. On the other hand, children simply tune out the teacher who talks her way aimlessly from one part of the lesson to another. As to the passing out and collecting of materials—felt staves, sticks, manuscript books, song books, etc.—this can be done, with the cooperation of the classroom teacher, just before the music teacher arrives; or, if this is not feasible, it may all be done by selected children during the greeting.

In classes where the recorder is used (as it frequently is in the lower grades of Kodály classes) it is placed at the end of the lesson in the 5 minutes shown as VII and VIII in the outline. It is usually tied into the notational work of step VI. The children play what they have just derived and written.

Thus far, in the preceding two chapters, the author has discussed broad goals and objectives of Kodály musical training and has presented one way of planning for skill and concept learning. At this point, perhaps, it would be interesting to take one rhythmic figure listed as part of the work of third grade (𝅗𝅥. ♪) and follow it from the early preparation stage, through the make conscious stage, to the reinforce and assess stages, to see what additional musical learnings can be drawn from a core of song material selected to teach one rhythm motive.

If the teacher were simply to teach thirty or so songs with 𝅗𝅥. ♪, music lessons would be dull indeed. Looking at only a few of the songs used to prepare, make conscious, reinforce, and assess the children's learning of the 𝅗𝅥. ♪ rhythmic figure, what are some of the other musical learnings that might be incorporated through these songs during the same time span?

Songs (Arranged by the Position of the Figure)

𝅗𝅥. ♪𝅘𝅥 𝅘𝅥	𝅘𝅥 𝅘𝅥 𝅗𝅥. ♪
"Chairs to Mend"	"Maria"
"Wind the Bobbin"	"Old Gray Goose" (+)[4]
"Riding in a Buggy"	

[4] The songs marked (+) may be found in the author's book *The Kodály Method* (Englewood Cliffs, N.J.: Prentice-Hall, 1974); the others are notated in Appendix E.

♩. ♪♩   ♩. ♪♩. ♪

                                            "Al Citron"

"Shady Grove"   "John Kanaka"

"Perry Merry Dictum" (+)

"Hymn to Joy" (+)   ♩   ♩. ♪

"Cradle Song" (+)   "London Bridge Do Lord"

Using these songs, and others, the teacher may work with students on moving accurately to a simple duple or quadruple beat, clapping, tapping, stepping, and gradually internalizing the beat. The game songs—"London Bridge Do Lord," "John Kanaka" and "Al Citron"—are particularly useful for this.

In addition, these songs are pentatonic. The class should be able to sing them all in *solfa* and with hand signs. They are within the known tonal and rhythmic vocabularies of the children, except for the pattern being prepared (♩. ♪).

Rhythmic ostinati may be performed with these songs and the others on the list. These should be pulled from songs and used in such a way that the ♩ ♫ figure is always being clapped as the ♩. ♪. is being sung: for example, the teacher could derive with the class the rhythm of the phrase "each sent a present" from the song "Perry Merry Dictum" or the phrase "bobbin a-wound up" from the song "Wind the Bobbin" (♩ ♫ ♩ ♩) and then have them use that pattern as an ostinato while singing "Chairs to Mend," "Wind the Bobbin," and "Riding in a Buggy."

This reinforces the musical ability to hear and perform two parts at the same time. It also sets the stage for making students consciously aware of the ♩. ♪ pattern and gives them the necessary tools for deriving this new rhythm, rather than being told about it. When students are performing rhythm and ostinato correctly, the teacher may concentrate their attention on one phrase of a song ("Wind the Bobbin") in which ♩. ♪♩ ♩ is being sung while ♩ ♪ ♪ ♩ ♩ is being clapped. (The ostinato should be shown on the board with separated eighth notes for this.)

The teacher might ask:

1. "Is our clapping rhythm the same as our singing rhythm?" [No!]
2. "How is our singing rhythm different from our ostinato?" [A longer beginning sound.]

3. "How can we change the notation of our ostinato so that it will sound the same as our singing rhythm?" [Students will use ties ($\downarrow$ $\downarrow$ $\downarrow$ $\downarrow\downarrow$) to extend the duration. The teacher may then show $\downarrow$. as an alternate way of notating $\downarrow$ $\downarrow$.]

Once the $\downarrow$. $\downarrow$ is taught (made conscious) it must be reinforced, it must be found, identified, and performed in previously known songs and in new songs. "Chairs to Mend" and "Riding in a Buggy" contain the $\downarrow$. $\downarrow$ figure in the same position in the pattern as does "Wind the Bobbin" (at the beginning). It will be necessary to find it also in other positions and patterns: "Old Gray Goose" ($\downarrow\downarrow$ $\downarrow$ $\downarrow$. $\downarrow$), "Al Citron" ($\downarrow$. $\downarrow\downarrow$. $\downarrow$), "London Bridge Do Lord" ($\downarrow$ $\downarrow$. $\downarrow$), "Cradle Song" and "Hymn to Joy" ($\downarrow$. $\downarrow\downarrow$).

Again, many other musical activities must be brought to bear on this song material if lessons are to be musical experiences rather than mechanical "programmed learning." With "Chairs to Mend," the students should both sing and clap in canon, i.e., the class may sing or three individuals may sing the three voices of the canon, but the students may also clap in canon to their own singing. This requires a far higher level of skill. It is a challenge youngsters enjoy.

Inner-hearing exercises may be applied to any of these songs. The class might sing "John Kanaka," for example, hiding the $\downarrow$. $\downarrow$ patterns in their heads, i.e., they would not sing aloud wherever $\downarrow$. $\downarrow$ occurred in the song.

Form could be derived through inner hearing with "Hymn to Joy." Have the class sing the first phrase aloud, the second aloud, the third inside, and the fourth aloud. Ask:

"Which phrases are similar?" (1, 2, 4)
"Are any exactly alike?" (2, 4)
"How are 1 and 2 different?" (Question and answer)
"Is any phrase completely different?" (3)
"How can we diagram this form?" (AABA)

A listening lesson can follow this, using the fourth movement of Beethoven's *Ninth Symphony,* from which the "Hymn" is taken.

Harmonic understanding can be prepared with "Cradle Song." The class may sing the melody and decide whether a sustained *do* (I chord root) or the *so* (V chord root) sounds best, and then may listen to and sing with the beautiful Bach harmonization of this melody in the *St. Matthew Passion*.

Discuss how Beethoven used dynamic levels and tempo to add interest and excitement to his theme. Compare this with the use of dynamics and tempo in a recording of the Bach chorale. Improvise a second voice part for "Cradle Song," using the I and V tones and the ♩. ♪ rhythmic figure.

All the above materials and techniques could be used in the teaching of ♩. ♪. But what else happened musically during the same period?

1. A variety of kinds of good music has been performed: singing games, dances, authentic American folk songs, composed music of Bach and Beethoven. If nothing else had been accomplished the time would have been well spent.

2. The level of the child's musical literacy has been increased in several ways. Not only has something new, ♩. ♪, been added to the child's known rhythm vocabulary, but also the known tonal vocabulary (*l s m r d l, s,*) has been reinforced through the singing of many songs in this tone-set, and preparation of the *m-f* half-step has been begun through three songs in which this was the only unknown interval ("Chairs to Mend," "Cradle Song," "Hymn to Joy").

3. The student's ability to perform more than one rhythm at a time has been increased through ostinato and canon.

4. His inner hearing skill has been reinforced and extended.

5. He has worked on deriving and understanding musical form.

6. He has been applying the expressive elements—dynamics and tempo—in his music making.

7. He has used his known tonal and rhythmic vocabulary not just in music reading and writing but also in improvising and creating.

The last two chapters have made an attempt to offer possible techniques for accomplishing some of these tasks—techniques compatible with the Kodály philosophy and based on the Kodály pedagogical method. One hopes that teachers will find these suggestions helpful, but that they will decide upon their own goals, determine their own sequences, write their own long-range plans, rather than simply use the ones offered here.

Kodály represents a body of living, growing thought about music education. It should not be frozen into one sequence, one rigid pedagogy. Within the clearly defined philosophy of Kodály many sequences, many teaching techniques should be possible.

SUMMARY

Planning for teaching must occur on many levels. There must be broad goals (p. 154) and more narrowly defined instructional objectives through which to achieve those goals (p. 154). There must be detailed long-range plans through which to achieve the instructional objectives (p. 156) and daily plans through which to implement the long-range plans (p. 172). Ways must be decided for assessing the students' learning and for evaluating teaching and curriculum content. Materials of instruction, songs, games, dances, and listening selections must be chosen and arranged into a teaching order. Skills must be sequenced in a way that is compatible with child development and with the musical materials. And throughout all these steps the teacher must not lose sight of the fact that it is the musical experience, the musical context, that is the single most important factor in child musical learning.

The best laid plans are pointless if that musical experience is not of the highest quality possible.

SUGGESTED ASSIGNMENT

1. Looking at the long-range plan you constructed as an assignment for Chapter 7, determine what musical activities may be experienced through each song you have listed.

2. The sequence given in this chapter is intended for students who begin music instruction at age five or six. Construct a similar hierarchy for older beginning students.

chapter 9

Problems in Kodály Practice, Unique to American Schools and Materials

In the years that the author has worked with teachers engaged in Kodály practice in American schools, a number of concerns have emerged repeatedly:

— How and when should compound meter be taught?

— Where does triple meter fit in a skill sequence based on American folk music?

— Should low *la* and *ti* be taught through the *do*-pentatonic or penta-chordal song literature or through the minor-mode *la*-pentaton or pentachord, as the Hungarians teach it?

— What shall we call 𝅗𝅥 , 𝅘𝅥. 𝅘𝅥𝅮, $\overset{\text{3}}{\overline{\text{♩♩♩}}}$, and various other rhythmic figures?

In this chapter some possible solutions to these problems will be offered.

THE $\frac{6}{8}$ PROBLEM

Kodály stated emphatically that the music used for teaching children must be drawn initially from their own cultural and lingual heritage; that through the familiar rhythmic stress of the mother-tongue may young children easily acquire the skills and concepts necessary for music literacy.

Most of the problems that have arisen in American Kodály practice have stemmed from ignoring this basic dictum. Hungarian folk music is being used to teach American children in Kodály programs in many parts of the United States. Hungarian sequence has been taken and superimposed on American folk song in others. Neither of these two practices is effective.

Language and music are inseparable in folk song. The Hungarian language is spoken with stress always on the first syllable:

Ha én ci–ca vol–nek,
>   >   >

while English is largely an iambic language in which sentences most often begin with an unaccented sound, as in the translation of the Hungarian sentence above:

If I were a pussy–cat.
>   >

To draw the analogy with music, it is as if the Hungarian language is spoken in simple duple meter, beginning always on the downbeat, while English is spoken in compound duple meter, beginning on an upbeat. This lingual difference between Hungarian and English has created some mammoth problems in American Kodály teaching of compound meter.

The Hungarians teach $\frac{6}{8}$ late—in the fourth year of a six-times-weekly music program. In terms of the number of music lessons, an American program of twice-weekly music would have to delay the teaching of $\frac{6}{8}$ until well into high school to ensure a musical background equivalent to that of the Hungarian fourth-grade special music school class. This is obviously impractical. More English-language folk music exists in $\frac{6}{8}$ than in any other meter. It is the most common meter of nursery rhymes, singing games, early childhood songs, and ballads. While the Hungarians must look to foreign song material to teach $\frac{6}{8}$, Americans are surrounded by rhyme and song in $\frac{6}{8}$ from early childhood. The frequency with which this occurs in the folk literature makes it not only possible but also imperative that teachers of English-speaking children introduce $\frac{6}{8}$ much earlier and in a very different way than it is introduced in Hungary.

In Hungary, $\frac{6}{8}$ is approached by having students first sing and see songs in $\frac{2}{8}$, $\frac{3}{8}$, and $\frac{4}{8}$. Very few English-language folk songs exist in these meters. Then, when $\frac{6}{8}$ is introduced in Hungary, it is done through comparison with triplets in $\frac{2}{4}$:

In English-language folk music, triplets occur very infrequently, and always as an exceptional measure in an otherwise straightforward simple duple setting. For example: ("Pretty Polly")

To use the infrequent ($\frac{2}{8}$, $\frac{3}{8}$, $\frac{4}{8}$) and the exception (triplets) to explain the frequent and common ($\frac{6}{8}$) seems contrived, to say the least, and certainly inappropriate for teaching English-speaking children.

If one decides in this instance to discard the Hungarian model—not the underlying principles, but just this particular pedagogical process—then the teaching of $\frac{6}{8}$ becomes quite a bit simpler. The teaching process must be drawn from the teaching material, and of that there is a great amount.

However, there are still some problems to be addressed:

1. What is compound meter? What is the underlying musical concept children should hold about compound meter?
2. When should $\frac{6}{8}$ occur in the skill sequence? Before or after $\frac{3}{4}$? Should it be "made conscious" all at one time, or should various aspects of it be "made conscious" over a span of years?
3. Exactly how should $\frac{6}{8}$ be presented? How should one organize song materials for teaching? Which rhythmic figures should be taught first?

In addition, there are some questions of theory that must be decided upon—questions on which no two theory texts seem to be in agreement:

1. What is the beat note in $\frac{6}{8}$? Is it ♪ or is it ♩. ?
2. If it is ♩. , why is 8 the bottom number in the time signature?

3. If it is ♪, how and when should one deal with the secondary accent?

The author should like to turn to each of these problems now and to suggest possible solutions.[1]

What Is Compound Meter?
How Is It Different from Simple Meter?
What Concept Should Children Hold of Compound Meter?

Since the Kodály approach is an experiential and aural one, any answers to these questions must be ones children can derive from singing, hearing, and feeling. Teacher explanations are neither necessary nor desirable. The difference that children can aurally perceive is that in simple meters the division of the beat is felt in *twos*, while in compound meters the division of the beat is felt in *threes*. Since all metric arrangements are in twos or threes or combinations of twos and threes, this basic understanding at an early age can lead to later understanding of even such asymmetric meters as $\frac{5}{8}$ and $\frac{7}{8}$; and the compound meters $\frac{9}{8}$ and $\frac{12}{8}$ become a natural compound counterpart of the $\frac{3}{4}$ and $\frac{4}{4}$ meters.

At the earliest level, however, what children must be able to hear is that in

the felt beat (♩) frequently has two even sounds over it, while in

the felt beat (♩.) frequently has three even sounds over it.

When Should $\frac{6}{8}$ Be Taught?

English-language infant songs and rhymes are more often in $\frac{6}{8}$ than in $\frac{2}{4}$. Young children making up their own tunes and rhymes switch freely back and forth from $\frac{6}{8}$ to $\frac{2}{4}$. In view of this, it is important that the

[1] The author should like to acknowledge the contributions of Daniel Chandler, Polly Walter, and Nadine Sample, graduate students in the Holy Names Kodály program, to the creation and testing of this approach to $\frac{6}{8}$ meter.

nursery school or kindergarten music teacher incorporate many ⁶⁄₈ songs and rhymes in the teaching material from the very beginning of the children's music experience. Moreover, when singing a "good morning" greeting (as many Kodály teachers do) the stress must be placed where it falls in a linguistically natural manner:

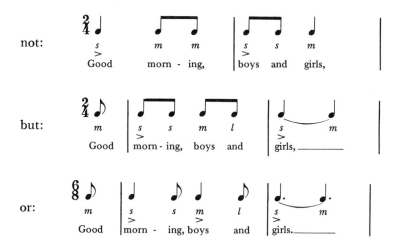

Whether this kind of greeting, and the response, are performed in simple or compound meter is not at issue. Whether it forces the language into an unnatural stress is. If the natural language stress is subverted at this early age, it will be very difficult for children to perceive compound metric stress and the feeling of upbeat correctly later.

The teaching of ⁶⁄₈ can follow the same procedure used in teaching ²⁄₄. Basic beat must be discovered—clapping and stepping the ♩ for ²⁄₄, swinging arms and swaying the ♩. for ⁶⁄₈. When the duple beat in ⁶⁄₈ can be performed accurately, children may be asked: "How many sounds do we hear on the beat?" This is the same question used to derive ♫ as two sounds over the ♩ beat in simple meter. Examples must be drawn from the rhymes and songs that begin ♫♩ ♫♩ so that the three sounds to the ♩. beat are obvious and easy to hear. This most basic lesson in compound meter should probably take place early in second grade, after children are secure in simple duple meter and have already identified ♩, ♫, and 𝄽.

By the end of first grade, children taught in this way have shown they can aurally distinguish between simple and compound meters in songs taught by rote. Since they know ♫ as two sounds on a beat, they have no difficulty in second grade in dealing with the notation ♫♪ for three sounds on a beat. Spoken, the first is *ti-ti,* the second, *ti-ti-ti.*

The overall order for teaching ⁶⁄₈ might be viewed as follows:

At the kindergarten and first-grade levels:

— Sing songs and play singing games both in simple and in compound meters.
— Have children distinguish between songs that step-march-walk and songs that sway-skip-gallop. Have them move with appropriate motions to songs in ²⁄₄ and ⁶⁄₈ meters,

At the second-grade level:

— Make children consciously aware that in both stepping music (²⁄₄) and swaying music (⁶⁄₈) one feels two beats to a measure; that the even divisions of sound over the beat are grouped in two (♫) in stepping music and in three (♫♪) in swaying music.
— Have them step the beat and clap the eighth-note subdivisions ♫ while singing in ²⁄₄. Have them sway the beat and clap the eighth-note subdivisions while singing songs in ♩..

At the third-grade level:

— After ♩. is taught in simple duple meter (through an ostinato ♪ ♪ ♪ ♪ in which eighth notes are tied to create the new rhythm: ♪ ♪ ♪ ♪ = ♩.   ♪)), the symbol ♩ may be introduced as the felt beat in ⁶⁄₈. That is, if they know the three small divisions of the beat as ♫♪ , the children should be able to derive the equivalent single sustained sound as ♩ . When this has been taught, meter and measure and simple notation for ⁶⁄₈ may be begun. Initially, the meter sign should be shown as ²/♩.. This is in keeping with the practice followed in first and second grade of showing simple duple and quadruple meters as ²/♩ and ⁴/♩ . (The felt beat in ⁶⁄₈ songs is ♩., not ♪. The eighth note is the felt beat in some composed ⁶⁄₈ music, but in no folk song of which the author is aware.) The most common ⁶⁄₈ rhythmic patterns (♩ ♪♩ ♪, ♩ ♪♩., ♩. ♩.)

should be introduced during this same period through songs learned in earlier years and through new songs.

At the fourth-grade level:

— Standard notation for $\frac{6}{8}$ may be shown and read from. The children will understand that there is no numerical equivalent for ♩. , so the eighth note must be used as the unit of measurement, even though it is not felt as the beat. Later, less frequent rhythmic figures should be dealt with as they occur in the songs: ♩. ♫ , ♩. , ♩♫♫ , ♫♫♩ , ♩♫♫ , ♪ 𝄾 ♪. Songs and rhymes must be carefully chosen at the beginning of the whole process for each step of the learning. The material suitable for dealing with the ♫♫♩ ♩♫♩ pattern in first grade is not always the best material for dealing with it in fourth. The teacher's long-range strategy for teaching must contain materials that clearly illustrate the meter and the rhythmic figure being studied, while still being appropriate to the age of the child. Nursery rhymes are excellent for teaching $\frac{6}{8}$ to kindergarten children. Sea chanteys are better for teaching the same rhythmic patterns to fourth graders.

At the levels above grade four, other compound meters $(\frac{9}{8}, \frac{12}{8}, \frac{6}{4})$ may be introduced as they are needed to deal with advanced song material. The underlying principle taught in first grade remains valid: in compound meters one feels the division of the basic beat into *three's*: in $\frac{9}{8}$ there are three basic beats, each with three smaller internal beats; in $\frac{12}{8}$ there are four basic beats, each with three internal beats; in $\frac{6}{4}$ there are two basic beats (♩.), each with three internal beats.

The question of terminology has been a persistent problem. The author prefers the terms *beat* (♩.) and *internal beats* (♩♫♩). However, various other terms have been used successfully: *beat* (♩.) and *pulse* (♩♫♩); *beat* (♩.) and *current beat* (♩♫♩); *big beat* (♩.) and *little beats* (♩♫♩). The last has the advantage of being most meaningful to very young children.

The most significant aspects of this approach to compound meters are that it is rooted deeply in the common usage and stress of the English language and that it is not something that happens just once in a "make conscious" lesson somewhere in third or fourth grade, but rather is developed gradually to the extent that children's maturity and musical experience will allow, over a period of more than 4 years.

The Triple Meter Problem

It has been the practice in most American Kodály programs to teach
$\frac{3}{4}$ after $\frac{2}{4}$ and $\frac{4}{4}$ and before $\frac{6}{8}$. This has developed in a rather logical
subject-oriented way. It has been dealt with at this point because teachers
have felt it a necessary prerequisite to $\frac{6}{8}$.[2] The old subject-logic approach
to education dies hard. Theoretically, simple triple meter should be
easier than compound duple meter. Theoretically, simple triple meter
should therefore precede compound duple meter in any skill hierarchy.

In practice, however, if one returns to the Kodály philosophy that
a child's musical experiences should be rooted in the folk music of his
mother-tongue, an altogether different ordering emerges. A vast number
of $\frac{6}{8}$ songs exists; relatively few songs may be found in $\frac{3}{4}$ in either the
Anglo-American or the Black folk heritages. This being the case, it ap-
pears rather obvious that compound duple should precede simple triple
as conscious knowledge. The author proposes pushing triple meter to
fourth or fifth grade, as a known meter.

In original American folk music, almost the only examples in triple
meter are the cowboy songs of the late nineteenth century, reflecting the
rather sentimental popular music of that day. There are some lovely old
English folk tunes in $\frac{3}{4}$, but these, for some reason, rarely found their way
into American usage with real American variants, as did many of the
tunes in simple and compound duple meter.

An additional problem is that almost all American songs in triple
meter begin with an anacrusis. From the standpoint of teaching a new
meter, the upbeat is definitely a problem. Even though youngsters will
have dealt with upbeats earlier in $\frac{2}{4}$, $\frac{4}{4}$, and $\frac{6}{8}$ songs, the material used
to make $\frac{3}{4}$ a conscious learning for students should ideally begin with an
accented beat since meter is derived through hearing and clapping the
pattern of accented and unaccented beats.

The biggest problem with existent practice in teaching $\frac{3}{4}$, however,
is that it is usually presented at a time when children are literate only
within the pentatonic tonal systems, while almost all American triple
meter folk music is diatonic. The obvious solution, again, is to delay the
introduction of triple meter until fourth or fifth grade, when youngsters
are singing, reading, and writing easily within the diatonic tonal systems.

All the above is intended for the children of Anglo-American and
Black cultural heritages. There are, of course, American communities of
Germanic, Hispanic, and other cultural heritages in which triple meter
is found frequently in the folk music. In Milwaukee or San Antonio the

---

[2] Many years ago the author felt this way too in her book *The Kodály Method*
(Englewood Cliffs, N.J.: Prentice-Hall, Inc., 1974), p. 92; since then she has
changed her mind.

order for presenting meters can and should differ sharply from the order in Boston or San Francisco.

The deciding factors must be, as for all sequence in a Kodály framework: the developmental level of the children to be taught, and the frequency of occurrence of the rhythmic figure, melodic turn, or meter in the folk music of the children's mother-tongue—the language spoken in their homes. Using these two measuring sticks, most American children will be able to comprehend compound duple meters, $\frac{6}{8}$ and $\frac{6}{4}$, both earlier and more easily than simple triple meters.

PROBLEMS INVOLVED IN TEACHING LOW la AND ti

Problems have arisen almost every time American teachers have used the Hungarian model rather than the "frequency of occurrence in the folk music" rule for determining teaching sequence. The teaching of low *la* and of *ti* (the leading tone) is a case in point.

In Hungarian songs of the adult folk heritage (as contrasted to infant songs), the most frequent tonal center is low *la*. Even the pentatonic songs have a distinctly minor-mode character. When low *la* is taught there, it is introduced through songs with the *la* tonal center. Children who have grown up with the sound of this modality in their ears have no difficulty at all learning the new note—low *la*—through songs in which it is the key note or tonal center.

American folk music and, for that matter, the largest amount of music of any kind heard in the United States is *do*-tonal centered, in a distinctly major character. The note low *la* is better introduced here through *do*-tonal centered material. If it is introduced through the minor pentaton: ("I Got a Letter")

$$\text{♪ ♩ } \quad \text{♪ ♫ ♩ ♩} \quad \text{♩} \quad \text{♩.}$$
$$m \quad m \qquad r \quad m \ r \quad d \qquad d \qquad l,$$

the children must deal with two unknowns at once: 1) the new note, low *la*; 2) the minor modal sound of the *la*-pentaton. It is the author's opinion that low *la* is far better approached with American children through *do*-tonal centered material: ("Rattlesnake")

$$\text{♩ ♩ ♫ ♩ } | \ \mathbf{o} \qquad ‖$$
$$m \quad r \quad d \ d \ l, \ | \ d$$

In this way, the security of the familiar surrounds the single unknown note.

There is no question that the latter approach is more effective. Recently, both were used, the first with children in an Oakland school, the second in two schools in San Jose. The teachers involved were all master teachers,[3] the children were similar in background and musical training. The children who were taught low *la* through *do*-tonal centered material were able to deal with the new note quickly and easily, while the children working with the *la*-tonal centered material had so much difficulty with the "make conscious" lesson that it had to be retaught at a later date.

When low *la* is securely learned as the note below *do* in the *do*-pentatonic tonal system, *la* as a tonal center in *la*-pentatonic songs may be introduced. There are a number of lovely American *la*-pentatonic songs. If children have been enjoying them as rote songs, they will not have difficulty aurally perceiving the difference in modality between the *do*- and *la*-centered songs.

The teaching of *ti* as the second in a pure minor scale (low *la* to *la*) or as the seventh and leading tone in the major scale (*do* to high *do*) presents a similar problem. The leading tone is not frequent in American *do*-tonal centered folk music. Much more music exists in the pentatonic tone-sets from low *so* to high *la* and in pentachordal (*d–r–m–f–s*) and hexachordal (*d–r–m–f–s–l*) tone-sets. When *ti* does exist in the tone-set, it may occur only once in a song as the next to the last note. It is a passing tone and, for that reason, sometimes difficult to direct attention to.

It might seem easier to deal with *ti* in a minor pentachord (*l,–t,–d–r–m*) setting. The second of a scale is surely more prominent than the seventh in most songs. Again, this is the pattern of a Hungarian sequence: *ti* is taught through minor pentachordal songs:

---

[3] In Oakland: Scott McCormick (St. Theresa's School). In San Jose: Mary Esposito (Cory School) and Kathleen Cain (Booksin School).

The strong position of *ti* in this and similar songs would seem to make it an ideal teaching vehicle, and indeed it is—in Hungary. It is not with American children. It is simply not the tonal vocabulary, the most characteristic melodic turn of English-language music.

Ti, like low *la,* is best taught to American children through familiar *do*-tonal centered material:

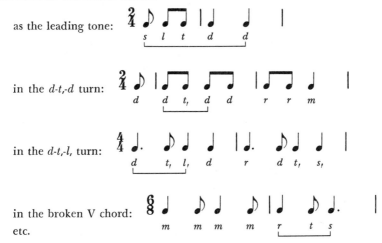

It should be taught in each melodic turn within the *do* scale before it is dealt with in the minor mode:

When a class is singing, reading, writing, and improvising well using *ti* in *do*-tonal centered settings and has sung a number of rote songs in the *la*-pentachord and hexachord, the latter may be examined and sung in *solfa* using the note *ti* as the second.

It is important that students experience other tonal centers. They should sing many songs in *la*-, *so*-, and *re*-pentatons. They should, later, become familiar with some of the beautiful Aeolian, Dorian, and Mixolydian folk songs of the American heritage. They absolutely should not be limited in their musical activity to *do*-centered songs. However, it is suggested that the *do*-centered material, being the most common musical heritage of America, is the best vehicle for teaching previously unknown notes and melodic turns.

DURATION SYLLABLE TERMINOLOGY

There is one other area that seems to present some difficulty to a number of teachers and that is what to call certain rhythms and rhythmic figures.

At the onset, the author should like to say that she does not think it matters in the least what one calls rhythmic figures, as long as the durations are sounded correctly. The object is to read melodies correctly in rhythm. Only at the earliest stages should the two aspects—rhythm and melody—be separated for students' music reading. By fourth grade, in a twice-weekly music program, youngsters should be able to keep the beat lightly with fingertips and read a song in *solfa* with rhythmic accuracy. If there are rhythmic problems, they should be anticipated and dealt with before the reading; but to continue to read every song in *ta*'s and *ti*'s before singing it is a self-defeating process.

One of the questions most often asked of the author is: "What do you call . . . [sixteenth notes, triplets, dotted rhythms]?" There is a Hungarian system of duration syllables adapted from the work of the French theoretician Chevé:

♩,	♫,	♩,	♩.,	𝅝 ,	♩. ♪,	♪♩.,	⟌³⟍ 𝅘𝅥𝅮𝅘𝅥𝅮𝅘𝅥𝅮,
ta	ti - ti	ta-	ta - -	ta - - -	ta - i - ti	ti - ta - i	tri - o - la

𝅘𝅥𝅮𝅘𝅥𝅮𝅘𝅥𝅮𝅘𝅥𝅮,	𝅘𝅥𝅮 𝅘𝅥𝅮𝅘𝅥𝅮,	𝅘𝅥𝅮𝅘𝅥𝅮 𝅘𝅥𝅮,	♪ ♩ ♪,	♩. 𝅘𝅥𝅮,	♫.
ti - ri - ti - ri	ti - ti - ri	ti - ri - ti	syn - co - pa	tim - ri	ti - rim

In practice, there have been problems with some of these in American schools.

♩ ♩. 𝅝 : if the quarter note is "ta," how may one differentiate between it and the half, dotted half and whole notes which also are "ta"? It is surely an unmusical practice to emphasize the second, third, and fourth beats of an extended duration: "ta-ah" or "ta-ah-ah-ah."
>   > > >

One solution is to have durations of longer than a beat performed on pitch rather than in spoken sound. It the pattern is chanted on pitch while the class keeps a fingertip beat, the unwanted and unmusical accents disappear.

The same problem recurs with dotted rhythms. When following

the Hungarian rhythm syllables $\underset{ta\ -\ i\ -\ ti}{\text{♩.}\quad\text{♪}}$, children tend to accent the

$(ta\ -\ ee\ -\ tee)$

second sound: $\underset{\underset{>}{ta\ -\ i\ -\ ti}}{\text{♩.}\quad\text{♪}}$, an absolutely incorrect emphasis.

This may be solved as above, by having youngsters sing rather than say rhythm patterns; however, the mere change of vowel phonetically from *ä* to *ē* causes an incorrect rhythmic emphasis on what should be a uniformly sustained sound.

Pierre Perron has devised a system of syllables for use in his radio musical education series *Making Music*,[4] which might prove useful to teachers who have encountered some of the difficulties mentioned above. In some instances they are the same as the Hungarian, but in some they are quite different.

Rhythm Names Developed by Pierre Perron

Simple meter:

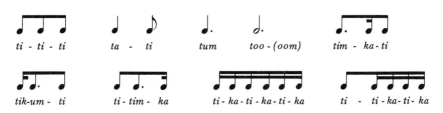

Compound meter:

4 Pierre Perron and Margaret Tse, Quebec Ministry of Education, Montreal, Canada.

ti- ka- ti- ka - ti

ti - ti- ka -ti

ti- ka- ti - ti

ti - ti - ti -ka

Even adults enjoy working with these involved and catchy rhythmic sounds. They can be an aid to teaching. Care must be taken, however, that any rhythm syllables do not become an end in themselves.

This chapter has dealt with certain problems encountered by teachers engaged in Kodály practice. They may not seem to be particularly important problems, but to the teacher wondering why her children are having difficulty with $\frac{3}{4}$ or what went wrong with the lesson on low *la,* they are very real.

The point the author has tried to make is that the solutions to these and similar problems will not be found by looking outward to Hungary, but by looking inward to American children and American music. Zoltán Kodály would have been the first to say this.

SUGGESTED ASSIGNMENTS

1. Construct a list of American folk songs, *do*-tonal centered for use in teaching *ti*. Categorize the list by the place of *ti* in the melodic teaching pattern in the song.

2. Determine the cultural and lingual heritage of the other students in your class. In the light of this heritage decide whether $\frac{3}{4}$ should be taught before or after $\frac{6}{8}$, and state your reasons.

chapter 10

American Folk Music for Teaching

Folk music is the mirror of the people's soul.

—KODÁLY

What is folk music? The International Folk Music Council, meeting in São Paulo, Brazil, in 1954, adopted the following definition:

> Folk music is the product of a musical tradition that has been evolved through the process of oral transmission. The factors that shape the tradition are: (i) continuity, which links the present with the past; (ii) variation, which springs from the creative impulse of the individual or the group; and (iii) selection by the community, which determines the form, or forms, in which the music survives.
>
> (i) the term folk music can be applied to music that has been evolved from rudimentary beginnings by a community influenced by popular or art music and it can likewise be applied to music which has originated with an individual composer and has subsequently been absorbed into an unwritten living tradition of a community.
>
> (ii) The term does not cover popular composed music that has been taken over ready-made by a community and remains unchanged; for it is the refashioning and recreation of the music by the community which gives it its folk character.

The particularly pertinent points in this rather long and carefully worded definition are that songs to be considered authentic folk songs:

1. must have been passed down by singing, not via printed music;
2. must be the product of evolution, i.e., have been changed, varied, and altered as they were passed down;

3. must have been around in one variant or another a certain number of years. (This time criterion adds the element of selection—the best, the most singable variants, are the ones that survive.)

Teachers should be concerned with the heritage of folk music for a number of reasons. The point has been made earlier in this book that as children have a lingual mother-tongue, so also do they have a musical mother-tongue—the folk music of their country, of their ancestors, of their ethnic groups, of their geographical regions. As children learn to speak their lingual mother-tongue before foreign languages, so also they should learn to sing in their musical mother-tongue—folk music—before other music.

Musically—folk songs are well suited to teaching because of their simple short forms, their frequent melodic and rhythmic repetitions, their small range, and simple scales.

Lingually—folk songs are well-suited to teaching young children because of their commonplace vocabulary and frequent repetition, and because they follow closely the stress patterns of the mother-tongue.

Most important, though, folk songs are a living art. They have not been composed for pedagogical purposes. They have intrinsic value as an art form. Further, through folk songs the teachers may help children reach the finest composed music. It is a much closer step from a beautiful, authentic folk ballad to a symphony than from a so-called "semi-classical" or "pops" work. This relationship of folk music to art music is sometimes very obvious (e.g., Beethoven's peasant dance in the *Pastoral Symphony*, Aaron Copland's use of cowboy tunes in *Billy the Kid*); at other times the relationship has been less obvious, but it has been there throughout history. Both folk music and art music have been influenced by the times in which they were created and each, in turn, has influenced and been influenced by the other.

"But the *pop* of today is the *folk* of tomorrow." This statement is often put forward. Perhaps this is so in some instances, but who can tell in which. A song like "Greensleeves" was a pop song in its day. It has lasted 400 years, and is now a folk song, and a beautiful one. But what of the thousands of pop songs of 400 years ago that have not lasted? "Greensleeves" and songs like it have been sifted through time. They have survived because of their unique beauty. What of today's music will be around in 400 years? It is too close in time to know.

Many children spend most of their waking hours immersed in a sea of bad music. Only when they are in the music class can the teacher be sure they are surrounded by good music. It is the responsibility of the teacher to do so. It is not necessary to denigrate popular music, but there is no need, either, to use it in the curriculum. One may teach only by example, and the quality of the music chosen for teaching is of the greatest importance.

The United States is experiencing a time of folk-song revival such as it has never before known. Beginning in the late 1800s with the pioneer work of Francis James Child in the collection of ballad texts, it gathered momentum with the work of Cecil Sharp and Maud Karpeles, who in the early 1900s compiled and published folk songs they found in the Appalachian mountains, and with the work of other serious ethnomusicologists important to the American scene: Phillips Barry, Frank Clyde Brown, Vance Randolph (Ozarks), B. A. Botkin. This revival continued into the 1930s with the labor and progressive movements (borrowing earlier folk tunes to present their causes) and the formation of the American Archive of Folk Song (A.A.F.S.) at the Library of Congress, by the efforts of D. K. Wilgus, George Korson, and the Lomax's. It then pushed into the 1940s, 1950s, and 1960s with the scholarly work of Bertrand Harris Bronson and with collector-performers such as Burl Ives, John Jacob Niles, Pete Seeger, and Peggy Seeger. The songs they sang and sing are ballads and southern mountain songs, Negro spirituals and blues, songs of cowboys, hobos and prospectors, of railroad men and sailors—songs based on the happenings of the time.

There are almost as many ways of categorizing American folk music as there have been people collecting it; there are books on folk songs organized by geographical area: Appalachian, Ozarks, New England, Texas, . . .; by song subject: work songs, spirituals, songs of courtship and marriage, children's songs,. . . .; by ethnic group: Anglo-American, Black-American, Indian, Hispano-American are the major ethnic groupings of American folk music, but one may also find whole volumes of songs of proportionately very small groups: the Pennsylvania Dutch, for example, or the Shakers.

Any comprehensive examination of the American folk tradition must be an examination of many folk traditions. For the purposes of this chapter the author should like to look briefly at just two of these: music of the Anglo-American heritage and the music of Black Americans.

ANGLO-AMERICAN

The Ballad

Ballad singing is an ancient tradition that came to America with the earliest settlers from the British Isles; Cecil Sharp and Maud Karpeles[1] found examples of ballads in the Appalachian mountains,

---

[1] Cecil J. Sharp and Maud Karpeles, *English Folk Songs from the Southern Appalachians* (London: Oxford University Press, 1932, 1960).

many of which they traced to the fifteenth and sixteenth centuries—songs that came to America with the very earliest settlers and survived in a very pure form.

Basically, a ballad is a song telling a story. Some ballads ran over 100 verses. Usually ballads were unaccompanied, although occasionally a dulcimer, guitar, or other plucked instrument was used. Essentially, there are three categories of ballads:

1. those in the *ancient tradition* that came from the British Isles and remained intact ("John Randolph");
2. *native American* ballads ("John Henry");
3. *broadside ballads* ("The Mary L. Macay")—these were sometimes hack pop tunes written and published to make money and, at other times, familiar folk tunes to which new words were added. They dealt with the disasters of the time—hangings, piracy, highwaymen, ship sinkings, etc. They were a popular medium through the seventeenth and eighteenth centuries. They were known as "Come All Ye's" [2] (Benjamin Franklin wrote two of them: "The Lighthouse Tragedy" and "Blackbeard"—neither has survived). Those songs in this category that have survived have been shaped and refined by the folk process and have earned their place in the ballad tradition.

The form of ballads was usually a four-phrase A-B-C-D with a four-line verse, the second and fourth lines rhyming.

It was a tradition in pioneer families, during the westward movement, to take the family "ballet [ballad] book" along with them. They sang their way West. The "ballet" book was a scrapbook, rather like a recipe book, full of songs hand notated and written.[3] (Usually, at least one member of the family could notate; musical literacy was not such a rare thing in those days.)

The ballad is the oldest and best known of Anglo-American folk forms, but numerous other types of songs flourished in the same tradition. There were:

1. *Cumulative songs*—such as "Twelve Days of Christmas" and "There Was a Little Oak."

[2] Alan Lomax, in his *Folk Songs of North America* (Garden City, New York: Doubleday & Co., Inc., 1960), gives thirteen of these, all of which begin with some variant of the phrase "Come All Ye."

[3] One of the most famous of these old ballet books: Almeda Riddle, *A Singer and Her Songs* (Baton Rouge, Louisiana: Louisiana State University Press, 1971), is an account which includes not only selections from her own ballet book, but also songs from the books of her family—parents and grandparents—as well.

2. *Folk lyric songs*—songs without a story, that were simply images held together by a pretty tune or mode: "Black Is the Color."

3. *Nonsense songs*—such as "The Good Old Man."

4. *Animal songs*—fanciful songs dealing with possums, roosters, hound dogs, frogs; songs designed to appeal to children: "Groundhog," "Rattlesnake," "Frog Went A-Courtin'."

5. *Play-party songs*—these were basically fiddle tunes in which voices were substituted for instruments as accompaniment for "games," which in reality were dances. They emerged wherever the church forbade instrumental music and dancing in the United States. Examples are "Alabama Gal" and "Shake Them Simmons Down." Sometimes these tunes were taken from minstrel shows: "Old Dan Tucker," "Old Brass Wagon." The minstrel tunes that have survived have earned their place in the folk heritage.

6. *Carols*—Christmas carols are the best known, but carols also exist for other seasons or times of the year: "May Day," for instance.

7. *Work songs:*
   a. *Sea chanteys*—the sea provided a true meeting ground of cultures; crews of the great merchant ships were English, Irish, Black, and Asian. The period of flowering was brief—mostly in the nineteenth century—although written reference to sea-songs has been found as early as in the fifteenth century. With the passing of the great sailing ships, the chanteys went also. Chanteys in their purest form were a simple singing-out of orders and responses as the crew worked. The solo line was sung by the "chantey-man" and the responses were sung by the crew. The chantey-man was hired for his ability to improvise both words and music with considerable variation. Choruses were sung by the crew in unison to the established melodic patterns. No accompaniment was used. An example is "Santy Anno."
   b. *Cowboy songs*—between 1867 and 1890, 40,000 cowboys sang as they drove 10 million cattle to Northern markets. The songs were lullabies to lull the cattle to sleep at night, rhythmic yells to get the cattle to move along, story accounts of stampedes, lonely complaints about night watch, sentimental ballads about the death of a comrade: "The Streets of Laredo."
   c. *Other work songs*—Railroad: "Pat Works on the Erie;" Lumbermen: "The Jam on Gerry's Rocks;" Canal boat songs: these were both serious, "The Erie Canal," and parodies [4] on sea chanteys, "The E-R-I-E."

8. *Revival songs and white spirituals*—such as "Wayfaring Stranger" and "Bound for the Promised Land." Although these two songs were originally white spirituals, they, and others like them, gradually became part

---

[4] An excellent source for these is: John A. Lomax and Alan Lomax, *Folk Song U.S.A.* (New York: Duell, Sloan & Pearce, Inc., 1947).

of a joint white–black culture. On this point Wilgus [5] said:

> To America from Africa the Negro brought a song tradition differing from, and yet in some respects resembling, the European folk tradition with which in fact it had some historic connections. From the songs of the whites the Negro borrowed what was congenial to him, and the whites were debtors as well as creditors. The resulting hybrid is a folk music which sounds African in the Negro tradition and European in the white tradition.

BLACK-AMERICAN

That Negro tradition, spoken of by Wilgus, contains a source of some of the most original and beautiful of all American folk music. The spiritual is probably the most widely known and accepted of all black-American music. Actually, the term "spiritual" is a sixteenth-century English one. The songs known today as Negro spirituals were called "shouts" or "jubilees" by the black people with whom they originated, and in the old days these shouts and jubilees were accompanied by circle dances which increased in intensity as the religious exultation increased. They were associated with inherited religious practices from West Africa. Later, the music was retained, but it was altered to suit white audiences. The texts were the folk poetry of the black people. Taking Bible stories, they made them a part of their own tragic history: in "When Israel Was in Egypt's Land" the words "let my people go" surely refer to the enslaved black people who were singing; in "Little David" it is not hard to realize the associations of the white masters as Goliath and the black slaves as David. It was the famous *Fiske Jubilee Choir,* touring the country to raise money for black education after the Civil War, that first used the term "spiritual" in connection with these songs, and it was through their somewhat toned-down choral versions that the spiritual became well-known throughout America.

Less well-known, but equally beautiful, are the many field hollers and work songs of the black people. These were songs for cutting down the sugar cane, loading the river boats, for ax teams and stevedores, and for picking the cotton. There were songs just for entertainment; patting songs and chants in which the voice was accompanied by a complicated rhythmic accompaniment of body slapping and tapping: "Juba," "Hambone." There were songs about the hardships of slavery: "Black Sheep,

[5] D. K. Wilgus, "The Negro-White Spiritual" in: *Anglo-American Folksong Scholarships Since 1888* (New Brunswick, New Jersey, Rutgers University Press, 1959).

Black Sheep," and about escape: "Slave Lament," "Follow the Drinkin' Gourd."

The development of blues from earlier black music was a gradual and natural one. Blues are a way of talking to oneself. In their simplest form, a first line is repeated twice, followed by a second (rhyming) line to complete the thought or verse. The verses may float, i.e., they may show up sometimes in one song and sometimes in another. The scale is usually a major one with a ♮7, although the third may be flatted also. Blues like these went on to become the foundations of jazz, and that jazz influenced some of the most serious works of twentieth-century composers.

MUSICAL CHARACTERISTICS OF AMERICAN FOLK MUSIC

Is there a set of musical characteristics common to the Anglo-American and black traditions of American folk songs? It appears so. A large number of these songs, black and white in origin:

1. have a range of from the fourth below the key note to the sixth above (producing a *s*, to *l′* scale rather than a *d* to *d′* one);
2. have as an important melodic turn *d l, s,—s, l, d;*
3. are duple in meter. Some are $\frac{6}{8}$, particularly those of Scottish-Irish origin, but this is duple too, compound duple. The only common exceptions are the cowboy songs (generally $\frac{3}{4}$) which reflect nineteenth-century sentimentality and the pop idiom of that day;
4. are often pentatonic in feeling—in terms of *solfa* almost as many songs exist without *fa* and/or *ti* as with these notes. The African modes brought to the United States were hemitonic and pentatonic. Later, Black music used the ♭7 and ♭3 also.

The white tradition was largely an unaccompanied one (although the dulcimer was used in Appalachia), while the black tradition made use of the banjo, brought from Africa, and of invented instruments, usually rhythm instruments, as accompaniment. However, neither tradition was a particularly harmonic one. When singing was accompanied, where the educated musician would have automatically introduced a subdominant chord in the harmonization, the folk musician would continue the tonic. Secondary chords were not used and even the dominant sevenths were rare. Variations in tempo and dynamics within a song were uncommon.

Folk music and scholarship has come into its own in the twentieth century. Almost every state in the union now has an Archive of Folk

Song. There is an American Society for Ethnomusicology, headquartered in Ann Arbor, Michigan, which publishes a good scientific journal. Folkways Records, under the direction of Moses Asch, has done much to make authentic folk songs available to all.

The material is available. All that remains for teachers is to select, sequence, and use it.

CHOOSING FOLK SONGS FOR TEACHING

How should the music teacher go about putting together a collection of folk songs for teaching? The tendency on the part of many teachers is to look for "*so-mi*" songs or "low *la*" songs. This way is fraught with danger. It is somewhat like building a house looking only at the nails rather than at the blueprint.

In earlier years, not knowing better then, the author, on finding a song that was almost right for a teaching purpose, would "bend" it a little. "Rain, Rain, Go Away" was taught as *s-m-ss-m, ss-mm-ss-m,* leaving out the inconvenient *la* in the second phrase, thus doing away with one of the most characteristic intervals of American infant songs—the *mi* to *la* perfect fourth on an unstressed beat. "A-Tisket A-Tasket" was taught without the initial anacrusis, in spite of the fact that in the English language almost every sentence begins with an unstressed sound, and to eliminate the upbeat destroys both the musical and the linguistic integrity of the piece.

To deliberately alter a folk song in a structural way for teaching purposes is an act of destruction. It can also be an act of destruction, albeit a lesser one, to alter words and word meanings to make them less offensive, to "pretty" them up ("I done lost dat closet key," as it appears on a Library of Congress recording, becoming "I have lost my golden key"). Of course, a teacher may alter words to be able to use a musically beautiful, pedagogically sound example in which some words or phrases are not suitable for children. Sometimes, though, teachers alter words not because they are unsuitable for children but because they offend their own sensibilities. More than one teacher has told the author that he or she would never use "Hangman, Hangman, Slack Up Your Rope," that it is not a good thing for children to sing this wonderful old Ozark ballad about a young man about to be hanged for his debts, who is saved at the last moment by his sweetheart bringing the gold to pay them off. Is it really necessary to protect a generation of young television viewers and movie goers from a song that describes a reality of America's past? More folk texts are useable than are generaly realized to be. In staying with the "safe" song material, teachers may be ignoring a whole part of folk tradition that reflects much of human life and the history of the American peoples.

About 3 years after the author did her first Kodály work, in 1966, she proudly showed her collection of teaching songs to Erzsébet Szőnyi of the Franz Liszt Academy. Professor Szőnyi was much kinder about them than the author would be today. In subsequent years, after several visits to Hungary, a year of study there, observations in the singing schools and discussions with the fine teachers there, and after work with Hungarian ethnomusicologist László Vikár, the author's collection of folk songs for teaching has altered drastically. Fewer than half the original songs remain. It is as important to discard as to collect. One must constantly be looking for better musical materials to replace the less good ones for teaching. But how may one recognize a good folk song for teaching when one finds it?

Folk music being considered for use in teaching should be examined in two ways: from the pedagogical viewpoint (What makes a good teaching song?), and from the ethnomusicological viewpoint (Is this really a folk song? Is it the best, the loveliest, the most authentic variant of this folk song?).

The pedagogical criteria are relatively easy to establish and follow. An examination of the Hungarian singing school texts *Ének-Zene* reveals that to make children consciously aware of any previously unidentified melodic or rhythmic element, the songs chosen:

1. are of small range. For example, in terms of American materials, although children are familiar with *la, so, mi,* and *do* when they are preparing for *re,* the preferable make-conscious song would probably be a *m-r-d* one ("Hot Cross Buns") rather than a *l-s-m-r-d* one ("Hush Little Minnie"). Fewer notes make it easier for children to focus on the new unknown one.

2. contain the new note or rhythm pattern in a place conspicuous to young children, e.g., the beginning phrase of the song, and usually contain it more than once. Such songs are made up of short, clear, independent phrases, easy to diagram and recall. For syncopation: "Alabama Gal" contains ♪ ♩ ♪ three times, once at the beginning of each phrase.

3. introduce, especially at the earliest levels, a new melodic turn in the context of simple quarter-note patterns in duple meter. For *la:*

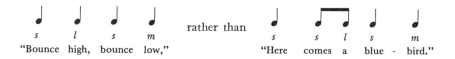

4. initially introduce the new note through a descending rather than an

ascending melodic line. For *re*:  before

"Old   Aunt   Di -   nah."   That young children sing descending patterns more easily and accurately than ascending ones is widely known. Anyone who doubts the truth of this should try to teach the minor third initially as *m-s,* with the *mi* consistently on the strong beat. In fact, try to find a *s-m* or a *l-s-m* song with the *mi* on the strong beat. The one exception in American folk music to this general rule of teaching initially from the descending interval is *la,* which in American infant songs occurs as a rising fourth on an unstressed beat:

Of course, songs can be found that do not conform to one or more of the above four points and still are excellent teaching songs. However, there is a fifth and last criterion that must be scrupulously observed:

5. [the songs chosen] contain no unknown notes or rhythms other than the new one being taught. It is a sore temptation sometimes to use a song with just the right melodic turns for a melodic make-conscious song, and overlook a small unknown rhythmic element in it, but this is bad teaching practice. How may one expect a child to concentrate on the unknown when there are two unknowns?

In the first-grade book in Hungary there are 30 different songs dealing with the teaching of the note *re.* Some are preparation, three are designated as make-conscious songs, and the rest provide reinforcement of the newly learned note in various intervalic combinations; they are the practice and reading songs. Almost without exception, these thirty songs follow the five criteria given above.

However, all the above rules can be followed faithfully and the teacher can still end up with poor musical material if the songs are not the best folk songs. What is a good folk song from a musical point of view?

Assuming that the teacher looks in places where there is some assurance of the authenticity of the material, there are some simple tests teachers may apply to help choose the best folk music for teaching.[6]

1. Read the text of the song.
   a. Is the language simple and direct?
   b. Does the subject matter have meaning for the children?
   c. Will it stimulate the imagination?
   d. Does it encourage creativity, role playing, games?
2. Sing the song.
   a. Do the text and music really fit together?
   b. Is there a pervasive mood that will speak to children emotionally?

If a song holds up well under these artistic judgements, as well as meeting the pedagogical requirements, it may be a winner—one with which children can grow.

Zoltán Kodály was linguist, ethnomusicologist, teacher, and artist—four persons in one. Few teachers can be that, and, short of being that, each must seek elsewhere the components missing from his own talents and training.

Folk Song Collections

Programs of collection and analysis are being carried out in various parts of the United States. At Holy Names College there is a resource center containing more than 1300 folk songs analyzed by tone-set, rhythm, and form, and characterized by teaching purpose. Collections have also been made by the Kodály Musical Training Institute at Watertown, Massachusetts, by teachers in the New Haven Ringer group, and by numerous Kodály-trained individuals around the country.

In addition, many teachers are delving into the ethnic music of the areas in which they teach: the Finnish music of Northern Michigan, the Navajo music of Arizona, the Mexican music of California. Others are digging into the vast and largely uncharted folk materials in the Archive of Folk Song at the Library of Congress. Perhaps one of the most potentially useful of these projects is a recently-completed index of some of the child-related materials housed in the Archive.[7]

[6] Suggested by Eleanor Locke, Director of the Folk Music Resource Center at Holy Names College, Oakland, California.

[7] This was compiled by Catherine Parnell as part of her Master's thesis at Holy Names College. A reference copy is available at the College's Folk Music Resource Center.

An increasingly vital need is a way of cross-referencing sources, eliminating duplication of effort, and making materials more accessible to teachers. With this in mind, the folk-music committee of the Organization of American Kodály Educators has investigated the possibility of computerizing the existing collections so that the teacher who needs thirty songs in the *re* pentaton, for example, could turn to one central source. Until this becomes a reality, it is the individual teacher who must continue to search out the best materials for teaching.

The easiest way to do this is to forget the phrase "for teaching." Read through fine song collections. Look through the State's Folk Song Archive. Listen to children on playgrounds and city streets. Talk to older people and ask them to sing the songs they sang as children. Whenever a song is found that has a lovely melody and a good text, it should be analyzed for its tone-set and rhythms and placed in the teacher's collection. Gradually, a sequence will emerge. It may be very similar to the sequence given in this book or it may be very different. However, if the music has been drawn from the cultural heritage of the children being taught, the sequence inherent in the music will be right for teaching those children.

Kodály said:

> The musical culture of a country is not created by individual musicians but by the whole population. Everyone has a share in it, even to the smallest. It is vain for individuals to work if they are not accompanied by the echo of millions.

It is to be hoped that American music teachers, through the quality music they choose for teaching, will help their children to hear that "echo of millions."

SUGGESTED READING

BRUNO NETTL, *Folk Music In The United States: An Introduction* (Detroit: Wayne State University Press, 1976). [Third Edition, revised and explained by Helen Myers.]

ALAN LOMAX, *Folk Songs of North America* (Garden City, New York: Doubleday and Co., Inc., 1975).

EILEEN SOUTHERN, *The Music of Black Americans: A History* (New York: W. W. Norton and Co., Inc., 1971).

HAROLD COURLANDER, *Negro Folk Music, U.S.A.* (New York: Columbia University Press, 1963).

WILLIAM MAIN DOERFLINGER, *Shantymen and Shantyboys: Songs of the Sailor and the Lumberman* (New York: Macmillan Publishing Co., Inc., 1951).

CECIL JAMES SHARP and MAUD KARPELES, *80 English Folk Songs from the Southern Appalachians* (London: Faber Music Ltd., 1968).

BERTRAND HARRIS BRONSON (Ed.), *The Singing Tradition of Child's Popular Ballads* (Princeton, New Jersey: Princeton University Press, 1976).

APPENDICES

Introduction
to the Appendices

About the notation of songs in this book. It has been the practice among some folk-song transcribers to use diatonic-scale key signatures for pentatonic, pentachordal, hexachordal, and other small-range folk songs. The feeling seems to have been that the tones used in such songs are in reality only fragments of eight-note major or minor scales and that the "missing" notes are in some way implied.

In terms of most American folk music this is simply not accurate. The scale of a pentatonic song—of which there are many American examples—is a five-note scale composed of major seconds and minor thirds. If constructed starting with *do* as the tonal center on F, its notes are F, G, A, C, D. To put a key signature of B-flat at the beginning of such a song, in which B does not exist, is to make nonsense of key signatures and to deny the reality of pentatony in American folk music.

The notational convention of folk songs in a Kodály framework is to give as key signature only those sharps or flats that *actually* occur as structural elements in the tone-set of the song. For example, a pentatonic song in C-*do*, F-*do*, or G-*do* placement requires no key signature at all. No sharps or flats occur in *do*-pentatonic scales constructed on these beginning notes. A song in dorian mode with D as the tonal center would likewise be shown with no sharps or flats in the key signatures rather than be shown, as such examples so often are, with a B-flat in the key signature and a natural sign before every B in the song. The latter implies that the song is in D-minor with "accidentals," while the Kodály notational technique clearly indicates its modality. There is nothing "accidental" about the raised sixth in the dorian mode; it is the characteristic interval of that mode.

For the reader's convenience tone-sets are given before each song, from highest to lowest *solfa* note, and the tonal center of each is circled (except in the infant *s-m-l* songs in which there is no clearly defined tonal center).

Songs to Accompany Chapter 2

1. BLUE BELLS

ls m

Blue - bells, cock - le - shells, Ee - vy I - vy o - ver

Blue - bells, cock - le - shells, Ee - vy I - vy Out, Now,

2. OLIVER TWIST

ls m

Ol - i - ver Twist you can't do this so what's the use of try - ing?

Touch your knees, touch your toes, Clap your hands and a - round you go.

3. LEMONADE

ls m

Here we come. Where from? Ten - nes - see. What's your trade?

Lem-on-ade! Get to work and give us some, if you're not a - fraid!___

4. WITCH, WITCH

s m

Witch, Witch, Could-n't sew a stitch Picked up a pen-ny and

thought she was rich! Are you my child - ren? Yes mam
(2x) Spoken: No! You Old Witch!

5. THE LANTERN MAN

ls m

Twen-ty, For - ty, Six - ty, Eight-y a hun -dred years a - go

All through the night with lan- tern bright the watch trudged through the snow.

And lit - tle boys tucked snug in bed would wake from dreams to hear

"Two in the morn- ing by the clock and stars are shin - ing clear."

6. BYE LO, BABY OH

s m

Bye - lo, Ba - by, Oh; Off to dream-land you must go.

7. BOUNCE HIGH

ls m

Bounce high, Bounce low, Bounce the ball to Shi - loh!

8. ICKA BACKA

ls m

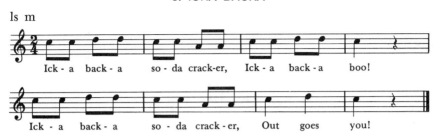

Ick - a back - a   so - da crack-er,   Ick - a   back - a   boo!

Ick - a back - a   so - da crack - er,   Out   goes   you!

9. DOGGIE, DOGGIE

ls m

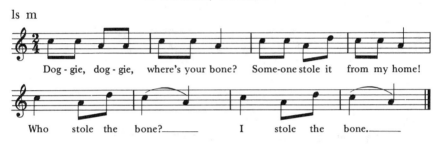

Dog - gie, dog - gie,   where's your bone?   Some-one stole it   from my home!

Who   stole the   bone?_____   I   stole the   bone._____

10. CUCKOO

ls m

I   hear a   cuck - oo;   Cuck - oo,   who   are   you?

11. BOBBY SHAFTOE

ls m

Bob - by Shaf - toe's gone to sea,   Sil - ver buck - les   on his knee,

He'll come back and   mar - ry me,   Bon - ny Bob - by   Shaf - toe.

12. BEE BEE

s m

Bee,   Bee,   bum - ble bee,   al - lee, al - lee   out's in free.

13. GOOD NIGHT

Good night, sleep tight, Friends will come to - mor - row night.

14. SEE SAW, MARGERY DAW

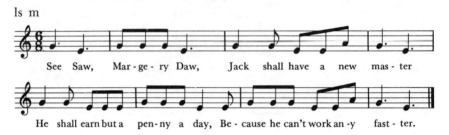

See Saw, Mar-ge-ry Daw, Jack shall have a new mas - ter

He shall earn but a pen-ny a day, Be - cause he can't work an -y fast - ter.

15. LITTLE SALLY WATER

Lit - tle Sal - ly wa - ter, sit - ting in a sau - cer,

Rise Sal - ly, Rise Sal - ly, Wipe a - way your tears Sal - ly,

Turn to the east Sal - ly, turn to the west Sal - ly,

Turn to the ver - y one that you love the best, Sal - ly.

16. KNOCK AT THE DOOR

Knock at the door, peep in, O - pen the door and walk in.

17. HERE COMES A BLUEBIRD

Here comes a blue - bird in through my win - dow

Hey,   did - dle - um - a   day,   day,   day.

Takes him - self   a   part - ner   hops   in   the   gar - den,

Hey,   did - dle - um - a   day,   day,   day.

18. BOW WOW WOW

s mr d

Bow - wow - wow!   Who's   dog   art   thou?

Lit -tle   Tom - my   Tuck - er's   dog!   Bow,   wow,   wow.

19. SALLY GO ROUND THE SUN

ls mr d

Sal - ly   go 'round   the   sun,   Sal - ly   go 'round   the   moon.

Sal - ly   go 'round   the   chim - ney   pot,   Ev - 'ry   af - ter - noon.

20. DEEDLE DEEDLE DUMPLING

s mr d

Dee - dle   dee - dle   Dump - ling,   my   son   John,

Went   to   bed   with   his   stock - ings   on.

One   shoe   off   and   one   shoe   on,

Dee - dle   dee - dle   dump - ling   my   son   John.

21. DOG AND CAT

Bought me a dog, Bought me a cat They both fight but
do not mind that Hi - Ho, my dar - ling.

22. POOR LITTLE KITTY CAT

Poor Lit - tle Kit - ty cat, Poor Lit - tle fel - ler
Poor Lit - tle Kit - ty cat, Lost in the cel - lar.

23. OLD KING GLORY

Old King glo - ry on the moun tain
The moun - tain was so high, it near - ly touched the sky,
The first one, the sec - ond one, the third fol - low me.

24. SKIN AND BONES

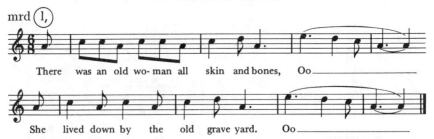

There was an old wo - man all skin and bones, Oo___
She lived down by the old grave yard. Oo___

2. One night she thought she'd take a walk. . . . .
3. She walked down by the old grave yard. . . . .
4. She saw the bones a-layin around. . . . .
5. She thought she'd sweep the old grave yard. . . . .
6. She went to the closet to get a broom. . . . .
7. She opened the door and BOO!

25. MIGHTY PRETTY MOTION

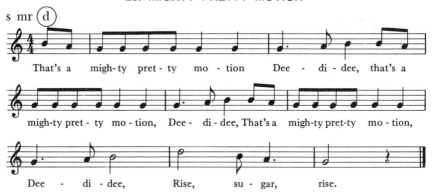

s mr (d)

That's a migh-ty pret-ty mo - tion Dee - di - dee, that's a
migh-ty pret - ty mo - tion, Dee - di - dee, That's a migh-ty pret-ty mo - tion,
Dee - di - dee, Rise, su - gar, rise.

Songs to Accompany Chapter 3

1. WALK DANIEL

2. Fly the other way Daniel.
3. Fly way back home Daniel.
4. On the eagle's wing Daniel.

2. WALK AND STOP

Oh well you walk and you walk and you walk and you stop!

Oh well you walk and you walk and you walk and you stop___

¹ The number in parentheses refers to the difficulty level of the song as discussed in Chapter 3, p. 50.

3. ALL 'ROUND THE BRICKYARD

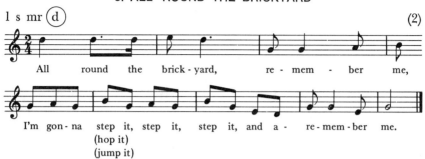

All round the brick-yard, re-mem-ber me,

I'm gon-na step it, step it, step it, and a-re-mem-ber me.
(hop it)
(jump it)

In the above movement songs any kind of motion may be substituted for "walk" or "step."

4. OATS, PEAS, BEANS AND BARLEY GROW

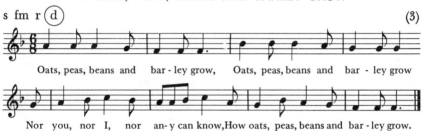

Oats, peas, beans and bar-ley grow, Oats, peas, beans and bar-ley grow

Nor you, nor I, nor an-y can know, How oats, peas, beans and bar-ley grow.

2. Thus the farmer sows his seed,
   Stands erect and takes his ease,
   He stamps his foot and claps his hands
   And turns around to view the land
3. Thus the woman churns her cheese
   Stands erect and takes her ease,
   She rocks to the left and rocks to the right
   And runs indoors to trim her light
4. Waiting for a partner
   Waiting for a partner
   Open the ring, take one in.
   As we all gaily dance and sing

5. HERE WE GO ROUND THE MULBERRY BUSH

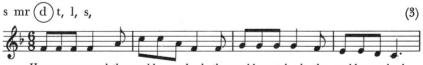

Here we go round the mul-ber-ry bush, the mul-ber-ry bush, the mul-ber-ry bush,

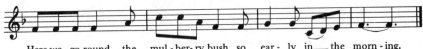

Here we go round the mul-ber-ry bush, so ear-ly in____the morn-ing.

> 2. This is the way we wash our clothes,
>   Wash our clothes, wash our clothes,
>   This is the way we wash our clothes
>   So early Monday morning.
> 3. (activities added for each day of the week)

In each of the above "acting-out" games the children step or skip in a circle on the chorus and stand in place and pantomime actions during the verses.

6. OLD ROGER IS DEAD

r' (d') tls m d   (3 and 6)

Old Ro - ger is dead and gone to his grave

H'm,   Ha!   Gone to his grave.

> 2. They planted an apple tree over his head
>   H'm, ha! Over his head.
> 2. The apples were ripe and ready to drop. . . .
> 4. There came an old woman a-pick-in them up. . . .
> 5. Old Roger jumped up and gave her a knock. . . .
> 6. Which made the old woman go hippity hop. . . .

Verse 1.	The children stand in a circle around "Roger", stretched out on the floor in the center of the circle.
Verse 2.	A child stands at Roger's head with arms out stretched. He is the "apple tree."
Verse 3.	The "tree" allows the apples to drop.
Verse 4.	A child from the circle walks around Roger, picking up the apples.
Verse 5. and 6.	Roger jumps up and chases the old woman around the outside of the circle. She becomes the next "Roger."

7. LITTLE SALLY WATER

mr(#) (d) l,s,   (3 and 4)

Lit - tle Sal - ly wa - ter,   Sit - ting in a sau - cer

Cry - in and a weep - in o - ver all she had done

Rise Sal - ly, Rise. Dry your weep - in' eyes.

Turn to the East, Sal - ly, Turn to the West, Sal - ly,

Turn to the ve - ry one that you love the best, Sal - ly.

8. GREEN GROWS THE WILLOW TREE

s fm r (d) s,   (4)

Green grows the wil - low tree, green - grows the wil - low tree,

Green grows the wil - low tree, Come my love and sit by me.

2. On the banks the rushes grow, (3x)
Shake her hand and let her go.

One child sits in the center while the group steps around her in a circle. On "Come my love" the child in the center pulls someone in from the circle to sit with her. On the words "shake her hand" the first child does just that, and on "let her go," the first child moves to the circle, leaving the second in the center as "it." In older variants it was "kiss your love" rather that "shake her hand."

9. JENNY JONES

sf mr (d) t, s,   (5 and 6)

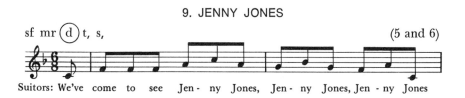

Suitors: We've come to see Jen- ny Jones, Jen- ny Jones, Jen - ny Jones

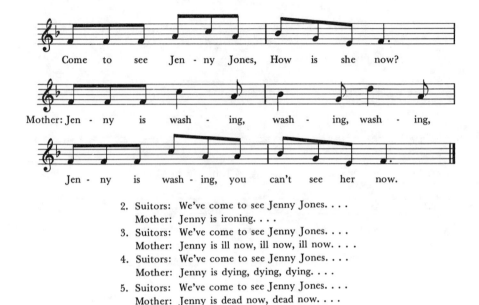

Come to see Jen - ny Jones, How is she now?

Mother: Jen - ny is wash - ing, wash - ing, wash - ing,

Jen - ny is wash - ing, you can't see her now.

2. Suitors: We've come to see Jenny Jones. . . .
   Mother: Jenny is ironing. . . .
3. Suitors: We've come to see Jenny Jones. . . .
   Mother: Jenny is ill now, ill now, ill now. . . .
4. Suitors: We've come to see Jenny Jones. . . .
   Mother: Jenny is dying, dying, dying. . . .
5. Suitors: We've come to see Jenny Jones. . . .
   Mother: Jenny is dead now, dead now. . . .

Verse
6.(in march tempo)

Red for the sol - diers and blue for the sail - ors

and black for the mour - ners of poor___ Jen - ny Jones.

This is a confrontation–chase game. In this variant, "Jenny" and "Mother" are on one side, the rest of the children in a line on the other. The line steps forward and back during the dialogue. "Jenny" acts out what "mother" says. On verse 6 the line marches around Jenny who is stretched out on the ground, arms folded across her chest, eyes closed. At the end of the verse, Jenny's "corpse" jumps up and gives chase.

10. CUT THE CAKE

d' ls fmr (d)   (6)

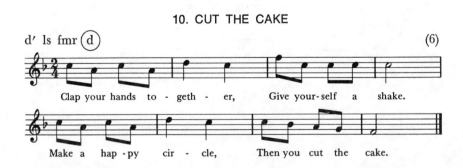

Clap your hands to - geth - er, Give your-self a shake.

Make a hap - py cir - cle, Then you cut the cake.

Circle formation. One child steps around the outside of the circle. On the words "cut the cake" the child brings his arms down between two children, breaking their clasped hands. The two whose hands were separated run in opposite directions while the first child takes their place in the circle. The runner who gets back to his place last is "it" next.

11. CHARLIE OVER THE OCEAN

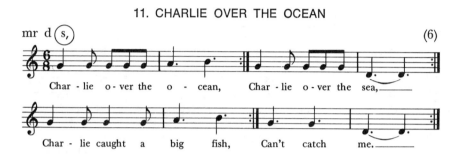

One child steps around the outside of the circle. On the final word "me," he taps a child in the circle who chases him around the circle. The one who gets back to the space first is "safe," the other one "it."

12. WIND THE BOBBIN

This is a winding game. The leader moves in smaller and smaller circles until the group is tightly wound. On the words "break it," all scatter. The most important things to remember for the success of this game formation are 1) all *must* hold hands except for the leader and the end of the line, and 2) all must continue to step in a forward direction.

The formation looks like this:

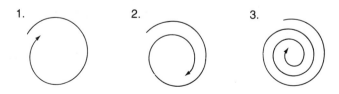

13. STOOPIN' ON THE WINDOW

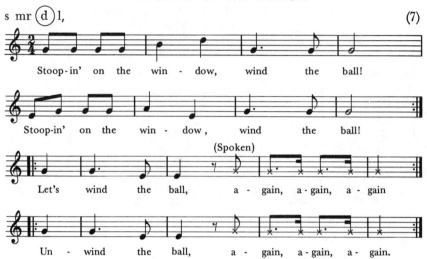

Stoop-in' on the win-dow, wind the ball!

Stoop-in' on the win-dow, wind the ball!

(Spoken)

Let's wind the ball, a-gain, a-gain, a-gain

Un-wind the ball, a-gain, a-gain, a-gain.

"Stoopin' On the Window" uses the same formation as "Wind the Bobbin," except that after the ball is wound, it is unwound. The leader must reverse direction.

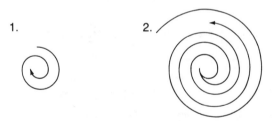

1.   2.

14. WIND UP THE APPLE TREE

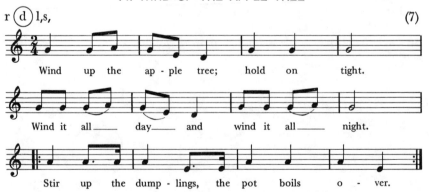

Wind up the ap-ple tree; hold on tight.

Wind it all___ day___ and wind it all___ night.

Stir up the dump-lings, the pot boils o-ver.

This is a reverse unwinding game. On the first two phrases the spiral is wound. On the last phrase the *end* of the line runs in a straight line to unwind the group.

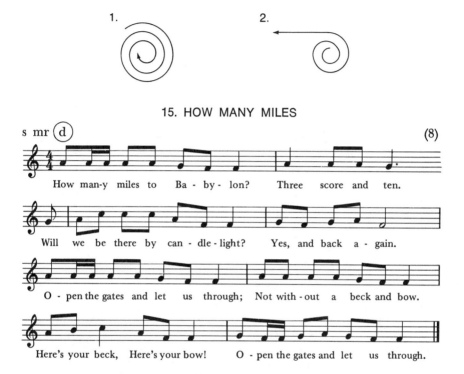

15. HOW MANY MILES

s mr (d)   (8)

How man-y miles to Ba - by - lon? Three score and ten.

Will we be there by can - dle - light? Yes, and back a - gain.

O - pen the gates and let us through; Not with - out a beck and bow.

Here's your beck, Here's your bow! O - pen the gates and let us through.

Two lines face each other. One group sings the questions, the other the answers. Both lines step forward and back while singing. On "Here's your beck, here's your bow" group 1 beckons and then bows. On the last phrase, "open the gates," group 2 forms arches with clasped hands and raised arms. Group 1 runs through the arches.

16. LONDON BRIDGE

ls fm r (d)   (8)

Lon - don bridge is fall - ing down, fall - ing down, fall - ing down

Lon - don bridge is fall - ing down, my fair la - dy.

2. Shake him up with pepper and salt. . . .
3. Off to prison you must go. . . .

Two players form an arch; a line of children pass through the arch. On "my fair lady" the two players forming the "bridge" drop their arms, capturing one of the players in the line. On "shake him up" they do just that, bouncing him around inside their joined arms. On "off to prison" they take him apart from the group and ask him "will you have silver or gold?" (The players forming the bridge have already decided which of them is silver and which gold.) According to his choice the prisoner lines up behind one side of the bridge. When all players have been captured, the two sides of the bridge have a tug of war.

17. GO IN AND OUT THE WINDOW

2. Now kneel before your partner.
3. Go in and out the window.
4. Now follow me to Boston
5. Now run and leave your partner.

Circle formation. Children stand with joined hands raised to form arches (Verse 1) while one child weaves in and out. The one who has been weaving then chooses a partner and kneels before her (Verse 2). On Verse 3, the first child and his partner take hands and weave the windows. On Verse 4 the two run around the outside of the circle and on Verse 5 the first child takes a place in the circle and the game begins again with the second child as "it."

18. BILLY BILLY

2. Step back Sally, Sally, Sally
   Steppin' down the alley all night long.
3. Here comes the second one just like the other one,
   Here comes the second one all night long.

Facing lines formation, boys in one line, girls in the other.

Verse 1: All join hands with the facing partner and move arms rhythmically back and forth while singing.

Verse 2: Girl #1 steps down between the two lines to the bottom of the set. She uses any kind of step she wishes to. It is to be an improvised motion.

Verse 3: Boy #1 steps between the lines to the bottom of the set. He must imitate the motions of girl #1.

The game repeats until all have had a turn.

19. AMASEE

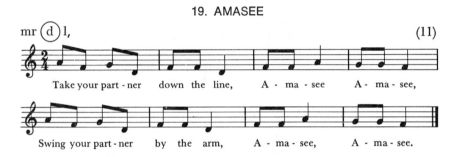

Take your part-ner   down the line,   A - ma - see   A - ma - see,

Swing your part-ner   by   the arm,   A - ma - see,   A - ma - see.

Facing lines formation, boys in one line, girls in the other. On the first phrase, boy #1 takes the hand of girl #1 and they walk down between the lines together. On the second phrase he links his right arm through her right arm and swings her once around. They then step into place at the end of the set and couple #2 repeat the motions, followed by #3 and #4, until all have stepped down the set, and couple #1 are again at the head.

20. SAILING ON THE OCEAN

Sail-ing on the o - cean the tide rolls high, Sail-ing on the o - cean the tide rolls high,

Sail-ing on the o - cean the tide rolls high;   You can get a pret-ty girl   by and by.

> 2. Got me a pretty girl stay all day (3x)
>   We don't care what the old folks say.
> 3. Eight in a boat and it won't go round (3x)
>   You can lose that pretty girl you just found.

Double-circle formation. A large circle on the outside, a circle of four boys on the inside. Outer circle walks clockwise, inner circle, counterclockwise while singing Verse 1. On the words "you can get a pretty girl" each boy in the inner circle changes direction, takes hands with a girl in the outer circle and walks beside her through the second verse. At the beginning of Verse 3, the boys pull their partners into the inner circle, change direction and walk in a circle of eight. On the words "you can lose" the boys step into the outer circle, leaving four girls in the center to begin the game again.

21. TURN THE GLASSES OVER

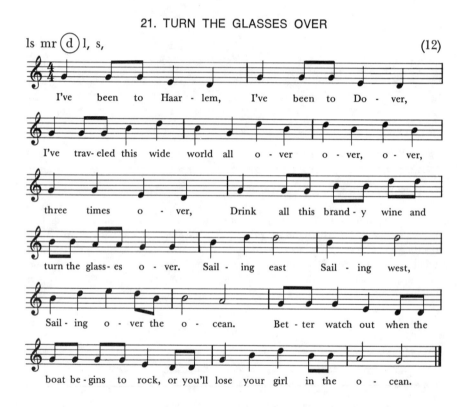

Double circle formation. Boys on the inside, girls on the outside. Hands are clasped in front in skaters position: left hands clasped under, right hands over. On the words "turn the glasses over" each boy lifts both hands. This automatically turns the girl so that she is facing in the opposite direction. Both circles continue to step, now in opposite directions. On the last note of the song each boy takes the right hand of the girl nearest him and the game begins again. This game is made more fun if there are more boys than girls. The extra boys remain in the center of the circle until "sailing east." Then they join the boys, circle, and try to get a girl on the last note. The process may be reversed if there are more girls than boys.

22. LEAD THROUGH THAT SUGAR AND TEA

s mr (d) l, s,   (13)

Lead through that su-gar and tea, O,   lead through that can - dy,

You lead through that su-gar and tea and   I'll lead through that can - dy.

2. You swing for sugar and tea and I'll swing for candy,
   We'll all swing for sugar and tea and we'll all swing for candy.

Facing lines formation—boys in one line, girls in the other. On "Lead through," boy #1 takes the hand of girl #1 and they walk down between the lines together. On "You lead" he links his right arm through her right arm and swings her once around. On "You swing" boy #1 links his left arm with the girl at the bottom of the girls' line and swings her while girl #1 does the same with the boy at the bottom of the boys' line. On "We'll all swing," boy #1 returns to swing his partner and all swing the person across with a right arm swing. Couple #2 then step down the set as the game begins again.

23. PAW PAW PATCH

s fm r (d) t, s,   (14)

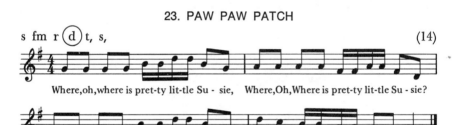

Where,oh,where is pret-ty lit-tle Su - sie,   Where,Oh,Where is pret-ty lit-tle Su - sie?

Where,oh,where is   pret-ty lit-tle Su - sie,   Way down yon-der in the paw paw patch.

2. Come on boys, lets go find her, (3x)
   Way down yonder in the paw paw patch.
3. Pickin' up paw paws, put 'em in your pocket (3x)
   Way down yonder in the paw paw patch.

Facing lines formation—boys in one line, girls in the other. On the words "Where oh where," girl #1 skips around behind the girls' line and up behind the boys' line, back into place. On "Come on boys," girl #1 repeats what she just did, this time with the whole line of boys following her. All must end up back in their original positions at the end of the verse. On Verse 3, the two lines "peel the orange"; that is, they turn to face the top of the set and the boys follow boy #1 around to the left while the girls follow girl #1 around to the right:

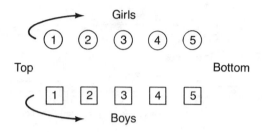

Boy #1 and girl #1 form an arch at the bottom of the set and the rest go through the arch and back to the top of the set. Couple #2 is now at the top of the set and the game begins again.

24. SHAKE THEM 'SIMMONS DOWN

2. Circle left, do, oh, do, oh.
3. Boys to the center, do, oh, do, oh.
4. Girls to the center, do, oh, do, oh.
5. Round your partner, do, oh, do, oh.
6. Prominade your corner, do, oh, do, oh.

Circle formation, alternating boys and girls. The girl on the boy's right is his partner, the one on the left, his corner. The words tell what actions to perform:

2. Circle left, do, oh, do, oh.
3. Boys to the center, do, oh, do, oh.
4. Girls to the center, do, oh, do, oh.
5. Round your partner, do, oh, do, oh.
6. Prominade your corner, do, oh, do, oh.

25. ALABAMA GAL

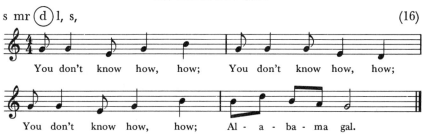

s mr (d) l, s,   (16)

You don't know how, how;   You don't know how, how;

You don't know how, how;   Al - a - ba - ma gal.

2. I'll show you how, how; (3x)
   Alabama gal.
3. Ain't I rock candy (3x)
   Alabama gal.
4. Come through in a hurry (3x)
   Alabama gal.

Facing lines formation: boys in one line, girls in the other as shown on "Paw Paw Patch." On "You don't know how," boy takes both hands of girl #1 and they sashay to the bottom of the set and back to the top. (Sashay: to slide to the side with a step–close–step–close–step.) On "I'll show you how," boy #1 swings girl #1 by the right arm, then girl #2 by the left arm, then back to girl #1 with the right and on to girl #3 with the left, and so on down the entire girls' line. Meanwhile, girl #1 is working her way down the boys' line. The important thing to remember at this point is *right* arm for swinging the partner, *left* arm for all others. The verse (#2) is repeated as often as necessary to get boy and girl #1 to the bottom of the set. Once there, they sashay back to the top of the set and "peel the orange" (see "Paw Paw Patch") on "Ain't I rock candy." They form an arch at the bottom of the set and the rest march through on "Come through in a hurry." Couple #2 are now at the top of the set, couple #1 at the bottom, and the dance begins again. This dance is a basic Virginia reel and may be performed with many other tunes, once learned.

26. OLD BRASS WAGON

mr (d) l, s,   (17)

Cir-cle to the left,   Old brass wa-gon,   Cir-cle to the left,   Old brass wa-gon,

Cir-cle to the left,   Old brass wa-gon, You're the one my   dar - ling.

2. Do-si-do, Old brass wagon
3. Into the center, Old brass wagon
4. Alamande left, Old brass wagon
5. Grand right and left, Old brass wagon
6. Swing, oh swing, old brass wagon
7. Promenade home, old brass wagon.

FORMATION: Square

head couple

side couple

side couple

head couple

Verse 1: All join hands and circle left.

Verse 2: Two dancers walk around each other passing right shoulders first and then back up into place, passing left shoulders. This may be done with the partner, the corner, or with another couple. In this verse of this song there is time to do-si-do the corner, then the partner.

Verse 3: All join hands and step toward the center, raising arms as they do so.

Verse 4: Alamande left—boys face left, girls face right so that each is facing the corner person. Turn the corner with a left arm swing, then back to the partner extending right hand to begin the grand right and left.

Verse 5: Grand right and left—boys move counterclockwise, girls clockwise, giving left hand to the next, right hand to the next, left to the next, until each dancer meets his partner and swings her on Verse 6.

Verse 6: Swing Oh Swing—swing partners with right arms.

Verse 7: Promenade home—move counterclockwise, boy on the inside, girl on the outside, hands in skating position.

27. DRAW A BUCKET OF WATER

(Six or Seven Year Olds)

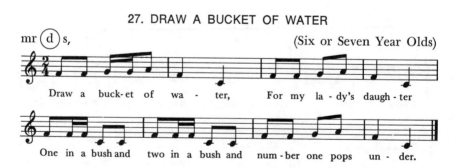

FORMATION:

3

1   2

4

Players 1 and 2 have both hands clasped. Players 3 and 4 have hands clasped above the hands of #1 and #2. All move backward and forward in a rhythmic body sway while singing. On the words "number 1 pops under," players #3 and #4 lift the clasped hands near #1, and #1 "pops" under them—into the space between the arms of #3 and #4. On the second verse, #2 "pops" under. On the third and fourth verses, #3 and #4 "pop" under the raised arms of #1 and #2. The result is a daisy-chain formation. One and two have hands clasped behind the backs of #3 and #4. Three and four have hands clasped behind #1 and #2. All hold hands tightly and leaning back against each other's arms, hop around very fast during the last verse. This usually results in great merriment and a number of children on the floor. Verses: All are the same except for a change in the number—

"number 2 pops under,"
"number 3 pops under,"
"number 4 pops under,"
"Everybody's under."

28. FOUR WHITE HORSES

mr (d) t(b) l, s,   (Eight or Nine Year Olds)

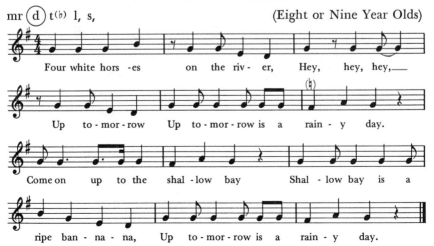

Four white hors - es   on the riv - er,   Hey,   hey, hey,___

Up   to - mor - row   Up to - mor - row is a   rain - y   day.

Come on   up   to the   shal - low bay   Shal - low bay is   a

ripe ban - na - na,   Up to - mor - row is a   rain - y   day.

FORMATION:

2

1   1

2

Two sets of facing partners. This is a clapping game involving clapping own hands, partner's hands across, and partner's hands beside.

The order of play is:

Clap—1. own hands together
    2. partner's hands across (ones above, twos below)
    3. hands of the people to the right and left
    4. own hands
    5. partner's hands across (twos above, ones below)

29. WEAVILY WHEAT

ls mr(d) l, s,   (Eight or Nine Year Olds)

Don't want your weav - ily wheat, Don't want your bar - ley,

Take some flour in half an hour and bake a cake for Char - lie

Five times five is twen - ty - five, Five times six is thir - ty

Five times sev'n is thir - ty - five, Five times eight is for - ty.

FORMATION:

$$\boxed{2}$$

$$\boxed{1} \qquad\qquad \boxed{3}$$

$$\boxed{4}$$

On "Don't want" all join hands and step clockwise. On "take some" they reverse directions. At "Five times five" all stand in place and layer hands in the center exactly on the beat: #1 puts his left hand in, #2 places his on top, followed by #3 and #4. All in turn then layer right hands; after which they pull out hands from the bottom of the pile and place on top.

Songs to Accompany Chapter 4

To Encourage Individual Singing

1. TELEPHONE SONG

ta l s m

Hey, Char-ley! I think I hear my name! Hey, Char-ley! I think I

hear it a-gain! You're want-ed on the tel-e-phone! If it

is-n't Ma-ry I'm not at home! With a rick-tick-tick-e-ty-

tick, Oh yeh! With a rick-tick-tick-e-ty tick, Oh yeh.

2. STEP BACK, BABY

Not last night but the night be - fore,   Step back, ba - by, Step back;

Twen-ty four rob-bers   at   my   door,   Step back, ba - by, Step back;

Open-ed up the door and let them in,   Step back, ba - by, step back;

Hit 'um on the head with a rol - lin' pin,   Step back, ba - by, Step back.

2. I picked up my fryin' pan, Step back, baby, Step back.
Should a seen the way those robbers ran, (etc.). . . .
Some ran east and some ran west. . . .
Some jumped over the cuckoo's nest. . . .

3. PAY ME

ls fm r (d) t,

Pay   me___   Pay   me___   Pay   me my   mon-ey down,

Pay   me___   Pay   me___   Pay   me my   mon- ey down.

4. CATEGORIES

s-m

(clap)   (swing)

One, two, ca - te - gor - ies, Tell   me the names of   (×   ×) cars___

(×   ×) Ford,___ (×   ×) Chev-ro- let   (×   ×) Ca - dil -lac   (×   ×) etc.___

5. LININ' TRACK

d' ls mr (d) ta, s,

Railroading Song

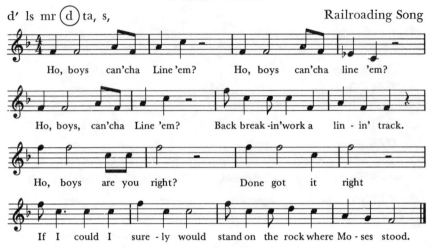

Ho, boys can'cha Line 'em? Ho, boys can'cha line 'em?

Ho, boys, can'cha Line 'em? Back break -in'work a lin - in' track.

Ho, boys are you right? Done got it right

If I could I sure - ly would stand on the rock where Mo - ses stood.

2. I got a woman on Jennielee Square,
If you want to die easy, let me catch you there.

6. "A" MY NAME IS ABBIE

s l (or d r)

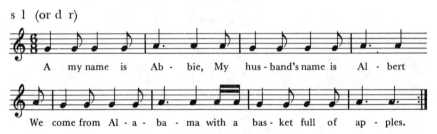

A my name is Ab - bie, My hus - band's name is Al - bert

We come from Al - a - ba - ma with a bas - ket full of ap - ples.

Rhythm—How Many Sounds on a Beat?

7. RAIN COME WET ME

s mr (d)

Rain, come wet me, Sun come dry me,

Keep a - way, pret - ty girls, don't come nigh me!

8. TRAIN IS A-COMIN'

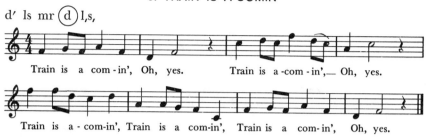

d′ ls mr (d) l,s,

Train is a com-in', Oh, yes. Train is a-com-in',— Oh, yes.

Train is a-com-in', Train is a com-in', Train is a com-in', Oh, yes.

9. DID YOU FEED MY COW

ls mr (d) s,   Spoken:

Spoken:

Did you go to the barn? Yes, mam!

Well did you feed my cow? Yes, mam!

What did you feed her? Oats and hay!

What did you feed her? Oats and hay!

2. Did you milk my cow? Yes Mam!
   Well did you milk my cow? Yes Mam!
   How did you milk her? Squish, squish, squish!
3. Did my cow get sick? Yes Mam!
   Was she covered in a tick Yes Mam!
   How did she die? um-um-um

10. BILLY BILLY

ls mr d — Texas

Here's the way we Bil - ly, Bil - ly, Bil - ly, Bil - ly, Bil - ly, Bil - ly,

Here's the way we Bil - ly, Bil - ly all night long.

2. Step back Sally, Sally, Sally,
   Steppin' down the alley all night long.
3. Here comes the second one just like the other one,
   Here comes the second one, all night long.

11. MY HOME'S IN MONTANA

d' ls fm r (d) — Cowboy Song

My home's in Mon - tan - a, I wear a ban - da - na

My spurs are of sil - ver my po - ny is grey.

When rid - ing the ran - ges my luck nev - er chan - ges

My foot in the stir - rup I gal - lop a - way.

12. WHO'S THAT YONDER

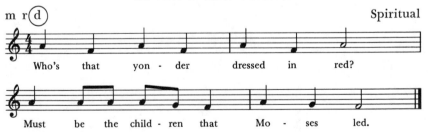

m r (d) — Spiritual

Who's that yon - der dressed in red?

Must be the child - ren that Mo - ses led.

13. THE BOATMAN

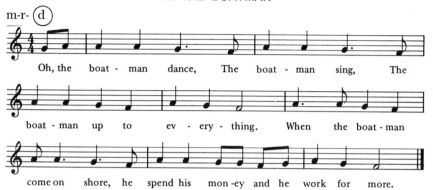

Oh, the boat - man dance, The boat - man sing, The boat - man up to ev - ery - thing. When the boat - man come on shore, he spend his mon - ey and he work for more.

2. Did you ever see where the boatman live?
   Got a house in the hollow with a roof like a sieve!
   The boatman say he got one wish,
   If it gets much wetter, gonna be a fish.
3. Oh the oyster boat should keep to shore,
   The fishing smack should venture more,
   The sailing ship go 'fore the wind,
   The steamboat leave a trail behind.

14. LONG LEGGED SAILOR

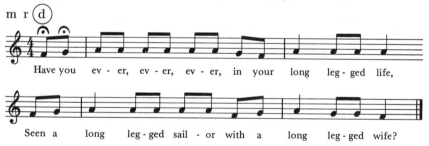

Have you ev - er, ev - er, ev - er, in your long leg - ged life,

Seen a long leg - ged sail - or with a long leg - ged wife?

2. No, I never. . . .   5. Bow legged. . . .
3. Short legged. . . .   6. No. . . .
4. No. . .   Action game.

15. BUFFALO BOY

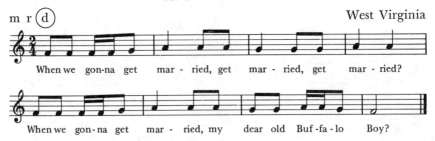

When we gon-na get mar - ried, get mar - ried, get mar - ried?

When we gon-na get mar - ried, my dear old Buf -fa - lo Boy?

2. I think it'll be next Sunday,
   That is if the weather be good.
3. What will you wear to the wedding?
4. Think I'll wear my overalls.
5. What will you drive to the wedding?
6. I think I'll drive my ox cart.
7. Why don't you come in the buggy?
8. My mule won't take to the buggy (not even if the weather be good)

16. GO ROUND THE MOUNTAIN

Go round the moun-tain; To - di - did-dle - um, To - di - did-dle -um,

Go round the moun-tain; To - di - did-dle- um, To - di - did-dle-um - dum.

2. Swing round your partner. . . .
3. Back 'round the mountain. . . .
4. Girls through the window. . . .
5. Boys through the window. . . .
6. Find you a new love. . . .

17. SWEET JOHNNY CUCKOO

Here comes sweet John-ny Cuck - oo, Cuck - oo, Cuck - oo.

Here comes sweet John-ny Cuck- oo on a cold and storm - y night.

2. What do you come for?
3. I come to be a soldier.

For ♩— m r (d) l,

18. SALLY IN THE KITCHEN

mrd l,

Pea's in the pot, Hoe - cake's a - bak - in',

Sal - ly in the kit - chen with her shirt - tail a shak - in'.

Wider-range Songs with m-r-d in a Strong Position.

19. OH WON'T YOU SIT DOWN

m r (d) l, s,   Spiritual

Oh, won't you sit down, Lord, I can't sit down

Oh, won't you sit down; Lord, I can't sit down

'Cause I Just got to heav - en got to look a - round.

20. EZEKIEL SAW THE WHEEL

mr (d) s,   Spiritual

E - ze - kiel saw the wheel_____ Way up in the

mid - dle of the air, E - ze - kiel saw the wheel_____

Way in the mid-dle of the air._____ Oh the big wheel run by

faith_____ and the lit - tle wheel run by the grace of God,

A wheel in a wheel,_____ Way in the mid-dle of the air.

21. RIVER BOAT CALL-SOUNDINGS

Mississippi River Song

s- m- (d)

And it's Quar - ter - less twain___ Mark___ twain___

Quar - ter twain___ Half twain___

And it's Quar - ter - less ta - ree. And it's Mark

ta - ree, Quar - ter ta - ree.

And it's Mark ta - ree. And it's No - bot - tom.

22. REMEMBER ME

s mr (d)

Come my love and go with me, re - mem - ber me.

Come go with me to Ten - nes - see, re - mem - ber me.

2. A horse and buggy to ride you round,
Your pretty little foot shan't touch the ground.

23. GOODBYE BROTHER

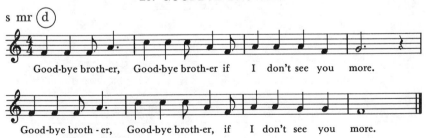

s mr (d)

Good-bye broth-er, Good-bye broth-er if I don't see you more.

Good-bye broth - er, Good-bye broth-er, if I don't see you more.

24. KANSAS BOYS

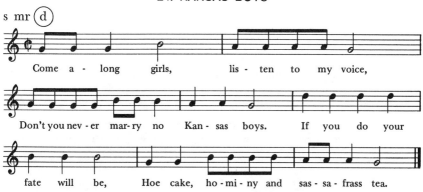

s mr (d)

Come a - long girls, lis - ten to my voice,

Don't you nev - er mar - ry no Kan - sas boys. If you do your

fate will be, Hoe cake, ho - mi - ny and sas - sa - frass tea.

2. When a young man falls in love, First it's "honey" and then "turtle dove."
After he's married, no such thing. "Get up and get my breakfast,
you good - for-nothing thing."

25. DINAH

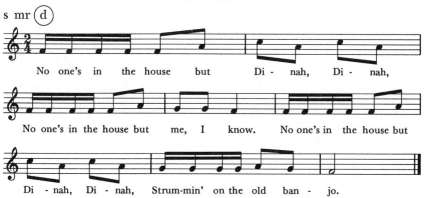

s mr (d)

No one's in the house but Di - nah, Di - nah,

No one's in the house but me, I know. No one's in the house but

Di - nah, Di - nah, Strum-min' on the old ban - jo.

26. HEY, BULLY MONDAY

s mr (d)

Hey, Bul - ly Mon - day, Hey, boy,

Gon - na walk down sal' pond, Hey, boy.

27. FED MY HORSE IN A POPLAR TROUGH

ls mr (d)

Fed my horse in a pop-lar trough, Fed my horse in a

pop-lar trough Fed my horse in a pop-lar trough,

There he caught the whoop-ing cough. Coy ma-lin-do,

Kill - Ko, Kill - Ko, Coy ma-lin-do, Kill - Ko me.

28. GREAT BIG HOUSE IN NEW ORLEANS

ls mr (d)

Play Party Song

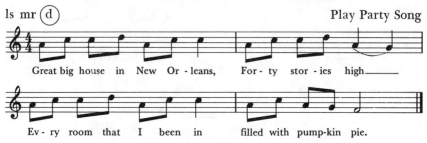

Great big house in New Or-leans, For-ty stor-ies high___

Ev-ry room that I been in filled with pump-kin pie.

2. Went down to the old mill stream to fetch a pail of water
   Put one arm around my wife, the other round my daughter.
3. Fare thee well my darling girl, Fare thee well my daughter,
   Fare thee well my darling girl with the golden slippers on her.

29. ROCKY MOUNTAIN

ls mr (d)

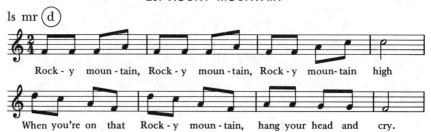

Rock-y moun-tain, Rock-y moun-tain, Rock-y moun-tain high

When you're on that Rock-y moun-tain, hang your head and cry.

Do, do, do, do, Do re - mem - ber me

Do, do, do, do, Do re - mem - ber me.

30. EYES OF BLUE

d' ls mr

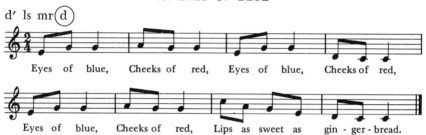

Eyes of blue, Cheeks of red, Eyes of blue, Cheeks of red,

Eyes of blue, Cheeks of red, Lips as sweet as gin - ger - bread.

31. DON'T LET THE WIND

d' ls mr(d)

St. Helena's Island

Don't let the wind, don't let the wind,

don't let the wind blow here no more Oh_____

don't let the wind, don't let the wind blow here no more.

32. GOOD-BYE LITTLE BONNY

d' ls mr(d)

Good - bye, lit - tle Bon - ny, Good - bye;

Good - bye lit - tle Bon - ny, Good - bye.

I'll see you a-gain___ but the Lord___ knows___ when;

Good - bye_____ lit - tle Bon - ny Good - bye.

33. RATLESNAKE

ls mr (d) l,

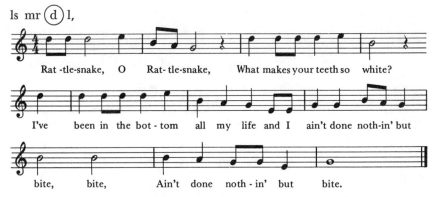

Rat -tle-snake, O Rat- tle-snake, What makes your teeth so white?

I've been in the bot - tom all my life and I ain't done noth-in' but

bite, bite, Ain't done noth - in' but bite.

34. JOHNNY'S GONE A LONG TIME

d' ls mr (d)

Run long my Lu - lu, John - ny's gone a long time;

John - ny is your sweet - heart, John-ny's gone a long time;

John - ny is your sweet - heart, John-ny's gone a long time;

John- ny is your sweet - heart, John-ny's gone a long time.

35. CEDAR SWAMP

d' ls mr (d) l,

Play Party Game

Way down low in the ce-dar swamp, Wa-ter's deep and mud-dy

There I met a pret-ty lit-tle miss, There I kissed my hon-ey.

Swing a la-dy up and down, Swing a la-dy home.

Swing a la-dy up and down, Swing a la-dy home.

36. CHICK-A-LI-LEE-LO

mrd (l,) s,

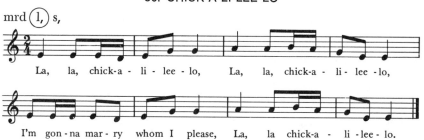

La, la, chick-a-li-lee-lo, La, la, chick-a-li-lee-lo,

I'm gon-na mar-ry whom I please, La, la chick-a-li-lee-lo.

37. OH JOHNNY

These— wars are a - rag - ing, And John-ny's got to fight;
I want to be with him From morn - ing to night.

Chorus:
"Oh, Johnny, my jewel
It seems as you're unkind.
It seems as I've loved you
From all other mankind

2. It seems as I've loved you
Which grieves my heart so.
Oh, may I go with you?
Oh, no, my love, no.

3. Tomorrow is Sunday
And Monday is the day
My captain commands me
And I must away.

4. You'll be standing on picket
Some cold snowy day,
Your red rosy cheeks
Will soon fade away.

5. Your red rosy cheeks
Which grieves my heart so,
Oh, may I go with you?
"No, my love no."

6. "Oh, daughter, dear daughter
You'd better stay at home,
You had better stay with mother
Till Johnny comes home.

7. "Oh, mother dear, mother
You need not talk to me,
I'll foller young Johnny
Across the flowing sea.

8. "I'll cut off my hair
Men's clothing I'll put on;
I'll pass as your messmate
As we march along."

38. THE BANKS OF THE OLD TENNESSEE

If I were a lit - tle fish—
I would - n't swim in the sea.—
I'd swim in the brook where my Kat - y baits her hook,
On the banks of the old Ten - nes - see.—

39. MY HORSES AIN'T HUNGRY (THE WAGONER LAD)

mr ⓓ l,s, m,

It's   dark   and   it's   rain-ing,   The   moon gives   no   light;

So__ stay   with   me   dar-ling   I   know   it's   all   right.

2. "Well sit down beside me; I'll tell you my mind:
My mind is to marry you and leave all behind.

3. "So put up your horses and feed them some hay,
For I cannot marry my parents both say."

4. "My horses are hungry, but they won't eat your hay;
So goodbye, my darling, I'll feed on my way.

5. "Your parents are against me; they say I'm too poor.
They say I'm not worthy to enter your door.

6. "So go with me, Molly; we'll drive till we come
To some little lone cabin; we'll call it our home."

7. "Yes, I will go with you, you're poor I am told;
But it's your love I'm after, not silver or gold.

8. "So fare-you-well, Mother, I'm going away;
His horses are hungry, but they won't eat your hay."

40. CUMBERLAND GAP

ls mr ⓓ l,

I   laid   down,   Took   a   lit-tle   nap,

For-ty-one   miles   from   Cum-ber-land   Gap.

2. Cumberland Gap's a mighty fine place,
Can't get water for to wash your face.

3. Cumberland Gap with its cliffs and rocks,
Home of the panther, bear and fox.

41. NINE HUNDRED MILES

ls mrd (1,)

Western Lament

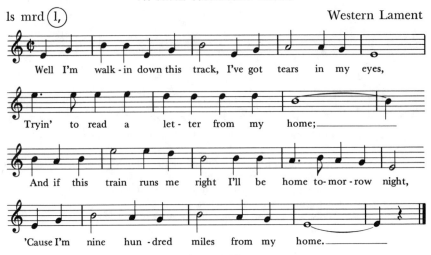

Well I'm walk-in down this track, I've got tears in my eyes,

Tryin' to read a let-ter from my home;

And if this train runs me right I'll be home to-mor-row night,

'Cause I'm nine hun-dred miles from my home.

42. TRAIL TO MEXICO

ls mr (d) l,s, m,

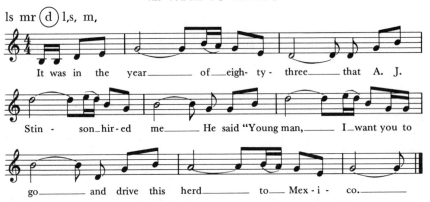

It was in the year___ of___eigh-ty - three___ that A. J.

Stin - son___hir-ed me___ He said "Young man,___ I___want you to

go___ and drive this herd___ to___ Mex-i - co.___

2. It was early springtime of the year
   When I set out to drive the steers,
   It was a long and lonesome go
   Along the trail to Mexico.

3. When I arrived in Mexico
   I missed the girl who loved me so,
   I wrote a letter to my dear
   But no word from her did I hear.

4. And so, I returned back to my home,
   To my beloved, no more to roam.
   I found her, wed, with a richer life,
   She hadn't cared to be my wife.

5. A curse on gold and on silver too,
   And on the gal who won't be true,
   I'll head right back to the Rio Grande
   And end my life an old cow hand.
6. Yes, I'll go back where the girls are true,
   I know one I can count on, too.
   I'm going back where the bullets fly,
   And follow the cow trail till I die.

Songs to Accompany Chapter 7

1. DO LORD

mr (d) l,s,   Spiritual

Do lord, O do lord, O do re - mem - ber me.

Do lord, O do lord, O do re - mem-ber me. Do lord, O do Lord O

Do re - mem-ber me. Way be - yound___ the blue.

2. GOIN' UP THE RIVER

ls mr (d) l,s,   River Boat Song

Go - in' up the riv - er, from Cat - lets - berg to Pike.

Work-in' on the push boat for old man Jef - fry Ike.

3. ZION'S CHILDREN

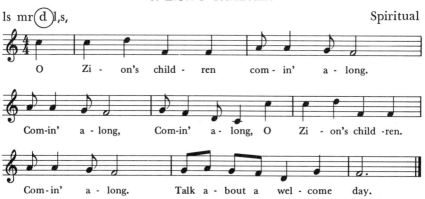

O Zi - on's child - ren com - in' a - long.
Com-in' a - long, Com-in' a - long, O Zi - on's child -ren.
Com-in' a - long. Talk a - bout a wel - come day.

4. THIS TRAIN

This train is bound for Glo - ry, This train is bound for glo - ry,
This train is bound for glo - ry, Child - ren get on board.

5. DON'T LET THE WIND

Don't let the wind, Don't let the wind,
Don't let the wind blow here no more, Oh, ——
Don't let the wind; Don't let the wind blow here no more.

9. I SAW THE LIGHT

10. CAPTAIN DON'T SIDE TRACK YOUR TRAIN

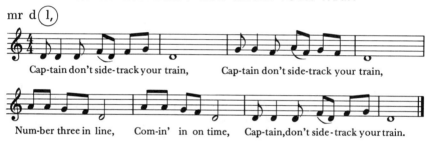

11. ALABAMA GAL [1]

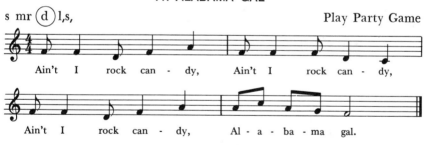

[1] Other verses to "Alabama Gal" may be found in the games and dances, Chapter 3.

Songs to Accompany Chapter 8

1. LONDON BRIDGE DO LORD

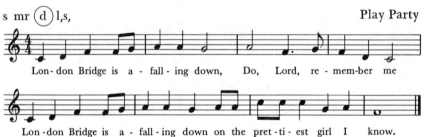

Play Party

Lon-don Bridge is a - fall-ing down,   Do,   Lord,   re - mem-ber   me

Lon-don Bridge is a - fall-ing down on the pret-ti-est girl I   know.

2. Choose your partner, honey my love,
   Do, Lord, remember me;
   Choose your partner, honey my love,
   You're the prettiest girl I know.
3. Shake his hand now, honey my love, ...
4. Send him home now, honey my love, ...
5. Choose you another one, honey my love, ...

2. SHADY GROVE

Shad - y Grove, My true love, Shad - y Grove I know,

Shad - y Grove, My true love, I'm bound for Shad - y Grove.

Verse:

1. Some come here to fiddle and dance,
   Some come here to tarry;
   Some come here to fiddle and dance,
   But I come here to marry.
2. Peaches in the summertime,
   Apples in the Fall,
   If I can't have the gal I love,
   I won't have none at all!

3. AL CITRON

Al cit - ron   de   un   fan - dan - go, San - go,   San - go, Sa - ba - ré.

Sa -ba - ré   de   la   ron - de - la Con su   tri - ki, tri - ki - trón.

Game for "Al Citron"

Children are seated in a circle on the ground. Each child has a pencil in front of him. On the upbeat each child picks up the pencil. On the first beat of each measure the pencil is put down with a bang on the ground in front of the neighbor on the right who on the following beat passes it on. This continues around the circle until the words "triki, triki, tron," when it is held and banged on the ground to the right and to the left of the child and then passed on to the right on the word "tron." The game is continued and any child breaking the rhythm is eliminated until only one is left.

4. THE OLD GRAY GOOSE

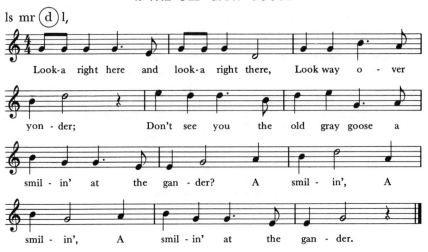

Look-a right here and look-a right there, Look way o - ver yon - der; Don't see you the old gray goose a smil - in' at the gan - der? A smil - in', A smil - in', A smil - in' at the gan - der.

5. JOHN KANAKA

I heard, I heard the old man say, John Ka - na - ka na - ka Too - la - ay, To - day, to - day is a hol - i - day, John Ka - na - ka na - ka Too - la - ay. Too - la - ay, Too - la - ay, John Ka - na - ka na - ka Too - la - ay.

1. Children form double circle—boys on outside, girls on inside.
2. Girls face the boys and establish partners.
3. On phrase one ("I heard, I heard. . . .") Boys do-si-do around their female partner.
4. On "John," children stamp foot.
   On "Kanaka naka," tap knees in rhythm.
   On "Toola," clap own hands twice.
   On "ay," clap partner's hands once.
5. On "Today, today . . .," repeat do-si-do with partner.
6. Repeat step 4.
7. On "Toolay, toolay," boys step to the left to establish a new partner (children may also do "Too-la-ay" clap pattern as they walk).
8. Children repeat step 4, and game begins again with the new partners.

6. CHAIRS TO MEND

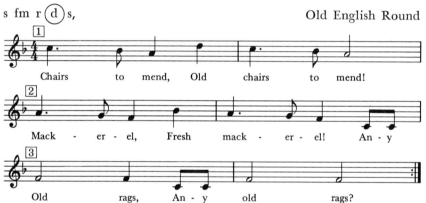

7. RIDING IN A BUGGY

Ma - ry Jane, You're a long way from home.

Who mourns for me? Who mourns for me?

Who mourns for me, my dar - ling? Who mourns for me?

8. MARIA [1]

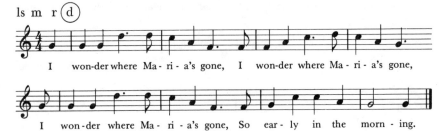

ls m r (d)

I won-der where Ma - ri - a's gone, I won-der where Ma - ri - a's gone,

I won-der where Ma - ri - a's gone, So ear - ly in the morn - ing.

2. She has gone and I can't go, (3x)
   So early in the morning.
3. Yonder she comes and "how do you do". (3x)
   So early in the morning.
4. Give her a kiss and wave on through. (3x)
   So early in the morning.

[1] The dance for this song is exactly the same as the one given for "Paw Paw Patch," Chapter 3.

9. DA PACEM DOMINE

s fm r (d²)

Early Anon.

Da pa - cem Do - mi - ne, Da pa - cem

Da pa - cem Do - mi - ne, Da

Do - mi - ne, in di - e - bus Nos - tris.

pa - cem Do - mi - ne in di - e - bus Nos - tris.

10. CRADLE HYMN

s fm r (d)

J. S. Bach

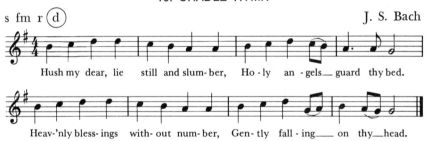

Hush my dear, lie still and slum- ber, Ho -ly an - gels guard thy bed.

Heav-'nly bless- ings with- out num- ber, Gen- tly fall - ing on thy head.

² Both voices may be solmizized as beginning on *do*.

11. JOYFUL, JOYFUL

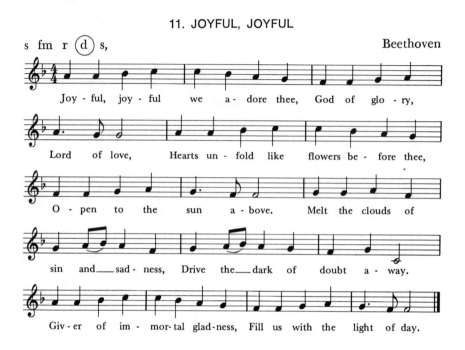

Beethoven

s fm r (d) s,

Joy - ful, joy - ful we a - dore thee, God of glo - ry,

Lord of love, Hearts un - fold like flowers be - fore thee,

O - pen to the sun a - bove. Melt the clouds of

sin and sad - ness, Drive the dark of doubt a - way.

Giv - er of im - mor - tal glad - ness, Fill us with the light of day.

appendix F

Songs to Accompany Chapter 10

1. JOHN RANDOLPH

s fm r dt, l (s) f

Ballad in the Ancient Tradition
(Mixolydian Mode) [1]

Where have you been a - rov - ing, John Randolph, my son?

Where have you been a - rov - ing, pray tell me lit - tle one?

I've been out a - court - ing. Go___ make my bed soon.

Moth-er I'm sick at the heart, and I want to lie down.

2. What did you have for your supper, John Randolph, my son
What did you have for your supper, pray tell me, little one.
Had eel soup and vinegar, Go make my bed soon.
Mother I am sick to the heart and I want to lie down.

[1] This version is an American variant of the old British ballad "Lord Randal," Child Ballad #12.

3. What color was it . . . .
   It was brown and speckled . . . .
4. What'll you will to your father? . . .
   My mules and my wagons . . .
5. What'll you will to your mother? . . . .
   My coach and six horses . . . .
6. What'll you will to your brother? . . . .
   My hounds and my musket . . . .
7. What'll you will to your sister? . . . . .
   My rings off my fingers . . . .
8. What'll you will to your sweet heart? . . . .
   A cup of strong poison . . .

2. JOHN HENRY

mrd ls m♭r (d)   Native American Ballad

John__ Hen-ry was just a lit-tle ba-by__

Sit-tin' on his dad-dy's__ knee__

He__ point his fin-ger at a lit-tle piece of steel,

"Steel gon-na be the death__ of me, me me

Steel gon-na be the death__ of me."__

2. They took John Henry to the mountain,
   That mountain was so high,
   That mountain was so tall and John Henry was so small
   He layed down his hammer and he cried, cried, cried.
3. Captain told old John Henry,
   'I believe this mountain's sinkin' in.'
   Says 'Stand back captain don't you be afraid,
   It's nothing but my hammer catching wind.'
4. Captain told old John Henry,
   "Gonna bring my steam drill round,
   Gonna take my steam drill out on the job,
   Gonna beat John Henry down . . . .

5. John Henry told his captain,
   "A man ain't nothin' but a man,
   Before I'd let your steam drill beat me down,
   I'd die with this hammer in my hand."
6. John Henry hammerin' on the right-hand side,
   Steam drill drivin' on the left,
   John Henry beat that steam drill down,
   But he hammered his fool self to death . . . .

3. THE MARY L. MACKAY

m′r′d′t ls fm(r)d

Broadside Ballad
(Dorian Mode)

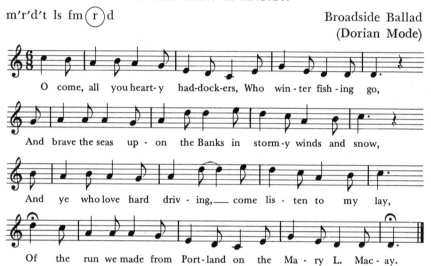

O come, all you heart-y had-dock-ers, Who win-ter fish-ing go,
And brave the seas up-on the Banks in storm-y winds and snow,
And ye who love hard driv-ing,— come lis-ten to my lay,
Of the run we made from Port-land on the Ma-ry L. Mac-ay.

2. We hung the muslin on her, the wind began to hum,
   Twenty hardy Nova Scotia men chock full of Portland rum,
   Mainsail, foresail, jib and jumbo, on that wild December day.
   As we passed Cape Elizabeth and slugged for Fundy Bay.
3. We slammed her by Monhegan as the gale began to scream,
   Our vessel took to dancing in a way that was no dream,
   A howler o'er the top rail we steered sou'west away,
   O she was a hound for running, was the Mary L. Macay.
4. The run was passing merrily and the gang was feeling grand,
   Long necks dancing in her wake from where we left the land,
   Our skipper he kept sober, for he knew how things would lay,
   And he made us furl the mainsail on the Mary L. Macay.
5. We laced our wheelsman to the box as he steered her through the gloom,
   A big sea hove his dory-mate right over the main boom,
   It tore the oil pants off his legs and you could hear him say,
   There's a power of water flyin' o'er the Mary L. Macay.
6. From Portland, Maine to Yarmouth Sound, twenty-two miles we ran,
   In eighteen hours, my bully boys, now beat that if you can.
   The gang said it was seamanship, the skipper he kept dumb,
   But the force that drove our vessel was the power
   of Portland rum.

4. THE GREEN LEAVES GREW ALL AROUND

s mrd 1, (s,)   (Cumulative Song)

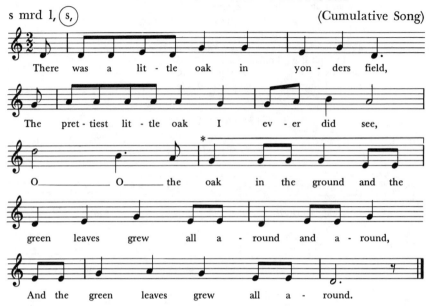

There was a lit - tle oak in yon - ders field,

The pret - tiest lit - tle oak I ev - er did see,

O_____ O_____ the oak in the ground and the

green leaves grew all a - round and a - round,

And the green leaves grew all a - round.

*This bar is sung twice in the second verse,
Three times in the third verse and so on.

> 2. And on that oak there was a limb.
>   The prettiest limb I ever did see,
>   O,O the limb on the oak
>   And the green leaves grew all
>   around and around.
>   And the green leaves grew
>   all around.
> 3. And on that limb there was a twig . . .
> 4. And on that twig there was a nest . . . .
> 5. And in that nest there was an egg . . .
> 6. And in that egg there was a bird . . . .
> 7. And on that bird there was a feather . . . .

* This bar is sung twice in the second verse, three times in the third verse and
so on.

5. BLACK IS THE COLOUR

ls fm r dt l⟨s⟩f

Folk Lyric Song
(Mixolydian Mode)

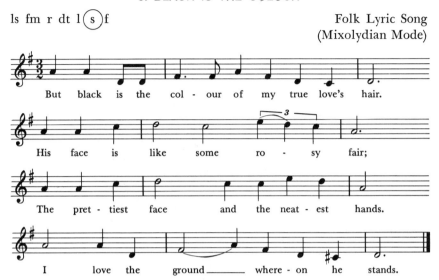

But black is the col - our of my true love's hair.

His face is like some ro - sy fair;

The pret - tiest face and the neat - est hands.

I love the ground_____ where - on he stands.

2. The winter's past and the leaves are green,
   The time is past that we have seen;
   But still I hope the time will come.
   When you and I shall be as one.

6. THE GOOD OLD MAN

s'f rdt⟨s⟩

Appalachian
(Mixolydian Mode)

Where are you go - ing, my good old man?_____

Where are you go - ing my hon -ey, my lamb?

Best old soul in the world. (Spoken) *Goin' huntin'*

Verse 2.
When will you be back, my good old man?
When will you be back, my honey, my lamb?
Best old soul in the world.

Spoken: Friday evenin'.

Verse 3.
    What'll you have for supper . . .
                         Eggs.
Verse 4.
    How many will you have . . . .
                     A bushel.
Verse 5.
    A bushel will kill you . . . .
                     Can't help it.
Verse 6.
    Where do you want to be buried . . .
                     In the chimney corner.
Verse 7.
    Why do you want to be buried there . . . . .
                     So's I can haunt you.
Verse 8.
    Haunt can't haunt a haunt, my good old man.
    Haunt can't haunt a haunt, my honey, my lamb.
    Meanest old devil in the world.

7. GROUNDHOG

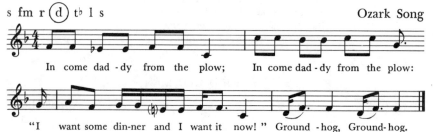

s fm r (d) t♭ l s   Ozark Song

In come dad - dy from the plow; In come dad - dy from the plow:

"I want some din-ner and I want it now!" Ground - hog, Ground- hog.

2. There's a piece of bread a laying on the shelf
   If you want anymore, you'll get it yourself ground-hog ground-hog
3. He picked up his gun and whistled to his dog
   Off to the wide woods to catch a ground hog ground-hog ground-hog
4. Two in a rock and two in a log
   Good lawd a mercy, what a big ground hog. ground-hog ground-hog
5. Run here, Sal, with a ten foot pole,
   Twist this ground-hog out of this hold. ground-hog ground-hog
6. Daddy returned in an hour and a half
   He returned with a ground-hog big as a calf. ground-hog ground-hog.
7. How them children whopped and cried,
   I love that ground-hog stewed and fried. ground-hog ground-hog
8. Took him home and tanned his hide
   Made the best shoe strings ever was tied. ground-hog ground-hog
9. Meat's in the cover and the hide's in the turn
   If that ain't ground-hog, I'll be durn, ground-hog, ground-hog
10. In come Sal with a snigger and a grin
   Ground-hog gravy all over her chin. ground-hog ground-hog

11. Come here, maw and look at Sam
    He's et all the meat and sopping up the pan. ground-hog ground-hog
12. Old Aunt Sal was the mother of them all
    She fed them on ground-hog before they could crawl ground-hog ground-hog

8. SANTY ANNO

s mrdt, (1,) s, m,   Texas Chantey

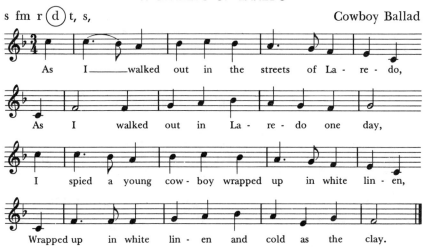

Oh, San - ty An - no gained the—day, Hoo -ray, San - ty An - no,

He lost it—once but— gained it twice all—— on the plains of Mex -i- co.

2. And General Taylor ran away, Hooray, Santy Anno
   He ran away at Monterey, All on the plains of Mexico.
3. Oh Santy Anno fought for fame . . . .
   And there's where Santy gained his name . . . .
4. Oh Santy Anno fought for gold. . . .
   The deeds he done have oft been told. . . .
5. Oh Santy Anno's days are o'er . . .
   And Santy Anno will fight no more . . . .

9. STREETS OF LAREDO

s fm r (d) t, s,   Cowboy Ballad

As I——walked out in the streets of La - re - do,

As I walked out in La - re - do one day,

I spied a young cow - boy wrapped up in white lin - en,

Wrapped up in white lin - en and cold as the clay.

2. "I see by your outfit that you are a cowboy."
   These words he did say as I boldly stepped by;
   "Come sit down beside me and hear my sad story,
   I was shot in the breast and I know I must die.

3. It was once in the saddle I used to go dashing,
   It was once in the saddle I used to go gay;
   First to the dram house and then to the card house,
   Got shot in the breast and I'm dying today.
4. Go get seven cowboys to carry my coffin,
   Get seven maidens to carry my pall,
   Put seven red roses on top of my coffin,
   My luckiest number when the dice used to fall.
5. Oh, beat the drum slowly and play the fife lowly,
   Play the dead march as you carry me along;
   Take me to the green valley, there lay the sod o'er me,
   For I'm a young cowboy and I know I've done wrong.

10. SLAVE LAMENT (LINK O'DAY)

11. FOLLOW THE DRINKING GOURD

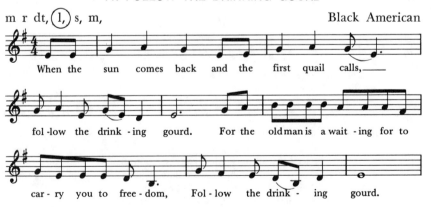

Fol - low_____ the drink - ing gourd, Fol - low_____ the

drink-ing gourd,___ For the old man is a wait - ing for to

car - ry you to free - dom, Fol - low the drink - ing gourd.

12. HANGMAN, SLACK UP YOUR ROPE

s mrdt, (1,) s,m,   Ozark [2]

Hang man, Hang man, slack up your rope; Slack it for a while,

I look o - ver yon -der and I see my Paw a com - in', He's

walked for man -y a - mile, "Say Paw, Say Paw,

Have you brung me an -y gold? An-y gold for to pay my fee?"

"No, my son, I have not an - y gold, you must

hang on the gal - lows___ tree."

Verse 2, 3,& 4: The words are the same with
only the relative changed:
I see my Maw, Brother, Sister.

[2] This is an American variant of a ballad that exists in numerous earlier English
variants.

Existing Kodály Programs and Organizations

Some institutions at which teacher-training in Kodály may be obtained.

1. Holy Names College: 3500 Mountain Boulevard, Oakland, California 94619
   - Full-year program leading to the degree of Master of Music Education with emphasis in Kodály.
   - Five-summer program leading to the same degree.
   - Shorter programs leading to the Kodály Certificate.
   - Hungarian and Hungarian-trained-and-certified American faculty.
   - Some fellowships available.
   Director: Sr. Mary Alice Hein

2. Kodály Musical Training Institute: 23 Main Street, Watertown, Massachusetts 02172
   - Summer courses and full-year programs leading to the Kodály Certificate.
   - Affiliation with several degree-granting institutions.
   - Hungarian and Hungarian-trained American faculty.
   - Some scholarships available.
   Director: Dr. David Jenness

3. Kodály Center of America: 1326 Washington Street, West Newton, Massachusetts 02165
   - Summer programs: Four summers, leading to the Kodály Certifi-

cate; three summers plus one year at an affiliated institution, leading to a Master's degree.
— Hungarian and Hungarian-trained American faculty.
— Some financial help available.
Director: Denise Bacon

4. Silver Lake College: Manitowac, Wisconsin 54220
   — Bachelor of Music degree in Music Education with major concentration in Kodály.
   — Master of Music Education with Kodály emphasis, in conjunction with University of Wisconsin—Green Bay.
   — Full-time, part-time, or summer study.
   — Hungarian-trained faculty.
   Director: Sr. Lorna Zemke

5. The University of Calgary (Department of Music): 2500 University Drive, N.W,. Calgary, Alberta, Canada T2N 1N4
   — Two-year program (one of which must be spent in residence), leading to the degree of Master of Music with a concentration in Kodály.
   — Summer programs in Kodály.
   The author is a member of the Faculty of Fine Arts at this University.

6. Kodály Institute: Kecskemet, Hungary
   — Full-year and summer courses leading to the Kodály Certificate.
   Director: Peter Erdei

7. Esztergom Summer University: Esztergom, Hungary
   — Introductory Courses and Lectures in Kodály.
   Director: Professor Erzsébet Szonyi, Franz Liszt Academy of Music, Budapest, Hungary.

Many additional summer programs exist. The author suggests that interested students carefully study summer faculty qualifications before registering for any summer course. There is at present no single standard of Kodály certification in the United States. Many teachers listing themselves as "Kodály trained" have indeed spent a year or more studying in Hungary or with Hungarian-trained American faculty. Others have not. It is up to the prospective student to determine the qualification of workshop clinicians and summer course teachers. In doing this it may prove helpful to write to the closest regional Kodály group. The names and addresses of those formally in existence as of April, 1979, are listed on pp. 277 and 278.

Kodály-Related Organizations

1. International Kodály Society (IKS): Budapest, Hungary
   An honorary society. Membership by invitation to Kodály educators who have shown significant contributions to the international Kodály movement.

2. Organization of American Kodály Educators (OAKE): 131 Second Street, Framingham, Massachusetts 01701
   Executive Secretary: Jonathan C. Rappaport.
   Membership open to all interested music educators.

3. Kodály Institute of Canada/L'institut Kodály du Canada: P.O. Box 20, Stn. A, Ottawa, Ontario, Canada K1N 8V1.
   Contact: Mae Daly.

Regional Affiliates of OAKE

1. AKTS—Arizona Kodály Teachers Society
   Contact: Jerry Jaccard, RR1, Box 1942, Show Low, AZ 85901
2. CAKE—California Association of Kodály Educators
   Contact: Eleanor Locke, Holy Names College, 3500 Mountain Boulevard, Oakland, CA 94619
3. EKA—Eastern Kodály Association
   Contact: Sarah Ferrebee, 873 West Boulevard, Hartford, CT 06105
4. KEEP—Kodály Educators of Eastern Pennsylvania
   Contact: Helen Henry, Media Elementary School, State and Munroe Streets, Media, PA 19063
5. KET—Kodály Educators of Texas
   Contact: Tom Kite, 8237 Glenview Drive, Houston, TX 77017
6. KMEET—Kodály Music Educators in East Tennessee
   Contact: Ben Coton, Box 24500, East Tennessee State University, Johnson City, TN 37350
7. Kodályans
   Contact: J. Gilbert Knapp, Associate Professor of Music, Oregon State University, Corvallo, OR 97331
8. MKMEA—Midwest Kodály Music Educators Association
   Contact: Harold Caldwell, School of Music, Ball State University. Muncie, IN 47306
9. MUSIK—Maryland United Specialists in Kodály
   Contact: Karen Taylor, 7707 Greenview Terrace, #60, Towson, MD 21204

10. NEO–OAKE–Northeastern Ohio–OAKE
    Contact: Margaret L. Stone, 960 Janet Drive, Kent, OH 44240

11. PNOAKE–Pacific Northwest–OAKE
    Contact: Shirley Linscott, Supervisor of Music, Seattle Board of Education, Seattle, WA 98101

12. SOAKE–Southwest Ohio Association of Kodály Educators
    Contact: Norma Hellen, Cameron Park School, 626 Waycross Road, Cincinnati, OH 45240

There will surely be others as time goes on. For more information see the *Kodály Envoy,* the official publication of OAKE, at the address given above.

Teachers wishing to observe the Kodály concept functioning in American schools can take advantage of many fine programs around the United States and Canada. The San Jose project has been discussed in the Preface to this book. Two others should be singled out.

The New Haven (Connecticut) Program. The oldest and the first to be completely authentic in its practice, i.e., offering music taught by Hungarian-trained American teachers. This unique program, the vision of ethnomusicologist Alexander Ringer, has been in continual operation since 1969.

Another exemplary program exists in the public schools of West Hartford, Connecticut, under the leadership of music supervisor Jack Alexander. This program is perhaps the most unique of the three mentioned, since it represents a public school music system that has, without support from outside funding agencies or institutions, committed itself to authentic Kodály practice in its schools.

Alphabetical List of Songs

Alabama Gal
Al Citron
All 'Round the Brickyard
Amasee
"A" My Name Is Alice

Banks of the Old Tennessee, The
Bee Bee
Billy Billy
Black Is the Colour
Blue Bells
Boatmen, The
Bobby Shaftow
Bounce High
Bow Wow Wow
Buffalo Boy
Bye Lo, Baby O

Captain Don't Side Track Your Train
Categories
Cedar Swamp
Chairs to Mend
Charlie Over the Ocean
Chick-a-li-lee-lo

Cradle Hymn
Cuckoo
Cumberland Gap
Cut the Cake

Da Pacem Domine
Deedle Deedle Dumpling
Did You Feed My Cow?
Dinah
Dog and Cat
Doggie, Doggie
Do Lord
Don't Let the Wind
Don't Let Your Watch Run Down
Draw a Bucket of Water

Eyes of Blue
Ezekiel Saw the Wheel

Fed My Horse in a Poplar Trough
Follow the Drinking Gourd
Four White Horses

Get Your Feet Out the Sand
Go In and Out the Window
Goin' Home on a Cloud
Goin' Up the River
Goodbye Brother
Goodbye Little Bonny
Goodnight
Good Old Man, The
Go Round the Mountain
Great Big House in New Orleans
Green Grows the Willow Tree
Groundhog

Hangman, Slack Up Your Rope
Here Comes a Bluebird
Here We Go Round the Mulberry Bush
Hey Bully Monday
How Long the Train Been Gone?
How Many Miles

Icka Backa
I Saw the Light

Jenny Jones
John Henry
John Kanaka
Johnny's Gone a Long Time
John Randolph
Joyful Joyful

Kansas Boys
Knock at the Door

Lantern Man, The
Lead Through that Sugar and Tea
Lemonade
Linin' Track
Little Sally Water

London Bridge
London Bridge Do Lord
Long-Legged Sailor

Maria
Mary L. MacKay, The
Mighty Pretty Motion
My Home's in Montana
My Horses Ain't Hungry

Nine Hundred Miles

Oats, Peas, Beans and Barley Grow
Oh, Johnny
Oh, Won't You Sit Down?
Old Brass Wagon
Old Gray Goose, The
Old King Glory
Old Roger Is Dead
Oliver Twist

Paw Paw Patch
Pay Me
Poor Little Kitty Cat

Rain Come Wet Me
Rattlesnake
Remember Me
Riding in a Buggy
River Boat Call-Soundings
Rocky Mountain

Sailing on the Ocean
Sally Go Round the Sun
Sally in the Kitchen
Santy Anno
See Saw, Margery Daw

Shady Grove

Shake Them Simmons Down

Skin and Bones

Slave Lament

Snail, Snail

Step Back Baby

Stoopin' on the Window

Sweet Johnny Cuckoo

Telephone Song

There Was a Little Oak

This Train

Trail to Mexico

Train Is A-Comin'

Turn the Glasses Over

Walk and Stop

Walk Daniel

Weavily Wheat

Who's That Yonder?

Wind the Bobbin

Wind Up the Apple Tree

Witch Witch

Zion's Children